FATHERS
TO
DAUGHTERS

Contributions in Legal Studies
Series Editor: *Paul L. Murphy*

FATHERS
TO
DAUGHTERS

The Legal Foundations of Female Emancipation

PEGGY A. RABKIN

Contributions in Legal Studies, Number 11

GREENWOOD PRESS
Westport, Connecticut
London, England

Library of Congress Cataloging in Publication Data

Rabkin, Peggy A
    Fathers to daughters.

    (Contributions in legal studies; no. 11 ISSN 0147-
1074)
    Bibliography: p.
    Includes index.
    1. Husband and wife—New York (State)—History.
2.   Married women—New York (State)—History.
3.   Women's rights—History. I. Title. II. Series.
KFN5124.R3 346.747'0134 79-6830
ISBN 0-313-20670-8 lib. bdg.

Library of Congress Catalog Card Number: 79-6830
ISBN: 0-313-20670-8
ISSN: 0147-1074

First published in 1980

Greenwood Press
A division of Congressional Information Service, Inc.
88 Post Road West, Westport, Connecticut 06881

Printed in the United States of America

10 9 8 7 6 5 4 3 2 1

To Samuel with gratitude and affection

CONTENTS

ACKNOWLEDGMENTS

As with most creative endeavors, more than one person played a part in the creation of this work. My benefactors were family, friends, and mentors whose support, encouragement, pointers, and constructive criticism led to the publication of this book. I am, however, particularly grateful to Clifton Yearley, Mitchell Franklin, William Greiner, Ellen DuBois, A. J. Slavin, and Samuel S. Rabkin, who read the manuscript and offered thoughtful advice, and to Lillian Williams, who was always on hand with a word of encouragement. I am also indebted to Joan Sant, who very professionally typed the manuscript and read it for clarity and style. The important chore of proofreading was taken on by Joan Sant and Gertrude Sant. For this I offer special thanks.

INTRODUCTION

I.

By 1850 a self-conscious women's rights movement, as distinguished from isolated acts by feminist individuals, had become a vocal force in American political life. Traditionally the rise of this movement has been explained as "an offshoot of the agitation against slavery,"[1] which had served as "the means of entry into American political life of a vast number of women who organized, attended and chaired meetings, prepared agenda, made motions, debated issues, [and] circulated petitions...."[2] To support this theory, it has been pointed out that the "founders of the women's rights movement were all abolitionists,"[3] who, when "in the 1830's began to organize to free the slave-,... learned the politics of agitation for human rights."[4] In sum, the traditional approach to the question of the origin of the women's rights movement holds that "[a]s some women tried to change the world, they changed themselves."[5]

Central to the substantiation of this traditional theory is the alleged impact of the World Antislavery Convention held in London in 1840. It has been described as the "really decisive factor...in the total development of the American woman's rights movement...."[6] "The rejection of the women delegates," one historian argued, was "vital for the organization of a political woman's movement *separate* from the antislavery movement [since] nothing succeeds in raising a rival like exclusion."[7] Agreeing with this viewpoint, another historian contended that the "point at which the antislavery movement turned into the woman's rights movement came in 1840 at the World Antislavery Convention where several dozen American women, among them Lucretia Mott and Elizabeth Cady Stanton, who had traveled across three thousand miles of ocean to attend were refused seating because of their sex."[8] Because of this outrageous exclusion, yet another historian concluded that "Mrs. Stanton and Mrs. Mott decided it was time to fight for the right to work for abolition and for other rights of women as well."[9] More specifically, the traditional approach dates the origins of organized nineteenth-century feminism with the first Women's Rights Convention held in Seneca Falls, New York, in 1848. Thus some historians have claimed that this convention was precipitated in 1840 by the rejection of seasoned political activists who had already developed a profound sensitivity to human rights.[10] Yet no historian has adequately explained the eight-year lapse between the World Antislavery Convention and the Seneca Falls Convention.

Perhaps the virtual consensus[11] among historians of nineteenth-century feminism can be explained by an overwhelming reliance on the same primary source, the six-volume *History of Woman Suffrage*.[12] The first volume of this source was published in 1881. It is a collection of papers compiled and edited with commentary by three of the feminist movement's most outstanding leaders: Elizabeth Cady Stanton, Susan B. Anthony, and Matilda Joslyn Gage. Traditionally historians have trusted these women to write their own history. An example of this tendency is the editorial note introducing a reprint of the Stanton-Anthony-Gage account of the World Antislavery Convention in a book of selected readings on women in American life. The reading was strategically placed in a section entitled "Feminism and Reform." The editorial note reads

> The massive, six-volume *History of Woman Suffrage* is an exhaustive account and analysis of the suffrage movement by three of its outstanding leaders. They identify the World Anti-Slavery Convention of 1840 as the first great turning point in the evolution of women's rights movement. A great debate arose at that conference when the English and French delegates refused to seat female delegates from the United States even though the women were duly certified representatives of the American Anti-Slavery Society. The American Society preceeded to lodge a formal protest with the convention officials. But the incident convinced some women that their position was no more secure than that of the slaves whose cause they were championing and that the time had come for an independent feminist campaign.[13]

Tempting as it is to let the participants of the movement tell their own story, it is not enough. The question of the origins of American feminism is too crucial to be left to one source. Too many questions remain unanswered. Foremost among these questions are the following: If abolitionism caused feminism, what caused abolitionism? Why did the abolitionist movement come when it did? Why not sooner? Or later? One must also ask: If the outrage felt by Stanton and Mott by exclusion from the World Antislavery Convention of 1840 was severe enough to "cause" the calling of the Seneca Falls Convention of 1848, why was there an eight-year delay? If reforming spirits lead to other reforming spirits, what convinces reformers that it is time for a change? Why did American life need to change? To what new economic circumstances did outmoded intergender social relations need to accommodate themselves?

The answers to these questions are not to be found in most historiographical literature. Yet some historians recognized that such questions are troublesome. William O'Neill, a social historian, candidly admitted that, "No one can speak with certainty of the reasons why women emerged in the early nineteenth century as a distinct interest group."[14] Indicating his dissatisfaction with traditional interpretations of the origins of feminism, O'Neill warned that:

knowing that libertarianism is infectious does not help us appreciate why specific groups make certain responses at particular times. Why, for example, did women wait for more than a century after the American Revolution before asking that the Declaration of Independence be applied to them as well as to men?[15]

Augmenting this lack of certainty was the fact that advancement of women's position had not followed an ever upward progression. Rather, as O'Neill pointed out, "Medieval woman enjoyed a considerable freedom.... [F]or noblewomen positions of great authority were not unusual, and even lower class women enjoyed substantial economic opportunities in certain crafts and trades."[16] O'Neill noted that some English women had the right to vote as late as the eighteenth century and were never specifically excluded from the franchise until 1832.[17] Thus O'Neill's observations raised the question of why it was that "by the early nineteenth century women, especially married women, possessed few legal or political rights of their own."[18]

Mary Beard, a feminist historian of the second quarter of the twentieth century, in her ground-breaking work, *Women as Force in History*, [19] was concerned with similar observations of the uneven course of female progress. She blamed Sir Edward Coke and Sir William Blackstone, two English jurists and legal text writers, for distorting the facts of the law of married women's status and causing such distortions to be mistaken as the true state of the law.[20]

Mary Beard cannot be too strongly commended for studying the history of law rather than merely assuming the law was forever the same until the women's rights movement changed it. Because of her approach, some light can be shed on why the women's rights movement came when it did, that is, after Coke and Blackstone had divested women of formerly existing rights. Moreover, Beard must be praised for the reasons she chose the history of law as the subject matter of her inquiry. Other historians merely accepted the feminists' own story of the origins of feminism, but Beard reasoned that the origins of feminism could best be determined by examining what the feminists were trying to accomplish. She noted that "American feminists have long laid emphasis on the alleged subjection of women by law.... "[21] For that reason she chose the history of women's legal status as the subject of her special attention.[22]

Despite the merits of Beard's breakthroughs, her work has some deficiencies. First, she overstated her theory. Beard believed that the idea of women's historic subjection is a myth originating with the nineteenth-century feminists themselves.[23] Although the history of women's legal status has been uneven, it would be a mistake to dismiss as a myth the fact that women have generally occupied a lower status than men. Beard tried to establish her theory that women historically had not been a subject class by arguing that they had equity as well as law.[24] But she failed to develop equity's shortcomings. As Leo Kanowitz, a professor of law, demonstrated in his work *Women and the Law: The Unfinished Revolution*,[25] the institution of the wife's equitable separate estate suffered from many deficiencies.

In the early days of American law, some states had no court of chancery. Often, where they existed, those courts had limited jurisdiction. The result was that no forum was available to which a wife could apply for recognition or enforcement of her rights to a separate equitable estate. Second, if a husband or his agent could manage to reduce a wife's [property rights] without resorting to a court of equity, no occasion would arise for a court to condition its aid upon the making of an appropriate settlement for the wife and family. Third, equitable relief was not a reality for women of limited financial means or limited education and intellect. In many respects the concept of the wife's separate equitable estate was designed to assist the rich who were troubled lest the property they had transferred to their daughters would fall into the hands of undeserving husbands.[26]

Nineteenth-century feminists, according to Beard, cited William Blackstone's *Commentaries on the Laws of England*[27] as authority for this so-called mythmaking. Beard surmised that this occurred because the feminist readers did not understand that when Blackstone spoke of married women's disabilities "in law," he meant only under the common law. Thus Blackstone, according to Beard, was commenting on only a married woman's status apart from acts of Parliament, private contracts, equity, and any other source of law or custom, but feminists mistakenly thought he was dealing with all law.[28] She attributed this overemphasis on the misleading account given by Blackstone to the fact that "few [men] were well trained in the technicalities of the law,"[29] and "[l]egal training was not available to women."[30] Moreover, this myth was taken seriously since, Beard argued, Blackstone actively attempted to, and succeeded in, deceiving lawyers and laymen of both sexes,[31] because he was in fact hostile toward modification of the common law by legislation or equity.[32] As evidence of Blackstone's bad faith, Beard pointed to the fact that Blackstone neglected to show "how the [common-law] disabilities of married women, in respect of their property, could be and were frequently nullified by uses, trusts, and other arrangements which were valid and enforced in equity."[33]

Beard's analysis is open to some criticism. In Blackstone's depiction of married women's status, he may have overemphasized the common-law treatment; however, he did not totally neglect to deal with women's status in equity or that body of law administered by chancery, an ecclesiastical court, and referred to as *civil law*. Blackstone did declare that "[b]y marriage, the husband and wife are one person in the law."[34] However, he also made some qualifying remarks. "In the civil law," Blackstone explained, "the husband and wife are considered as two distinct persons."[35] Consequently, Blackstone fairly pointed out, they "may have separate estates, contracts, debts, and injuries: and therefore, in our ecclesiastical courts, a woman may sue and be sued without her husband."[36] Furthermore, although Blackstone was widely read, other descriptions of married women's property and status were known, too. Other treatises on law in general and on the law of married women's property in particular were available and read. Elizabeth Cady Stanton, the daughter of a judge, was well studied in the law. She read the works of James Kent and Joseph Story as well as Blackstone[37] and, along with all but one of her sisters, married into the legal profession.[38] In addition to Stanton, Lucy Stone, another nineteenth-century feminist, demonstrated a knowledge of all aspects of the law of married women's property. Her famous alternative marriage contract is evidence of a knowledge of the distinction between law and equity that went unnoticed by Beard. By point 3 of this "contract," drawn more for its political fuel than for its protection to the parties, Stone specifically rejected the trust and marriage settlement and demanded ownership of all separate property by married women as a legal right.[39]

In short, Beard's analysis is ambiguous. On the one hand, she accounted for the feminists' deception by Blackstone as a product of their ignorance of the law. On the other hand, she admitted their use of his doctrines because the "chance for oratory was irresistible."[40] Despite the ambiguity of Beard's analysis, the questions she raised were crucial and the approach she took to understand them was basically sound. More likely than not, at least some feminists, notably Elizabeth Cady Stanton, whose father was a judge and husband was a lawyer, were in fact well informed on legal matters. Consequently Beard's refusal to take this feminist's own account of the origins of the women's movement at face value was correct. Her implication that feminists used Blackstone for political purposes and her suggestions that legislation and equity were also important factors in the history of women's legal status[41] must be reckoned with by historians of feminism.

One historian who attempted to deal with the questions raised by Beard was Keith Eugene Melder. A historian of the origins of the feminest movement, Melder understood the historic importance of the changes in women's legal status wrought by the revision of property law. He suggested that these changes were one of the major factors in the inauguration of the nineteenth-century women's rights movement. He found it significant that "[t]he married women's property act was passed [in New York State]...more than three months before Mrs. Stanton stood before the little congregation at Seneca Falls to announce that man had made women 'civilly dead,' that he has taken from her all right in property..."[42]

Clearly influenced by Beard, Melder shared her ambiguous treatment of the evidence. After citing Beard's analysis of Blackstone's impact, Melder accepted her conclusion. He found it "not surprising that Blackstone represented *the law* to most feminists."[43] On the other hand, Melder noted that Blackstone's assertions "provided an ideal focus for polemical attacks"[44] even as "the law was growing distinctly more liberal with respect to women."[45]

Melder was correct to make use of the hints left him by Beard. He was also correct to question the conventional starting point of the majority of the works treating the history of the women's rights movement. Rather than beginning with 1840 or 1848, Melder chose to concentrate on the "hazy years preceding." Moreover, Melder pointed out that "Elizabeth Cady Stanton's massive compilation, the *History of Woman Suffrage,* has been the basic source for all works dealing with American feminism, but Mrs. Stanton, who was converted to the cause in 1840, devotes only a few pages to the *Preceding Causes* of women's rights agitation."[46]

Furthemore Melder wisely distrusted historical literature coming "from the pens of feminists."[47] After several years of research into the precise origins of the women's rights movement, he decided that "changes in women's lives and activities between 1800 and 1840 . . . contributed directly to the movement for women's emancipation."[48] He found much historical evidence "suggesting that the status of American women had actually been undergoing a profound transformation for decades preceding the movement dedicated to women's emancipation."[49]

Melder was concerned with the critical question of what caused reform in women's status and the impact of a hitherto almost exclusive reliance by historians on the history written by the participants themselves. He pointed out

The historian is thus confronted with a paradox; the feminists explained and justified their attacks on traditional practices by pointing at the injustices of these practices; at the same time many participants in the movement had taken advantage of new opportunities available for the sex, and new attitudes toward woman's role in society. Reformers are seldom aware of the dimensions of reform: regarding themselves as the instruments of change, as the active opponents of the status quo, they often assume that social institutions do not change, except when attacked by organized crusades dedicated to reform. In their voluminous writings, their records and correspondence, the femininsts assumed that their battle arose out of a sudden realization of injustice, and that only through a campaign against their oppressors could American women be freed.[50]

Melder believed that too much reliance on feminists' feminist history resulted in a misunderstanding of the origin of feminist reform. On the contrary, he discovered that "to some extent the movement itself grew out of changes in women's legal status, in their economic and occupational positions, and in the values and attitudes which governed their status in society."[51] Thus he rejected the "older view that agitation for women's legal rights itself brought 'emancipating' legislation."[52]

Melder's work was written in 1964. At that time he concluded that the passage of Married Women's Property Acts ranked high among the changes in women's legal status out of which the women's movement grew.[53] But he unhappily noted that "this important subject has never been investigated by a modern scholar."[54] Consequently he could relate only a "brief and necessarily superficial account."[55]

Since 1964, however, several studies of the Married Women's Property Acts have been made by legal scholars. One of the most comprehensive of these studies is *"The Married Women's Property Acts,"*[56] by Kay Ellen Thurman.

Her study is divided into two parts: the Married Women's Property Acts and the social system, and the Married Women's Property Acts and the legal process. The social institutions Thurman examined were the family and the market. The scope of her research spanned all fifty states from the date of adoption of their first married women's property provision to the present. Because of its sheer scope and breadth, this study is clearly an important research tool. Yet its weakness lies in the fact that little attention is paid to the effect of the acts on the nineteenth-century feminist movement or of the movement on the acts. Moreover it lacks a close analysis of any one state, leaving the impression that the forces behind passage of the Married Women's Property Acts were identical in each state. The process of legal change resulting from an interaction of private disputes, judicial decisions, and further legislation is missing from Thurman's work. Instead, the reader is left with broad generalizations supported only by citations to isolated cases.

In 1972 a Symposium on the Law School Curriculum and the Legal Rights of Women was held at New York University Law School. At that symposium John D. Johnston, Jr., professor of law at New York University, delivered a paper, subsequently published as an article, entitled *Sex and Property: The Common Law Tradition, The Law School Curriculum, and Developments Toward Equality*.[57] At the outset Professor Johnston must be commended for his observation that private law can affect public power and that "concepts of ownership and power are directly and inseparably linked."[58]

After discussing married women's property rights under the feudal common law and in equity, Johnston tried to determine the nature of the reform wrought by the Married Women's Property Acts. "[R]ather than a coordinated and unified effort to replace 'male supremacy' with equality as the guiding principle in determining the legal status of marital partners," he observed that the reform consisted of "only a series of piecemeal changes in the marital property laws of the various states affected."[59] After examining nineteenth-century treatises, Johnston concluded that "[a]lthough each liberalization of the law contributed to the emancipation of married women, such could not have been the legislators's primary motivation."[60] However, he offered no explanation of what possibly could have motivated the legislators in the various states he had examined superficially. Even his closer examination of the New York Married Woman's Property Act of 1848 shed little light on questions of why the act was passed when it was. Also unclear to Johnston was the question of why judicial interpretations of the Married Women's Property Acts were so restrictive.[61]

Although answers to these important questions were not forthcoming, Johnston's work insightfully raised them while correctly faulting the legal profession for not having framed them sooner for law school property classes. Johnston provided a *point d'appui* for subsequent scholarship. His disappointment caused by the "paucity of published research regarding the development of new marital property law in several states,"[62] the absence of which makes it "foolhardy to offer any generalized hypotheses about the underlying motivation and philosophies that shaped the married women's legislation,"[63] presents an invocation to scholars that should not be ignored. So, too, does his observation that our knowledge is too limited for us to be able "to reach firm conclusions about the interplay between the legislative and judicial processes with respect to the early married women's legislation."[64]

Johnston's and Thurman's works shed little light on the questions of the relation of the Married Women's Property Acts to the nineteenth-century feminist movement and of the movement to the acts. But these questions were the main focus of a 1973 work by Richard Rapaport entitled "Relationship of the Women's Movement to the Passage of the Married Women's Property Acts in the Mid-Nineteenth Century."[65] However, this work suffers from the same deficiencies as prior historical works about the origins of the women's rights movement. That is, it relies too much on pens of the participants. The work also oversimplifies the process into primarily a single dynamic: interest group (feminists) putting pressure on legislatures and the latter responding positively to such pressure. More seriously, it ignores the fact that the Married Women's Property Acts were part of a long series of legislation that aimed to defeudalize real property and convert it to an item of commerce thereby offering no explanation for the enigma of why these acts were passed with so little resistance while the demand for suffrage by the feminists met such great opposition.[66] In some cases, particularly with regard to the earliest bills, feminist agitation slowed the passage of the acts because of the fear of changes in intergender relationships,[67] while it was their appeal to commercial necessity that ensured their passage.[68] Furthermore the methodology of Rapaport's work intensifies these difficulties. Because the author emphasized the passage of the later acts and did not investigate the reasons for and impact of the first act, his pressure-group explanation acquires more apparent logic than it deserves. Consequently the reader learns only of the impact of feminism on the acts and nothing of the impact of the acts on feminism.

II.

The instant work in a general sense explores the origins of the women's rights movement. Specifically, it is a study of the origins and impact of the Married Women's Property Acts in New York State. As such it is an answer to the questions left open by Melder and Johnston. These acts had a profound impact on the status of women. In addition, they gave impetus to the women's movement by providing a focus for presuffrage demands. Moreover, the polemics that could be used in feminist activities were secure from any serious opposition as long as they related to the removal of common-law disabilities. Almost everyone realized that these disabilities were feudal and out of place in an increasingly commercial America. Yet once married women's property rights were won, it was a logical step to demand the suffrage—the recognized instrument for the protection of property.

The intellectual or jurisprudential origins of the Married Women's Property Acts is one subject of Part One of this book. Ultimately these New York acts can be traced to the codification movement—an early nineteenth-century movement, led by forces hostile to feudal English common law, aiming to defeudalize, reform, and codify law on the method of the French civilians. Economic and political origins are a part of this movement, too. The codifiers were more often than not Francophiles and Anglophobes who favored legislative, or what was to them democratic lawmaking, while opposing judicial lawmaking. Politically they aligned themselves with the Puritan, French, and American revolutions and with the philosophers of the Enlightenment. Their economic goal was to make land more accessible to greater numbers of persons by making it more easily alienable, that is, more transferable, or by transforming it into an ordinary item of commerce.

The interaction between statutes and cases within New York State, the state whose law reform provided the nation with a model for change, was not thoroughly explored by Thurman, Johnston, Rapaport, or other scholars. Significantly, therefore, the study of the important question of what the Married Women's Property Acts provided and how the courts interpreted them is the subject of Part Two. It is important to note that the subject matter of Part Two is more than a lawyer's legal history. Although drawn chiefly from statutes and cases, the evidence is presented within a social and economic context. It goes beyond a discussion of whether the courts were liberally or narrowly construing the acts, inquiring instead: what was really the crux of this dispute before the court? With this goal, the material not only answers Johnston's plea for data concerning the restrictive judicial interpretation, but also becomes a tool for understanding the social and economic impact of the changes in married women's property on the lives of real people—the parties before the court. Particular attention is placed on the procedural posture or on identifying the party who is invoking the doctrine of expanded married women's property rights and for what reasons. It is important that despite the radical change in family law brought by these acts, few husbands and wives were ever before the courts as adverse parties. More often they were joined in a common legal struggle against a creditor or employer.

As is always the problem with the use of appellate decisions as evidence, little can be discovered about conflicts settled out of court. The extent to which husband-wife relations were strained by the changes is impossible to know if disputes between them never reached the courts. Also impossible to know is the extent to which a husband could coerce his wife into renoucing her new property rights in his favor. Nevertheless, the evidence is of value in determining the kinds of issues raised and the way the courts put gloss on the statutes as an adjunct to their principal goal of rendering justice. This line of inquiry also contributes to an understanding that the process of legal change encompasses more than pressure groups and legislatures.

In a broad sense this is a study of legal process valuable to the student of both law and social change. In a narrow sense it is a tool for understanding marital property. Its history of struggle between common law and civil law suggests possibilities for further changes consistent with that history. Perhaps a community property system of equal partners is in store for the future,[69] especially as notions of alimony become increasingly disfavored. Finally, it is of value in understanding the origins of the nineteenth-century women's movement as something more than an outgrowth of abolitionism. Although not the subject of this study, it might nevertheless be surmised that abolitionism and feminism shared common roots. Rather than the one "causing" the other, the desire to commercialize property law might be said to have precipitated both of them, making the reforming spirit of the Enlightenment easier to embody into law.

III.

Thomas Jefferson maintained that the world belonged in *usufruct* to the living.[70] "Usufruct" being a property law term indicating a right to use or enjoy the property of another. It can be argued that the world Jefferson envisioned included the world of civil society as well as the world of politics. That is, enlightened reformers, such as Jefferson, viewed as necessary changes in the realm of private law as well as in public law—in the law of property as well as in the form of government. Consequently such reformers saw the need to defeudalize property law by making real property into an item of commerce owned outright by the living rather than tied by feudal traditions to those already in their graves. As such, land would be easier to sell and therefore to buy. Without such a reform, political freedom, won by the American Revolution, it was believed, would be less meaningful. The political reform would occur without abolishing prerevolutionary social relations such as *primogeniture*, whereby the first son inherits everything, slavery, and married women's civil incapacity.

In short, it is the thesis of this book that the movement to reform the law of property though legislation that would sweep feudal relations and concepts out of the law of real property initiated the first American women's rights movement. More precisely, this work demonstrates that the enlightened legislative reform, which was centered in New York State after the American Revolution, triggered the demand for female suffrage and not vice versa as prior scholarship suggested.

Although the passage of the Married Women's Property Acts can unquestionably be linked to the need to make property law conform to the realities of a commercial economy rather than to the fictions of the feudal order, abstract economic forces were not the only factors related to the passage of these acts. As noted above, politics played a role as the Francophile republicans achieved support for their mission of attaining a democratic legal system.

Also corollated to the passage of the acts that began the process of female emancipation was the very significant role that fathers were to play. This role was significant because although postrevolutionary America might have been ready for the idea that property law ought to be defeudalized, the notion that the time was right for female emancipation was not so widely accepted. As the story of the passage of the New York Married Women's Property Acts enfolds in the following pages, it will be demonstrated that these acts passed not in an attempt to modernize family law along with property law, but despite the fact that legislators wanted to leave the law of husband and wife unchanged. Although there is no doubt that some of the men of power who worked for the passage of these acts were advocates of equal rights for women, it is also clear that most of those whose support ensured passage of the first New York Married Women's Property Act were not profeminist in their thinking. Since it cannot be demonstrated that the ideology of feminism created the necessary consensus among legislators, what then united all ideologies into one camp when the legislative role was called in the spring of 1848? Among the factors that comprise the answer to this question was the existence of something common to men of all ideologies. The significant something that both profeminist and antifeminist legislators had in common was their daughters.

Notes

1. P. SMITH, DAUGHTERS OF THE PROMISED LAND 104 (1970) [hereinafter cited as P. SMITH, DAUGHTERS].

2. *Id.* at 111.

3. A. KRADITOR, THE IDEAS OF THE WOMAN SUFFRAGE MOVEMENT 1890-1920, at 1 (1965) [hereinafter cited as A. KRADITOR, IDEAS].

4. A. SINCLAIR, THE EMANCIPATION OF THE AMERICAN WOMAN 39 (1966) [hereinafter cited a A. SINCLAIR, EMANCIPATION].

5. A. SCOTT, THE AMERICAN WOMAN 88 (Spectrum ed. 1971) [hereinafter cited as A. SCOTT, AM. WOMAN].

6. R. RIEGEL, AMERICAN FEMINISTS 21 (1963) [hereinafter cited as R. RIEGEL, AM. FEMINISTS].

7. A. SINCLAIR, EMANCIPATION 57 (emphasis in original).

8. P. SMITH, DAUGHTERS 111.

9. A. KRADITOR, IDEAS 2.

10. *See, e.g.,* E. FLEXNER, CENTURY OF STRUGGLE 71-73 (1968); A. KRADITOR, IDEAS 1-3; G. LERNER, THE WOMAN IN AMERICAN HISTORY 82 (1971); R. RIEGEL, AM. FEMINISTS 21-22; A. SCOTT, AM. WOMAN 88; A. SINCLAIR, EMANCIPATION 57-58; P. SMITH, DAUGHTERS 111-13.

11. The word *consensus* is qualified by the word *virtual*, because occasionally a historian can be found who notices that the problem is somewhat more complex. *See, e.g.,* M. BEARD, WOMAN AS FORCE IN HISTORY (Collier paper ed. 1971) [hereinafter cited as M. BEARD, FORCE]; K. Melder, The Beginnings of the Women's Rights Movement in the United States 1800-1840 (1964) (unpublished Ph.D. dissertation in Yale University Library) [hereinafter cited as K. Melder, The Beginnings]; W. O'NEILL, EVERYONE WAS BRAVE (Quadrangle ed. 1971) [hereinafter cited as W. O'NEILL, EVERYONE]; W. O'NEILL, THE WOMAN MOVEMENT (Quadrangle ed. 1971) [hereinafter cited as W. O'NEILL, WOMAN MOVEMENT].

12. 1 E. STANTON, S. ANTHONY, & M. GAGE, THE HISTORY OF WOMAN SUFFRAGE (1881-1922).

13 A. SCOTT, WOMAN IN AMERICAN LIFE 61 (1970).

14. W. O'NEILL, WOMAN MOVEMENT 15.

15. W. O'NEILL, EVERYONE 4.

16. W. O'NEILL, WOMAN MOVEMENT 17.

17. *Id.*

18. *Id.*

19. M. BEARD, FORCE.

20. *Id.* at 87-132. *Cf.* Fenberg, *Blame Coke and Blackstone*, 34 WOMEN LAWYERS J. 7 (1948).

21. M. BEARD, FORCE 9.

22. *Id.*

23. *Id.* at 88, 155.

24. *Id.* at 155.

25. L. KANOWITZ, WOMEN AND THE LAW (1969).

26. *Id.* at 39 (footnotes omitted).

27. W. BLACKSTONE, COMMENTARIES ON THE LAWS OF ENGLAND (4 vols. 1765-69) [hereinafter cited as BLACKSTONE].

28. M. BEARD, FORCE 92-93.

29. *Id.* at 94.

30. *Id.* at 125.

31. *Id.* at 97.

32. *Id.* at 90-96.

33. *Id.* at 97.

34. 1 W. BLACKSTONE 430.

35. *Id.* at 432.

36. *Id.*

37. E. STANTON, EIGHTY YEARS AND MORE: REMINISCENCES 1815-1897, at 50 (Schocken paper ed. 1971) [hereinafter cited as E. STANTON'S REMINISCENCES].

38. *Id.*

39. Blackwell & Stone, *Marriage Document* (1855), *reprinted in* A. KRADITOR, UP FROM THE PEDESTAL 149-50 (1968):

> We protest especially against the laws which give to the husband: . . . The sole ownership of her personal, and use of her real estate, unless previously settled upon her, or placed in the hands of trustees. . . .

40. M. BEARD, FORCE 127.

41. *Id.* at 133-55.

42. K. Melder, The Beginnings 27-28.

43. *Id.* at 28 (emphasis in original).

44. *Id.*

45. *Id.* at 29.

46. *Id.* at x.

47. *Id.*

48. *Id.* at xii.

49. *Id.* at 6.

50. *Id.* at 5.

51. *Id.* at 6.

52. *Id.* at 30.

53. *Id.* at 23-30.

54. *Id.* note 46, at 24. Actually quite a good study had been conducted in 1960. *See* E. Warbasse, The Changing Legal Rights of Married Women, 1800-1861 (1960) (unpublished Ph. D. dissertation in Radcliffe College Library).

55. *Id.*

56. K. Thurman, The Married Women's Property Acts (June 6, 1966) (unpublished LL.M. thesis in University of Wisconsin Law Library).

57. Johnston, *Sex and Property: The Common Law Tradition, the Law School Curriculum, and Developments Toward Equality,* 47 N.Y.U.L. Rev. 1033 (1972) [hereinafter cited as *Sex and Property*]. *See also* Younger, *Community Property, Women and the Law School Curriculum,* 48 N.Y.U.L. Rev. 211 (1973), for a discussion of the elements of sex discrimination that existed in community property systems.

58. *Sex and Property* 1039.

59. *Id.* at 1061-62.

60. *Id.* at 1062.

61. *Id.* at 1069.

62. *Id.* at 1062.

63. *Id.*

64. *Id.* at 1069.

65. R. Rapaport, Relationship of the Women's Movement to the Passage of the Married Women's Property Acts in the Mid-Nineteenth Century (May 25, 1973) (unpublished manuscript in Stanford Law School Library).

66. *See generally,* Walker, *The Legal Condition of Women,* in The Golden Age of American Law 316, 318 (C. Haar ed. 1965), which Professor Johnston cited as support for the suggestion that advocacy of marital property reform did not also connote support for the then developing suffrage movement. *Sex and Property* note 120, at 1062.

67. Fear of changes in the family helped defeat a proposed constitutional provision for married women's property rights at the 1846 New York Constitutional Convention.

68. *See, e.g.,* Note, *Married Women Acts,* 14 Am. L. Rev. 788, 789 (1880), where a nineteenth-century female commentator analyzed the growth of married women's legislation:

> Indeed, it would be very curious if, after the rapid development of the modern system of commercial law, it should not be found that the immense mass of facts and extensive complications of interests which render the new laws of commerce possible and necessary, did not in some important ways affect the pecuniary interests of the wives of men whose business, whether small or great, belongs to the vast scale of changes of a commercial age.

69. *Cf.* Foster & Freed, *Marital Property Reform in New York: Partnership of Co-Equals?* 8 Family Law Quarterly 169 (1974); Glendon, *Matrimonial Property: A Comparative Study of Law and Social Change,* 49 Tul. L. Rev. 21 (1974).

70. Letter from Thomas Jefferson to James Madison (Sept. 6, 1789), *reprinted in* 15 Papers of Thomas Jefferson 392 (Boyd ed. 1958).

PART ONE

The Passage of the First New York Married Women's Property Act

Fog everywhere. Fog up the river, fog down the river. Fog on the Essex marshes, fog on the Kentish heights. Fog creeping into the cabooses of collier-brigs; fog lying out on the yards and hovering in the rigging of great ships; fog drooping on the gunwales of barges and small boats....

The raw afternoon is rawist, and the dense fog is densest, and muddy streets are muddiest, near that leaden-headed old corporation, Temple Bar. And hard by Temple Bar, in Lincoln's Inn Hall at very heart of the fog, sits the Lord High Chancellor in his High Court of Chancery.

CHARLES DICKENS,
BLEAK HOUSE (1853)

The legislature... has in good degree adopted the policy of the Roman and French law in constituting the wife a feme sole as to the property owned by her at the time of her marriage, and that given or devised to her during coverature.

JOHN BRIGHT,
A TREATISE ON THE LAW OF HUSBAND AND
WIFE AS RESPECTS PROPERTY (1850)

The law of the status of women is the last vestige of slavery. Upon their subjection it has been thought rests the basis of society; disturb that, and society crumbles into ruins. By the married women's property acts, the first blow has been struck. The cheek of the idol has fallen to the ground; the thunder is silent, and the earth preserves its accustomed tranquility. The huge idol will sooner or later be broken to pieces.

6 THE AMERICAN LAW REVIEW
73 (1871-72)

1 THE LEGAL STATUS OF MARRIED WOMEN BEFORE THE MARRIED WOMEN'S PROPERTY ACTS

I. The Status of Married Women at Common Law: Feudal Vestiges in Social Relations

Before 1848 the legal status of married women in New York State was bifurcated: one status for married women at common law and another, in equity.[1] At common law, the husband and wife were regarded as one person, and marriage resulted in the "civil death" of the woman.[2] Out of this fictional "unity" and "death" arose all of the common-law disabilities of married women.[3] Such common-law restrictions were harsh, but their impact was alleviated somewhat in that they did not extend to a married woman's equitable separate estate and obligations arising from this separate estate.[4]

Under common law, a married woman was unable to contract with her husband[5] or with third parties.[6] Similarly she could not convey real or personal property to or from her husband or acquire or dispose of property from third persons without her husband's consent.[7] Since a married woman was unable to contract or convey, it followed that she could not at law engage in trade or business[8] or sue or be sued without *joinder* of ("joining or unifying with") her husband.[9] However, a wife could engage in trade if she had the consent of her husband, for such consent implied authority for her to contract debts in conducting trade or business.[10] Also at common law, as a consequence of the fiction of unity, the marriage of a male debtor to his female creditor extinguished the antenuptial debt.[11] The theory underlying these rules was that by marriage, the husband and wife became one person and one could not owe oneself money.

Complementing the wife's disabilities was a correspondingly increased legal capacity for the husband at common law. Within the feudal hierarchy, each person had a particular status, and the common law expressed the various status relationships. At common law, the husband had the status of head and master of his household. A wife was required to render obedience, domestic service, and submission to her husband—duties analogous to the relation of a vassal to his lord.[12] Feudal law incorporated these status relationships into its law of real property. Ultimate ownership of land was in the king. Interests in land were parceled out in exchange for loyalty and military service upon demand. All land had to be held by someone capable of rendering such services.

The principle of seisin facilitated the operation of this feudal system. *Seisin* meant possession of land with an intent to claim a freehold interest in it in exchange for performing the feudal duties of homage and fealty. To facilitate this system of landholding in exchange for military protection, it was necessary for the land to be possessed or seized by a male. Thus common law gave a husband a freehold estate in real property held by his wife so the seisin would be in a male who could perform the required feudal duties. Whether the wife's interest arose before or after marriage, the husband was entitled to the possession, use, and income of her estate[13] for the duration of the marriage and their joint lives.[14] In accordance with this right to possession, the husband could bind the property by contract for the duration of his estate,[15] or he could grant, convey, or mortgage this interest.[16] At common law, if children were born, the husband became entitled to *tenancy*, or holding, of a deceased wife's land for the rest of his life; if there were no children, the husband's interest in his wife's estate ended with her death.[17]

Even though no military necessity existed, at common law, a wife's *personalty*, or movable property, was treated the same as her realty.[18] That is, all personal property owned by the wife before marriage was placed, or vested, absolutely in the husband's possession, as was any property acquired by her after marriage.[19] Likewise, the husband was entitled to his wife's choses in action, personalty, with a right of possession in the future, as long as he reduced them to possessions subject to the jurisdiction of the court whose function it was to ensure that he provide for his wife under the "doctrine of settlement for the wife's equity."[20] This doctrine compelled the husband to make a suitable provision for his wife and her children.

The common-law relationship between husband and wife had ramifications for relationships with third parties as well. At common law, the husband was responsible for all debts of the wife, which she contracted with third parties,[21] even if these obligations were incurred before marriage.[22] Because of the wife's incapacity to be sued without joinder of her husband, at common law, a husband was jointly liable for her *tortious*, that is, wrongful, injurious acts, toward third parties, whether committed by her before or after marriage. If the wife's *tort*, or legal wrong, was committed in the presence of the husband or by the husband and wife jointly, common law held the husband alone liable.[23] As a corollary to these principles, the common law also held the husband's estate *jure uxoris* in the real property of his wife.[24] A *jure uxoris* estate was an estate entitling the husband to the possession, use, income, and usufruct of his wife's property for the life of them both and was, therefore, liable for his debts.[25] Since he also owned absolutely his wife's personal property, such property could also be held liable.[26] Even a wife's paraphernalia, or her apparel and ornaments, could be claimed by her husband's creditors after his death.[27]

The disabilities incident to, or restrictions associated with, the legal status of women at common law were particularly debilitating in a commercial society. Common law had evolved to meet the needs of a feudal society in which one's legal status was in effect an expression of a property relationship between political superiors and inferiors within the feudal hierarchy. The reason for the system was military necessity in a landed economy.

It is a truism that once the reason for a rule ceases to exist, the remaining naked rule becomes irrational. So it was with the rules comprising the common-law status of married women, whose irrationality became increasingly clear as the economy became more commercial. The first inroads against the feudal legal status were made through equity, and further changes by legislation were to be extensions of equity principles.

II. The Status of Married Women in Equity: The Legal Foundations of Bourgeois Social Relations for Married Women

Before the 1848 Married Women's Property Act was passed in New York State, the common-law disabilities of married wommen were relieved by equity, which allowed a married woman an equitable separate estate.[28] Equity courts also provided for a married woman through a doctrine that created a right to a suitable allowance or settlement from her choses in action, interests in a decedent's estate, and other personalty that at common law became the property of her husband when he reduced them to his possession.[29]

The "equitable doctrine of a married woman's separate estate" was developed to correct the injustice and to alleviate the hardship created by the common-law merger of the legal beings of husband and wife that resulted in his legal rights in her property.[30] Under this doctrine of a married woman's equitable separate estate, property could be set aside for the separate use of a married woman, and if this were done, she was not burdened with common-law disabilities with respect to this property.[31] In such property the married woman had an equitable title while another person had a legal title. This other person was a trustee who was under a fiduciary duty to use the property for her benefit alone. This duty was enforced by chancery. If not restrained by the terms of the trust instrument, the beneficiary, or married woman, could act as a *femme sole*, or single woman, in the disposition of this equitable separate estate by sale, gift, or devise "gift by will".[32] Moreover, the married woman, and not her husband, was entitled to the sale, exclusive use, rents, and profits of this equitable separate estate.[33] Such an equitable estate could be established by the husband himself, who would voluntarily divest himself of his wife's estate and hold it as trustee for her separate use or beneficial enjoyment;[34] or a wife's separate estate could also arise by a conveyance from a third party directly to the married woman for her sole and separate use.[35]

A major advantage of this equitable mitigation of the strict common law was that a husband could not be compelled by equity to reduce his wife's choses in action to his possession in order to pay his creditors,[36] and a wife's separate equitable estate,[37] as well as any property settled on her by equity, for support of herself and family, was similarly secure from her husband's creditors.[38] Instead, the wife herself was free to encumber her separate estate as long as she was not specifically restrained by the terms of the trust instrument.[39] Moreover, a contract of a wife to a husband could be enforced in equity to the extent that repayment of the loan could be made out of the wife's separate property,[40] and the repayment of a loan made by a wife to her husband out of her separate property was enforceable in equity.[41] Significantly, in such a case, the wife's title to money or property received from the loan was good as against the creditors of her husband.[42]

Along with equity's disregard of the fictional unity of husband and wife, courts of this branch of jurisprudence gave full recognition to transactions or contracts between husband and wife when they were fair, just, and equitably ought to have been enforced.[43] Likewise, due to the disavowance of this common-law fiction, each spouse could sue or be sued by the other.[44] Moreover, equity recognized the validity of contracts with third persons if they were for the benefit of, or were a charge upon, the wife's separate estate, or if they did not conflict with the trust instrument.[45]

Thus equity did indeed mitigate the strict law of married women's property. The Married Women's Property Acts of 1848 and 1849 codified this law. The question then is: if equity so operated, why were these acts passed? The answer points out the limitations of equity as a method of law reform. Equity was a judge-made law. Its source was not in the people, but in the Crown. Since American law reformers, who were to pave the way for the passage of the Married Women's Property Acts, were Anglophobes as well as Francophiles, to them a system of law reform that was founded on judicial discretion emanating from the king's prerogative was destined to be challenged, despite positive inroads made against the feudal content of the common law. In contrast, American law reformers favored reform by legislatures that received their powers from the people. To this end, they looked to the codification of law by the French republicans as a model for reform.

Notes

1.

> As distinguished from equity law, [common law] is a body of rules and principles, written or unwritten, which are of fixed and immutable authority, and which must be applied to controversies rigorously and in their entirety, and cannot be modified to suit the pecularities of a specific case, or colored by any judicial discretion, and which rests confessedly upon custom or statute, as distinguished from any claim to ethical superiority.

BLACK'S LAW DICTIONARY 346 (4th ed. 1951).

[Equity is a] system of jurisprudence collateral to, and in some respects independent of, "law"; ... the object of which is to render the administration of justice more complete, by affording relief where the courts of law are incompetent to give it.... It is an elaborate system of rules and process, administered ... by distinct tribunals, [termed "courts of chancery,"] and with exclusive jurisdiction over certain subjects.

BLACK'S LAW DICTIONARY 634 (4th ed. 1951).

2. *See, e.g.,* Whiton v. Snyder, 88 N.Y. 299 (1882).
3. *See, e.g.,* Bennett v. Bennett, 116 N.Y. 584, 23 N.E. 17 (1889).
4. *See, e.g.,* Yale v. Dederer, 18 N.Y. 265 (1858).
5. *See, e.g.,* Winter v. Winter, 191 N.Y. 462, 84 N.E. 382 (1908).
6. *See, e.g.,* Dickerson v. Rogers, 114 N.Y. 405, 21 N.E. 992 (1889).
7. *See, e.g.,* Hunt v. Johnson, 44 N.Y. 27 (1890).
8. *See, e.g.,* Abbey v. Deyo, 44 Barb. 374 (Sup. Ct.) *aff'd*, 44 N.Y. 343 (1871).
9. *See, e.g.,* Bennett v. Bennett, 116 N.Y. 584, 23 N.E. 17 (1889).
10. *See, e.g.,* Cropsey v. McKinney, 30 Barb. 47 (N.Y. Sup. Ct. 1859).
11. *See, e.g.,* Power v. Lester, 23 N.Y. 527 (1861).
12. *See, e.g.,* Coleman v. Burr, 93 N.Y. 17 (1883).
13. *See, e.g.,* Hiles v. Fisher, 144 N.Y. 306 (1895).
14. *See, e.g.,* Bradley v. Walker, 138 N.Y. 291, 33 N.E. 1079 (1893).
15. *Id.*
16. *See, e.g.,* Jones v. Patterson, 11 Barb. 572 (N.Y. Sup. Ct. 1852).
17. *Id.*
18. *See, e.g.,* DeBrauwere v. DeBrauwere, 203 N.Y. 406, 96 N.E. 772 (1911).
19. *See, e.g.,* Whiton v. Snyder, 88 N.Y. 299 (1882).
20. *See, e.g.,* Westervelt v. Gregg, 12 N.Y. 202 (1854).
21. *See, e.g.,* Mygatt v. Coe, 124 N.Y. 212, 26 N.E. 611 (1891).
22. *See, e.g.,* Lennon v. Eldred, 65 Barb. 410 (N.Y. Sup. Ct. 1873).
23. *See, e.g.,* Vanneman v. Powers, 56 N.Y. 39 (1874).
24. *Jure uxoris* technically translates "in right of a wife." BLACK'S LAW DICTIONARY 990 (4th ed. 1951). Actually it meant that a wife did not lose title to real property formerly held by her solely in fee, but her husband acquired an interest known as *jure uxoris*, entitling him to sole possession and control during marriage.
25. *See, e.g.,* Van Duzer v. Van Duzer, 6 Paige 366 (1837).
26. *See, e.g.,* Westervelt v. Gregg, 12 N.Y. 202 (1854).
27. *See, e.g.,* Whiton v. Snyder, 88 N.Y. 299 (1882).
28. *See, e.g.,* Yale v. Dederer, 18 N.Y. 265 (1858).
29. *See, e.g.,* Westervelt v. Gregg, 12 N.Y. 202 (1854).
30. *See, e.g.,* Yale v. Dederer, 18 N.Y. 265 (1858).
31. *See, e.g.,* Martin v. Martin, 1 N.Y. 473 (1848).
32. *See, e.g.,* Yale v. Dederer, 18 N.Y. 265 (1858).
33. *See, e.g.,* Martin v. Martin, 1 N.Y. 473 (1848).
34. *See, e.g.,* Ryder v. Hulse, 24 N.Y. 372 (1862).
35. *See, e.g.,* Yale v. Dederer, 18 N.Y. 265 (1858).
36. *See, e.g.,* Westervelt v. Gregg, 12 N.Y. 202 (1854).
37. *See, e.g.,* Shirley v. Shirley, 9 Paige 361 (1841).

38. *See, e.g.,* Smith v. Kane, 2 Paige 302 (1830).
39. *See, e.g.,* Yale v. Dederer, 18 N.Y. 265 (1858).
40. *See, e.g.,* Gardner v. Gardner, 22 Wend. 526 (1839).
41. *See, e.g.,* Savage v. O'Neil, 44 N.Y. 298 (1871).
42. *Id.*
43. *See, e.g.,* Hendricks v. Isaacs, 117 N.Y. 411, 22 N.E. 1029 (1889).
44. *See, e.g.,* Moore v. Moore, 47 N.Y. 467 (1872).
45. *See, e.g.,* Yale v. Dederer, 18 N.Y. 265 (1858).

2 THE ROLE OF EQUITY IN LAW REFORM

I.

The role of equity in law reform was first pointed out by Aristotle.[1] For Aristotle equity was that form of justice that is a "correction of legal justice."[2] He saw that strict law becomes unjust when it is deemed universal, that is, applicable to every set of circumstances. About some things, Aristotle contended, "it is not possible to make a universal statement which shall be correct."[3] Thus the error is not in the law or in the legislator but in "the nature of the thing"[4] toward which the law must be applied. When such an unusual case arose, Aristotle thought it was the role of the jurist to use "sympathetic judgment"[5] and refrain from applying the letter of the law formulated by legislators who are "unable to define things exactly, and are obligated to legislate as if they held good always which in fact only holds good usually."[6] That judgment is equitable.

Aristotle likened the need for equity to the need for the decree. Both are used when it is "impossible to lay down a law"[7] and the rule must adapt itself to the facts of the particular case.[8] In fact, these two methods of legal modification were, in the initial stages of English equity, the same thing. When the maxims of common law became so rigid that strict conformance to their letter would not result in a just end, persons so adversely affected would address petitions to the king in council who was the "Fountain of Justice." When the king had more cases than time or desire to consider them, he turned the petitions over to the chancellor who issued a decree to do justice in the name of the king. Such was the origin of equity as a body of law separate from common law.[9] The chancellor was the king's secretary of state and under him were clerks, the highest of whom were ecclesiastics.[10]

The process of which such developments were a part was summarized in 1861 by Sir Henry Maine, a nineteenth-century legal historian and scholar of comparative law, in his *Ancient Law*,[11] a classic of legal literature written from the perspective of the historical school of jurisprudence. Maine's thesis was that societies progress in historical sequence through periods of legal development. These periods Maine characterized as dominated by legal fiction, equity, and legislation—instrumentalities of legal change. Law reform through legal fiction, equity, and legislation, Maine believed, culminated in a steady advancement from status to contract in private legal relationships.[12] Status was a feudal concept, contract a bourgeois device.

Although the absolute accuracy of Maine's thesis, in light of his bias in favor of nineteenth-century contract law, is open to question,[13] his study of Roman equity remains among the best. According to Maine, the Romans had a dual conception of law. First there was the *civil law*, or the law that a people enact. Second, there was the law that natural reason appoints for all mankind. This was called the *law of nations*, because all nationals were subject to its jurisdiction. Its rules were to be dictated by the principles of equity expounded by the praetor.[14] The praetor stood in Roman law midway between the juris consul and the legislature. That is, this official had a limited right to reform the law. His function was to determine in what cases the letter of the law was to give way to natural justice or equity. Such discretion was limited by public opinion, for he was viewed as the keeper of the conscience of the Roman people. If he did not exercise his discretion to modify the law within the conscience of the people, he was subject to dismissal from office.[15]

The function of this law of nature, and thus of equity, was to maintain legal jursidiction over commercial relations with foreigners who were excluded from Roman civil law.[16] This inclusion of foreigners within a legal system helped maintain domestic tranquility by ensuring that dispute settlement would have a peaceful alternative to armed conflict. The substance of this law of nature was defined by those elements of the various foreign people's civil laws that were common to "all of the nations," that is, to a large number of separate races.[17] Maine traced the ideas of this jurisprudence to Greek Stoic philosophers.[18] In line with this philosophy, the praetor issued edicts to restore technical legal anomalies to the way nature had governed man in his primitive state.[19]

Maine proposed that the law of nations and the law of nature "touch and blend through Aequitas or Equity."[20] This result obtained because the Roman juris consuls, to justify the improvement of their jurisprudence by the praetor, used the Greek doctrine of a "Natural state of man—a Natural society—anterior to the organization of commonwealths governed by positive laws."[21]

The Greco-Roman concept of equity reached England by the reign of Henry II (1154-89).[22] This was the same period in which new royal courts were created especially to administer the equitable prerogative.[23] However, equity did not reach its full significance until the Tudor age. At this time the chancellor administered law in the same way as did the Roman praetor, that is, as a method of construing the law using procedures different from common law. These new procedures created a new jurisprudence, the body of law that was adjudicated in chancery.[24] That jurisprudence was equity. But equity had another meaning as well. It still meant the judicial principle expressed by Aristotle that allowed for substantive modification of the letter of the law by applying its spirit to the irregular case. This principle allowed for great discretion in the hands of the chancellor.

The role of equity as an agent of law reform was noted by Maine.[25] A.K.R. Kiralfy, professor of law at King's College in London, subsequently refined

Maine's work.[26] In 1966 Kiralfy pointed out that equity, as an agent of law reform, could devise its own concepts and principles. Thus devices such as the trust, the injunction, and a remedy for breach of contract, specific performance, were developed.[27] Equity has a dual role in law reform, according to Kiralfy. One is procedural, the other substantive. However, procedure and substance are not always clearly severable. The very invention of procedures such as the trust, injunction, and specific performance in fact become substantive changes. A married woman who has property held in trust does in fact have property.

In 1966 the bifurcation of equity was traced by Stuart E. Prall[28] to the distinction between Greek and Roman concepts of equity. *Greek equity* was expounded by Aristotle. It was a method of judicial reform of substantive law by injecting justice to ensure the correct, although not the legal, result. On the other hand, *Roman equity* was a method of procedural change. Prall determined that the Roman idea eventually triumphed in England. Equity in England, unlike on the continent, became merely that body of law adjudicated in chancery.

Both the Greek and the Roman concepts of equity play a part in reforming strict law, which is unjust if applied to all cases. Prall attributed to Christopher St. Germain, a sixteenth-century barrister of the Inner Temple, the formal attempt in England to bring about a reconciliation between the two systems.[29] St. Germain had a thorough knowledge of canon law, common law, and equity.[30] He used his knowledge of canon law as the basis for his two *Dialogues Between Doctor of Divinity and a Student of the Common Law,* [31] published in the early sixteenth century. In this work he dealt with Greek equity in terms of "an equity derived upon certain statutes."[32] This meant that the general principles of a statute could be extended by the jurist to include certain exceptional cases that the framers, had they anticipated them, would have reasonably provided for in the original statute. Therefore the jurist was conceived to be at liberty to expand the statute by analogy. Thus Greek equity came to mean both the exclusion of a particular case from the letter of the law, when the result would be unjust or not within the spirit of the law, *and* the expansion of the strict law by analogy, to fit a similar, although unprovided-for, case.[33]

Edmund Plowden, another important English sixteenth-century jurist, also applied Aristotle's definition of equity to statutory interpretation, finding part of the jurist's role to be an expander of the statute through the method of supposing that "the law-maker [were] present, and that [the jurist] asked [the legislator] the question... touching the equity then... give... such an answer as... he would have done, if he had been present."[34]

Mitchell Franklin, a twentieth-century legal philosopher, described this bifurcation of equity as "positive" and "negative."[35] Both aspects of equity have a role to play in law reform. *Negative equity* contradicts the existing law in the name of a higher law, what Aristotle would call "correct justice." Only after negative equity has done its job does positive equity come into play. *Positive equity* regards the work done by negative equity as a "fresh starting point" from which "it rectifies, by extension (analogy) the existing law," and "by excluding overthrown, archaic and archaistic legal conceptions when they present themselves unexpectedly for recognition, as well as to deepen or to advance the new policies into new and unanticipated situations."[36]

Following this model, it can be said that equity as an instrument of legal change first acted negatively to block the strict feudal common law that did not allow a married woman to own property. It did this by developing the trust and by the doctrine of a married woman's separate estate in equity, that is, by developing a new procedure. After the new procedure was developed, equity could be used positively. If a married woman is able to hold a separate estate, by analogy or extension, she should be able to contract with respect to that estate. Franklin would agree with Maine that the next stage of law reform is codification of equity by the legislature.[37] The Married Women's Property Acts could be characterized as a codification of those equity principles that had been developed to alleviate effects of the common-law restrictions on married women.

II.

Equity is a Roguish thing, for Law we have a measure know what to trust too. Equity is according to ye conscience of him yt is Chancellor, and as yt its larger or narrower soe is equity. Tis all one as if they should make ys Standard for ye measure wee call a foot, to be ye chancellors foot; What an uncertain measure would this be; One chancellor ha's a long foot another a short foot a third an indifferent foot; tis ye same thing in ye Chancellors Conscience.[38]

If equity acted as it was supposed to, it modified the strict law. The goal was justice. Justice, however, is not the only possible consequence of unfettered judicial discretion. The strict law is a rule, a precedent, a standard, by which to make a decision. The idea of leaving the decision of a case to the conscience of the judge, unhampered by an overbroad rule or precedent, is satisfactory only as long as the judge's idea of justice corresponds to that of the litigants. But ideas of justice vary. This makes law unknowable, not only to the litigant but also to the lawyer, whose job it is to forecast a judicial decision to prevent unnecessary litigation or litigation that is likely to result in the client's defeat. Unknowable law is *ex post facto* (after the fact) and therefore illegitimate. It is all the more illegitimate if the conscience of the judge is filled with religious or political preconceptions that become the standards for decisions and if these standards are contrary to those of the majority of the people. It is not merely the unknowability of the rule of law to be pronounced and a lack of agreement on standards that makes such decisions seem *ex post facto* and illegitimate. The source of these standards is also at issue. The question is:

should the source of such jurisdiction be in the Crown or in the people, that is, in the legislature? This question remained a controversy in prerevolutionary New York.[39]

Notes

1. 5 ARISTOTLE, NICOMACHEAN ETHICS chs. 10 & 11; 6 ARISTOTLE, NICHOMACHEAN ETHICS ch. 22; 1 ARISTOTLE, THE RHETORIC ch. 13 [hereinafter cited as ETHICS; RHETORIC].

2. 5 ETHICS ch. 10.

3. *Id.*

4. *Id.*

5. 5 ETHICS ch. 11.

6. 1 RHETORIC ch. 13.

7. 5 ETHICS ch. 10.

8. *Id.*

9. *See*, Adams, *The Origin of English Equity*, 16 COLUM. L. REV. 87 (1916).

10. 1 F. POLLOCK & F. MAITLAND, THE HISTORY OF ENGLISH LAW BEFORE THE TIME OF EDWARD I 193 (2d ed. 1898).

11. H. MAINE, ANCIENT LAW (Beacon paper ed. 1963) [hereinafter cited as ANCIENT LAW].

12. *Id.* passim.

13. *See, e. g.,* W. FRIEDMANN, LEGAL THEORY 217 (5th ed. 1967); C. FRIEDRICH, THE PHILOSOPHY OF LAW IN HISTORICAL PERSPECTIVE 141 (2d ed. 1963).

14. ANCIENT LAW 41.

15. *Id.* at 54.

16. *Id.* at 44-46.

17. *Id.* at 47.

18. *Id.* at 53.

19. *Id.* at 54.

20. *Id.* at 55.

21. *Id.* at 68.

22. *See* H. RICHARDSON & G. SAYLES, LAW AND LEGISLATION FROM AETHELBERTH TO MAGNA CARTA 71-87 (1966), for a discussion of early English students of Roman law and their scholarship.

23. G. ADAMS, COUNCIL AND COURTS IN ANGLO-NORMAN ENGLAND 202 (1926).

24. Prall, *The Development of Equity in Tudor England*, 8 AM. J. LEGAL HIST. 1, 2-3 (1964) [hereinafter cited as *Tudor Equity*].

25. ANCIENT LAW 24, 27.

26. Kiralfy, *Law Reform by Legal Fiction, Equity and Legislation in English Legal History*, 10 AM. J. LEGAL HIST. 3 (1966).

27. *Id.* at 12-14.

28. *Tudor Equity* 2-3.

29. *Id.* at 3.

30. T. PLUCKNETT, A CONCISE HISTORY OF THE COMMON LAW 279 (5th ed. 1956).

31. *Id.*

32. C. ST. GERMAIN, DOCTOR AND STUDENT 50 (18th ed. 1792).

33. *Accord, Tudor Equity* 4-5.

34. 2 E. PLOWDEN, THE COMMENTARIES 467-68 (1972 ed.).

35. Franklin, *A New Conception of the Relation Between Law and Equity*, 11 PHILOSOPHY AND PHENOMENOLOGICAL RESEARCH 474 (1951).

36. Franklin, *The Ninth Amendment as Civil Law Method and Its Implications for Republican Form of Government*, 40 TUL. L. REV. 486, 494, (1966).

37. Franklin, *Some Considerations on the Existential Force of Roman Law in the Early History of the United States*, 22 BUFFALO L. REV. 69, 79 (1972).

38. J. SELDEN, TABLE TALK ON JOHN SELDEN 43 (F. Pollock ed. 1927).

39. *See* Katz, *The Politics of Law in Colonial America: Controversies over Chancery Courts and Equity Law in the Eighteenth Century,* 5 PERSPECTIVES IN AM. HIST. 257 (1971); Wilson, *Courts of Chancery in the American Colonies*, in 2 SELECT ESSAYS IN ANGLO-AMERICAN LEGAL HISTORY 779 (1909), for detailed accounts of the struggle in New York.

3 OTHER FORMS OF LAW REFORM AND THEIR POLITICAL RAMIFICATIONS

I.

In addition to equity, two other instruments of law reform are widely used. These are legal fictions[1] and legislation. Henry Sumner Maine, writing in 1861, was among the first to point out how these different forms of legal change were interrelated.[2] A.K.R. Kiralfy, as professor of law, King's College, London, England, tested Maine's theory.[3] Kiralfy believed that the type of law being changed dictated which agent of law reform would come into operation. In this respect he differed from Maine who, according to Kiralfy, believed that chronology dictated which method of law reform would dominate at each historical moment. Kiralfy presented Maine as advocating the idea that first legal fictions are developed, and next equity mitigates the law, and then equitable principles are codified.[4]

Kiralfy, disagreeing with a strict chronological approach, demonstrated that in the history of the law of real property, legislation came earlier than fictions and dictated the form these fictions were to take.[5] Not all of the statutory changes were steps toward modernization, however. When the statutes did not operate to enhance the greater alienability, or transferability, of land, which would have made land similar to any other item of modern commerce, legal fiction often came into operation. Kiralfy referred to this as the "cause and effect"[6] order (as opposed to chronological order) of succession of the agencies of "reform."

If one were to apply these concepts to the history of married women's right to convey property, one would discover that fiction preceded legislation, as Maine would have predicted. At common law, a married woman had no power, by her act alone, to convey real property by deed.[7] This was due to the fictional unity of the wife with the husband.[8] Thus one way a married woman could convey her property at common law in New York State was by uniting with her husband in levying a fine or suffering a common recovery.[9] The fine and common recovery were fictions. They were first made unnecessary by statutory reform in the form of the Married Women's Property Acts and later were abolished by statutory reform.[10]

Where Kiralfy's study of legal change reinforces Maine's is more significant than his critique. The relevant point is that law reform took one of these forms. Either the common-law judge could create a fiction to decide a case for which no precedent existed, or the chancellor could make a decision based on his conscience, or the legislature could pass a statute. By the midnineteenth century, debate over which of these forms of legal change should predominate had developed into a political battle. It was a battle with a two hundred-year history, which was begun in England in the days of King James, Sir Edward Coke, and Sir Francis Bacon. The history of the struggle against the prerogative courts resulted in the supremacy of Parliament in England.[11]

II.

The supremacy of the legislature over the domain of lawmaking and law reform, which existed in England, was also to dominate legal and political thinking in America until *Marbury* v. *Madison*[12] was decided in 1803. In this case, Chief Justice Marshall reasserted the theory put forth by Coke that cases and controversies were ultimately to be decided by courts. One explanation for the acceptance of parliamentary supremacy was that historically Parliament was less thought to be a legislature and more often considered the highest common-law court.[13] Thus in the early seventeenth century, when Parliament carried on the struggle, it was as one of the common-law courts. Only later did the theory of parliamentary supremacy become a theory of legislative supremacy over all courts—common-law as well as prerogative courts.

Stuart Prall, a historian of English legal history, suggested that the duality of equity caused much of the controversy over prerogative jurisdiction in seventeenth-century England.[14] Equity was both the substantive law that was adjudicated in the Court of Chancery (e.g., family law, merchant law, trusts) and the judicial principle that allowed judges the discretion to modify, interpret, set aside, or even extend by analogy a law in the name of "reason" or "justice." In the second sense, equity was also practiced in common-law courts. This was the Aristotelian concept of *epieikeia* espoused by Christopher St. Germain, a barrister of the Inner Temple who had a remarkable knowledge of legal philosophy and canon law, in his widely read sixteenth-century work *Doctor and Student*. It was around this point, according to Prall, that the controversy over equity raged.[15]

This concept of equity was in reality judicial lawmaking, something in opposition to the concept of parliamentary supremacy that was the eventual outcome of the struggle Coke led. Coke and the common lawyers eventually joined forces with the parliamentarians. Thus by the end of the seventeenth century, the struggle against the prerogative became a struggle against judicial lawmaking. This occurred partly because one effect of the St. Germain classic was to encourage common-law discretion by the new definition of the principle "the equity of the statute."[16] This meant that judges were able to expand the general principles of a statute beyond the scope of the statute by including within the statute's scope particular unprovided-for cases that presumably would have been covered had the legislators been aware of them, or if they had been conscious of the dictates of reason.[17] This is, however, judicial lawmaking supported by the fiction of the presumed intent of the legislature.

Theodore Plucknett, a historian of English common law, explained the reason for the survival of chancery.[18] Unlike the other prerogative courts, which were fated for doom, chancery was a civil court with a highly developed body of precedents and procedures. It was relied upon by those who were engaged in commerce. If chancery were abolished, much confusion would have resulted. Even the Statute of Uses,[19] passed in 1536 to destroy the trust by turning equitable estates immediately into legal estates, was not successful in obviating the need for chancery. The gentry greatly benefited from uses as administered by chancery because they were able to devise lands more freely than common law allowed.[20] Furthermore it has been suggested that Coke, with a bias toward free trade and economic liberalism, failed in his attempt to take commercial law from the prerogative courts that administered the law merchant, a law based on the Roman law of nations and quite different from the feudal law of real property as administered by the common-law courts,[21] thus making chancery too useful to destroy.

III.

Law reform by means of codification was initially advanced by all branches of the English legal system. In the interest of brevity and certainty, it was proposed in the Parliaments of 1593 and 1597.[22] Even Sir Francis Bacon, the prerogative jurist, was an agent of this movement. He drafted three hundred legal maxims or generalizations from which to begin the legal reasoning process. This was a start toward codification. Coke, too, was a systematizer. His *Reports* and *Institutes* were almost a code. Coke's objective was to draw together bodies of principle from a series of cases.[23] This Coke did, according to Christopher Hill, a scholar of English legal history, with bias toward free trade and economic liberalism.[24] Thus Coke wanted to see feudal tenures abolished[25] and the law merchant made a part of common-law jurisdiction.[26] This was necessary if common-law courts were to maintain control over the legal business of the commercial bourgeoisie. Until this time the prerogative Courts of Chancery and Admiralty had monopoly over the disputes of merchants,[27] a class of increasing wealth and power.

Gerard Malynes, another seventeenth-century law-reform advocate, in seeking to adapt the common law to an increasingly commercial society, argued that law must first become a "science" without "ambiguities and dark sentences."[28] This demystification of the law, Malynes suggested, could be accomplished through codification.[29]

Before this codification was seriously attempted, the common lawyers attempted to usurp jurisdiction. Coke was not alone in this effort. Judge

Hobart warned that "the custom of merchants is part of the common law of this kingdom, of which the [common-law] judges ought to take notice.... "[30] Judge Holt, a century later, agreed that if common law was to be made "the overriding jurisdiction of the realm," it must subsume law merchant.[31] Lord Holt, who presided over the King's Bench from 1689 until 1710, had been a student of Roman law.[32] He carried on the struggle to lay the foundation of modern commercial law.[33]

Coke took the matter of law reform to Parliament after his judicial services were terminated by King James. In the Parliament of 1621 he proposed a whole program of law reform and modernization. He introduced bills against monopolies and in favor of subordinating chancery to the common-law judges.[34] Thus Coke's program for law reform was a continuation of his struggle against the prerogative.[35]

Although Coke clearly favored law reform, he, unlike Malynes, never meant it to include the goal of demystifying law for the layman. He wanted the systematic revision for the jurist only. As Hill pointed out, Coke attributed the confusion in the law to laymen making conveyances, assurances, instruments, and wills without proper legal advice and to acts of Parliament being drafted by laymen.[36] The fact that Coke believed only jurists could know the law is manifested by his statements regarding the mysterious nature of the legal process:

[T]he reason of the law so too our own reason, that we perfectly understand it as our own, and then, and never before, we have such an excellent and inseparable propriety, and ownership therein, as we can neither lose it nor any man take it from us.... The law is unknowable to him that knoweth not the reason thereof.... Reasonableness in these cases belongeth to the knowledge of the law.[37]

By this Coke probably meant discretion. However, it was a discretion based upon judicial reasoning. This reasoning or method was a monopoly. Not only were laymen estranged from legal method, but so, too, was the Crown. Coke declared that "no man out of his own private reason ought to be wiser than the law, which is the perfection of reason."[38] This reason, or "the secrets of the law," could only be developed, according to Coke, through a legal education.[39] Thus when King James asserted his right to use his private reason, which was also the reason of a monarch who by divine right was given reason enough to render justice, Coke disagreed. Although he conceded that the king had natural reason, Coke responded that the law was not based on natural reason but upon an "artificial reason... which requires long study and experience."[40]

Radicals were bound to take Coke's ideas further than he intended. Despite his lack of intent, Coke in fact gave laymen reason to think the law should be demystified and synthesized for them as well as for jurists. Moreover, seventeenth-century religious dissenters believed that any person could know the grace of God without institutions. If anyone could know God's law, surely anyone should be able to know man's laws. If this were not so, the law was needlessly uncognizable. Hence it was argued by William Penn, defendant in the famous trial credited for securing the right to a jury independent of the judge:

[C]ertainly, if the common law be so hard to understand, it is far from being very common; but if the Lord Coke in his Institutes be of any consideration, he tells us, that common law is common right, and that common right is the Great Charter—Privileges.[41]

During the English Revolution, many believed law reform to be the reason the Civil War was fought.[42] They wanted the mysteries of the mumbo-jumbo men (i.e., lawyers and judges) made available in their vernacular, and they wanted local courts, trials by laymen, an elected judiciary, and codification.[43] Their aim was to have law without lawyers.[44] To John Warr, a seventeenth-century radical and legal-reform advocate, the aim was to

free the clear understanding from the bondage of the Form and to raise it up to Equity, which is the substance itself. For though the dark understanding may be restrained or guided, yet the principled man hath his freedom within himself, and walking in the light of Equity and Reason (truly so called) knows no bounds but his own, even Equity.[45]

Bacon, the spokesman for the royal prerogative, also advocated demystification and thought that the beneficiaries of law should not be the practicing lawyer; rather the end of law is "the happiness of the citizens."[46]

Stuart Prall[47] examined the writings of both the learned scholars and the unlearned pamphleteers who attacked or defended the English legal system during the English Civil War. He concluded that the future of both the common law and the prerogative courts was at issue, the common law for its inadequacies and the prerogative courts for their Romanism. He, like Hill, pointed out that one reason for the extension of the powers of the prerogative courts was the failure of feudal common law to keep pace with the changes in economic and social relations.[48] Equity was a necessary ingredient of a mature legal system as were devices such as the *use* or the *trust*, two devices, whereby one person uses the land while another legally owns it, Prall explained that the increased resort to the use or trust to escape feudal obligations connected with landholding, or to escape the requirements of *primogeniture*, whereby the first son inherits everything, and make it easier to transfer land, had been one of the most notable causes for the expansion of chancery jurisdiction. Thus common law was vulnerable because of its feudalism.

Chancery, although functional in the new economy, was subject to hatred, especially by the Puritans, because of its similarity to Roman canon law and because of the king's political control over the workings of these courts.[49] After the Court of Star Chamber, the Court of Requests, and the High Commission were abolished, chancery, the lone survivor of the prerogative courts, became the target of attack. Prall contended that "Chancery was to become the embodiment of all that was considered evil not only in prerogative and monarchy, but in the common law and in the entire legal system."[50]

Prall demonstrated his theory with thorough documentation.[51] He presented evidence of the inadequacies of the law. Law reform was demanded to solve the new problems of an increasingly commercial society. Debt collection and the conveying of property were the problems. A legal system based on feudal relations was the cause of these problems. Pamphleteers, such as William Leach, advocated the end of entails,[52] or limitations on inheritance, to solve both problems. Since debtors could not dispose of entailed estates, their creditors went unpaid.

The pamphleteers also attacked chancery. Although chancery provided for easier conveyance of real property through deeds, this prerogative court proved unsatisfactory in policing secret and fraudulent deeds. The pamphlet called for a system to register titles to stop the practice of selling estates to more than one buyer.[53] Attendant upon these reforms was a threatened legal profession. The goal was to have a legal system simple enough for litigants to plead their own cases.[54] The result was a counterattack by jurists and lawyers who were members of the propertied classes.[55]

More than a hundred years later, these issues were destined to be raised again by analogous parties in the New World.[56] Equity was needed to bring relief from the feudalism of common law; yet chancery was associated with royal interference and unfettered judicial discretion. The American Revolution was fought and the New York State legislature struggled against both chancery and common law for hegemony over the reforms that had to be made to adjust the law to the commercial economy. The result was that New York women were to be both agents and beneficiaries of the struggles among common law, equity, and legislation. The history of the struggle must be told so Mary Beard's contention that married women had equity at their disposal and were therefore not a subject class under the law can be successfully challenged. Several questions must be answered: If equity for women existed, why did the events of 1848 occur? Why were the Married Women's Acts passed, and why was the Seneca Falls Convention called?

Notes

1. A legal fiction is:

   An assumption or supposition of law that something which is or may be false is true, or that a state of facts exists which has never really taken place-
   . . . these assumptions are of an innocent or even beneficial character and are

made for the advancement of the ends of justice. They secure this end chiefly
by the extension of procedure from cases to which it is applicable to other
cases to which it is not strictly applicable....
BLACK'S LAW DICTIONARY 751 (4th ed. 1951).

Maine used the term fiction in a wider sense than this. He employed the term

to signify any assumption which conceals, or affects to conceal, the fact that a
rule of law has undergone alteration, its letter remaining unchanged, its
operation being modified...the fact is...that the law has been wholly
changed; the fiction is that it remains what it always was.

H. MAINE, ANCIENT LAW 25 (Beacon paper ed. 1963) [hereinafter cited as
ANCIENT LAW].

2. ANCIENT LAW 24.
3. Kiralfy, *Law Reform by Legal Fictions, Equity and Legislation in English Legal
History*, 10 AM. J. LEGAL HIST. 3 (1966) [hereinafter cited as Kiralfy].
4. *Id.* at 3-4.
5. *Id.* at 8.
6. Kiralfy 9.
7. Martin v. Dwelly, 6 Wend. 9 (1832).
8. *Id.*
9. Bool v. Mix, 17 Wend. 119 (1842); Martin v. Dwelly, 6 Wend. 9 (1832); Jackson
ex dem. Clowes v. Vanderhyden, 17 Johns 167 (1820) 1 A. L. R. 1080.
The fine was:

An amicable...agreement of a suit...by which...lands...become, or are
acknowledged to be, the right of one of the parties.
BLACK'S LAW DICTIONARY 759 (4th ed. 1951).

A common recovery was:

A mode of conveying lands by matter of record....It was in the nature and
form of an action at law, carried regularly through, and ending in a *recovery*
of the lands against the tenant of the freehold; which recovery, being a
supposed adjudication of the rights, bound all persons, and vested a free and
absolute fee-simple in the recoverer.
BLACK'S LAW DICTIONARY 347 (4th ed. 1951).

10. The Married Women's Property Acts allowed a married woman to convey
directly so the fiction was unnecessary. The fiction was finally abolished by N.Y. REAL
PROP. LAW §241 (McKinney 1896).
11. For a history of this struggle, *see* C. BOWEN, THE LION AND THE THRONE: THE
LIFE AND TIMES OF SIR EDWARD COKE 359 (1957). C. HILL, INTELLECTUAL ORIGINS OF
THE ENGLISH REVOLUTION (1965), especially note ch. 5 *Sir Edward Coke—Myth-
Maker* [hereinafter cited as HILL, ORIGINS OF REVOLUTION]. C. HILL, SOCIETY AND
PURITANISM IN PRE-REVOLUTIONARY ENGLAND ch. 11 *From Oaths to Interests*

(Schoken ed. 1964). Philips, *The Last Years of the Court of Star Chamber*, in TRANSACTIONS OF THE ROYAL HISTORICAL SOCIETY (1939). T. PLUCKNETT, A CONCISE HISTORY OF THE COMMON LAW (5th ed. 1956) [hereinafter cited as PLUCKNETT]. R. USHER, THE RISE AND FALL OF THE HIGH COMMISSION (1913).

12. 1 Cranch 137, 2 L.Ed. 60 (1803).

13. *Cf*, F. MAITLAND, *Introduction to Memoranda de Parliamento, 1305*, in SELECTED HISTORICAL ESSAYS OF F. W. MAITLAND 52 (1957).

14. Prall, *The Development of Equity in Tudor England*, 8 AM. J. LEGAL HIST. 1, 3 (1964) [hereinafter cited as Prall, *The Development of Equity*].

15. *Id*. at 6.

16. *Cf*. Franklin, *A New Conception of the Relation Between Law and Equity*, 11 PHILOSOPHY AND PHENOMENOLOGICAL RESEARCH 201 (1955).

17. Prall, *The Development of Equity* 5.

18. PLUCKNETT 195, 299, 685.

19. 27 Hen. 8, c. 10 (1536).

20. Prall, *The Development of Equity* 10.

21. Wagner, *Coke and the Rise of Economic Liberalism*, 6 ECONOMIC HIST. REV. 30 (1938).

22. HILL, ORIGINS OF REVOLUTION 230.

23. *Id*. at 232.

24. *Id*. at 233.

25. *Id*. at 235.

26. *Id*. at 237.

27. *Id*.

28. Cited in HILL, ORIGINS OF REVOLUTION 239 from G. MALYNES, *Consuetudo, vel Lex Mercatoria* (1626).

29. *Id*.

30. Cited in HILL, ORIGINS OF REVOLUTION 239.

31. Cited *id*. at 240.

32. PLUCKNETT 300.

33. *Id*. at 246, 664, 669.

34. HILL, ORIGINS OF REVOLUTION 243.

35. *Id*. at 247.

36. *Id*. at 250-51.

37. Quoted *id*. at 252.

38. Quoted *id*. at 253-54.

39. *Id*. at 254.

40. *Id*.

41. Trial of William Penn and William Mead, 6 STATE TRIALS 951 (1670).

42. *See* C. HILL, THE WORLD TURNED UPSIDE DOWN; RADICAL IDEAS DURING THE ENGLISH REVOLUTION 217 (1972).

43. *Id*.

44. *Id*. They also wanted law without lawyer's fees.

45. Quoted *id*. at 220.

46. Cited in HILL, ORIGINS OF REVOLUTION 263.

47. S. PRALL, THE AGITATION FOR LAW REFORM DURING THE PURITAN REVOLUTION 1640-1660 (1966) [hereinafter cited as S. PRALL, AGITATION FOR LAW REFORM].

48. *Id.* at 4.
49. *Id.* at 5-7.
50. *Id.* at 11.
51. *See e.g., id.* at 50-78.
52. An *entail* was:

> A fee . . . limited to . . . certain classes of issue, instead of descending to all the heirs.
> BLACK'S LAW DICTIONARY 624 (4th ed. 1951).

53. S. PRALL, AGITATION FOR LAW REFORM 60-62.
54. *Id.* at 62.
55. *Id.* at 67 and 145-48.
56. Actually these issues surrounding unfettered judicial discretion were vibrant even in colonial days. *See* Nelson, *The Legal Restraint of Power in Pre-Revolutionary America*, 18 AM. J. LEGAL HIST. 1, 10 (1974).

4 THE IDEOLOGY OF LAW REFORM THROUGH LEGISLATION

Roscoe Pound, jurist and legal historian, rhetorically posed and answered the question,"What did legislation achieve for American law in the height of legislative leadership from the Revolution to the Civil War?"[1]

For the most part it did away with survivals in seventeenth-century English law which had not been eliminated in the wake of the Puritan Revolution, and for the rest formulated what jurists of the school of natural law and courts of equity had worked out and made ready for legislative adoption...It abrogated rules and institutions which had come down from feudal England. It pruned away restrictions on free individual activity which spoke from the relationally organized society of the Middle Ages and had ceased to be applicable to society organized on the basis of free individual competitive self-assertion. What it reshaped, as for example in the Married Women's Acts, was mostly reshaped to the patterns laid out by equity.[2]

If the legislative reform movement, by reshaping the law of married women's legal status as laid out by equity jurisprudence, brought about the acts that set off the women's rights movement, it is important to examine the law reform movement in depth. This can best be accomplished by scrutinizing first the ideas of the codification movement's theoreticians and then changes in the law that resulted from their activities. The goal of the codifiers was defeudalization through legislation. Because their goal was antithetical to feudalism, they believed the common law, which was feudal in method, should not be the instrument used to modernize the content of law. In fact, the bench and bar feared the impact of defeudalization—the demystification of the legal system—with a resulting threat to their vocational existence.[3]

I. The Contributions of Jeremy Bentham

If the intellectual roots of legislative supremacy can be traced in part to the Puritan Revolution and in part to the French Enlightenment, these sources can be said to merge in the philosophy of Jeremy Bentham. Bentham is the acknowledged originator of the ideal of legislation as a scientific method of law reform in the Anglo-American common-law world.[4] Intending to eradicate the evils of judge-made law, his theme was double-edged—simultaneously intended to attack judicial discretion and to advance the theory of scientific law reform.

To Bentham, "discretion of a judge" and "common law" were interchangeable expressions.[5] The method he advanced as an alternative to common law was codified law.[6] Because Bentham believed that what had been referred to as "legal reasoning" was in fact judicial lawmaking, the alternative to common law that he proposed was codification and what was to be named the "civil-law method." According to Bentham, judicial lawmaking occurs when law becomes outmoded and the judge, while deciding a case, perceives the anachronism and the need to mitigate the harsh effect of the outmoded rule by the use of fictions. To Bentham such "reasoning" is illegitimate and not truly law.[7] He characterized fictions as an assumption of arbitrary power and a stealing of legislative power by the judiciary. Thus fictions were politically dangerous weapons in Bentham's eyes, for by the use of this technique of "willful falsehood," judges could usurp this power openly, since the delusion produced by the fiction prevents the usurpation of power from being made lucid and more easily thwarted.[8]

To Bentham, one of the most dreadful of all fictions was the "fictitious person ... called the common law."[9] This dread stemmed from Bentham's conception of the nature of law. As a positivist, he believed law was a command. For law to be legitimate, therefore, it must be a command from a legitimate source of power, and it must not be ad hoc or *ex post facto.* For Bentham the legitimate source of the command is the legislature that represents the people and the proper form of the command is a formulated statute, the point of which is sufficiently visible.[10] Since the judge is not a legislator, and would not admit to being one, Bentham believed, he creates a fictitious legislator called the common law to disguise the fact that the command he issues with every decision is actually his own decree.[11] This procedure Bentham characterized as "sham law" and, therefore, illegitimate despite the pretext offered to justify it, "that it is but a copy of a proposition ... delivered on some former occasion by some other judge...."[12]

Bentham's hostility toward common law was aroused because it manifested three truly discretionary and arbitrary features: (1) uncertainty,[13] (2) an *ex post facto* character,[14] and (3) unknowability by the common people who, nevertheless, are subject to the presumption that they know the law.[15] He described it as "law which is uncertain in its essence—law without beginning and without end—law by which animals are governed ... disgraceful to men."[16] He equated a judge making common law to a man making law for his dog:

When your dog does anything you want to break him of, you wait till he does it, and then beat him for it. This is the way you make laws for your dog: and this is the way judges make law for you and me.[17]

In place of this *ex post facto* and illegitimate common law, Bentham proposed a complete code written as clearly and simply as possible.[18] He thought that, "Whatever is not in the Code of Laws, ought not to be a law.

Nothing ought to be referred either to custom, or to foreign law, or to pretended natural law, or to pretended law of nations."[19] Thus Bentham's attack would also apply to equity as a method of law reform, since, as Henry Maine explained, equity's source was in the law of nations.

Although Bentham insisted on a complete and written law, he did acknowledge that it was not possible for the legislator to foresee every case that could arise.[20] Nevertheless, Bentham maintained that it was possible to codify every "species" of case that might occur.[21] In this way the codification comes "before events instead of following them."[22] Thus because the general principles of behavior are recorded before the facts, and because the source of those principles are in the representative legislature, the code and decisions based on it are legitimate.

The role of the judge as interpreter of the code was narrowly defined by Bentham. The introduction of any unwritten law, that is, judge-made law, should be strictly forbidden. According to Bentham's blueprint:

If a new case occur, not provided for by the code, the judge may point it out, and indicate the remedy; but no decision of any judge, much less the opinion of any individual, should be allowed to be cited as law, until such decision or opinion has been embodied by the legislator in the code.[23]

Thus Bentham was adverse to applying *stare decisis*, or the use of precedent provided by prior analogous decisions, to the code. He stated that:

If any commentary should be written on this code . . . all men should be required to pay no regard to such comment; neither should it be allowed to be cited in any court of justice in any manner whatsoever, neither by express words, nor by any circuitous designation.[24]

The judge's function, under Bentham's plan, is never to tell what he thinks the code means, but only what the "legislator had in view and intended to express, but failed to express. . . . "[25] and do this with "as little explanation or comment as possible."[26] If the substance of the law required revision, the legislature should do it at least every 100 years. This, Bentham hoped, would keep the terms and expressions from becoming obsolete and too remote from the common people who should always have a cognizable code.[27]

II. The Contributions of William Sampson

The Enlightenment's influence on the codification movement also can be seen in the work of William Sampson, a rebellious Irish Jacobean lawyer. Sampson wrote extensively in *The Northern Star*, a biweekly newspaper founded in Belfast in 1792 to spread the reform ideas of the French and American Revolutions.[28] Viewing legal obscurity as a major threat to popular government, his theme became the interrelations of legal demystification and democracy. In a 1794 satire, widely read on both sides of the Atlantic, he demonstrated the harsh consequences of criminal laws that both the accused and the jury could not know or understand. He portrayed a trial in which a hurdy-gurdy was charged with criminal libel for playing the politically inflammatory "ça Ira." Because the jury was exposed to the mystification caused by procedural formalities, injustice resulted.[29]

Sampson's thinking was most important in demonstrating that the ambiguity of law could be used as a political weapon. His satire effectively showed the way the ambiguous principles of oral common law could be transformed, shifted, or veered at the discretion of the judge who thereby gained the power of legislator while in the office of jurist. Just as the strict law could be alleviated in the name of equity or justice, the law could also be intensified by a politically partisan judge.

The evils of judicial legislation could be perceived by its opponents with particular clarity in times of political dissent. The rebellion in Ireland probably sharpened Sampson's perceptions. His work as an attorney for dissenters accused of libel, sedition, and treason was more activist and less theoretical than Bentham's. Soon he was branded a rebel himself and forced into exile. Sampson's exile status was destined to bring him to New York State, but before his arrival in America, he was a refugee in France. While there he became familiar with the French Civil Code and the jurists who supported it. In the code system, Sampson saw an answer to the problems of the ambiguities and uncertainties inherent in a system of judicial precedent.[30]

Sampson arrived in New York in 1806 and was admitted to the bar. While in America he waged a constant campaign for a national code, both through pamphlets[31] and in arguments before courts on behalf of his clients.[32] His ideal national code was to originate in the legislature, which represented the people. The code was to replace precedent as the source of any decision made by a court. Judicial lawmaking would be ended by this code, Sampson believed, because judges would no longer be permitted to rely on *stare decisis*, which Sampson felt had resulted in arbitrary, highly personal, inconsistent, and unpredictable decisions. Sampson saw the precode decisions as personal, because the outcome could not be predicted by the litigant. It was personal, because where the facts of a case were unique, that is, without precedent, the judge had been able to render a decision without legislative standards. Moreover the case with unique facts was the one most often before the courts, because only in a unique case would the parties endure the expense and trouble of litigation. Cases in fact similar to precedental ones would rarely be litigated. Faulting the entire system, Sampson proposed a new system that more closely suited postrevolutionary society.

Sampson's arguments in support of this new system reflected an Enlightenment optimism, a desire to make the American Revolution—the

Enlightenment's political expression—complete, and an intense Anglophia.[33] His *Anniversary Discourse*,[34] delivered before the Historical Society of New York in 1823, exemplified his arguments and the ideas behind them. In an expression of undaunted, almost religious, faith in "natural reason," science, and progress, he attacked the common law for being a "pagan idol,"[35] a "mysterious essence,"[36] and an "antique altar... worshipped by ignorants and superstitious voltaries."[37] As such it embodied "artificial reason"[38] or "judicial astrology"[39] not suited to the realities of the new scientific age.[40] Common law, he argued, was developed for barbarians in a time of universal darkness.[41] To advance the interests of a new commercial bourgeoisie, what was needed was a code of "written reason"[42] for an age of commerce, science, and progress.[43]

For Sampson the American Revolution meant the birth of democracy through the deaths of feudalism and its corollary, aristocratic privilege. As a warm supporter of the Revolution, Sampson, not satisfied with feudalism's death, sought also the demise of the common law, which he regarded as a prerevolutionary atavism. He advocated the codification of the new nation's private law as the way to make the postrevolutionary legal system into "a model of judicial polity equal to that already exhibited in our political institutions."[44] Until common law was replaced by a code, he declared, Americans would be "still dragging at their heels the fragments of their broken chains."[45]

Sampson, in advancing his position, was always ready to "twist the lion's tail." He argued that common law was "made for us" rather than "by us" and was made by a foreign people.[46] As such, it was "imported law,"[47] unfit for "our own independent condition."[48] Because of its feudal rules and procedures, it was, he believed, unsuited for a commercial state.[49] He hoped that with codification we would no longer import this foreign law since "English judges... are not fit persons to legislate for us."[50] All English judges, he claimed, were "appointed by a king, and he is the fountain of their justice...."[51] Thus the law made by these judges should not become the basis of American law.

Sampson's plan was to discard English reports as "rubbish" and to replace them with an unambiguous, regulated, and systematized form of American substantive law supplemented with a plainly and intelligibly written statement of the general principles and standards on which it ought to depend. *Stare decisis* would be replaced by these general standards in order that

[p]articular cases will not then be resorted to instead of general law. The law will govern the decisions of judges, and not the decisions the law. Judgments will be *ligibus non exemplis*. And it will not be necessary that at least one victim should be sacrificed to the making of every new rule, which without such immolation would have no existence.[52]

Thus Sampson aimed to eliminate judicial lawmaking and its consequent evil, *ex post facto* uncertainty.

Sampson, like Bentham, refused to acknowledge the legitimacy of legal fictions as a method of law reform. He claimed that his method would also end the system of judicial lawmaking through fictions, as a result of which litigants are subjected to "precedents composed before the party was in being, and which, in no one single instance, conform to the truth insomuch, that he who dares to tell his case according to the simple and honest truth, will for that very reason, if for no other, fail in his suit."[53]

Sampson's *Anniversary Discourse* was widely reported in contemporary newspapers and periodicals.[54] This and other articles and correspondence by him intensified the popular interest in law reform.[55] One result of this increased interest was the commissioning of those who were to revise New York's statutes in the 1820s and 1830s.[56]

III. The Contributions of James Humphreys

In Part II of his 1827 work, *Observations on the Actual State of the English Laws of Real Property; with Outline for a Systematic Reform*,[57] James Humphreys, a prominent nineteenth-century English real estate lawyer, suggested remedies for what he considered to be a defective state of property law. Inspired by Bacon's scientific method and the French Civil Code, he advocated framing an entire system of the laws of real property.[58] Humphreys, like Bentham before him, was hostile to fictions and like David Dudley Field, a codifier who was to follow him, was hostile to two separate jurisdictions (law and equity) for distinct modifications of the same property.[59] Humphreys's attack was against feudal common law, but neither did he accept equitable solutions to the problem. As he put it:

The three great causes to which I would attribute the redundancy of these laws are:—1. The technicalities of *tenure in general*, with the entire mass of *customary tenures*; 2. *Uses* and 3. *Equitable interference*, comprising passive and constructive trusts, with the various other instances and the peculiar rules of this interposition...."[60]

Humphreys's hostility toward equity as a means of law reform stemmed from a hostility toward both its origin and the reason for its survival. He disliked uses or trusts because they were introduced into the law "by churchmen for sinister purposes."[61] Churchmen, Humphreys maintained, invented the use to circumvent their vows of poverty through the creation of a trust relationship with another, which allowed them an equitable interest in property while legal title was in the other party. The reason for the continuance of uses and for the development and retention of passive and constructive trusts was that they were successful modes to avoid the intractableness of feudal tenures.[62] Yet to Humphreys, a trust was merely another fiction by which equity judges assumed the functions of a legislature.[63] His plan called for the removal of the tenures and, therefore, the removal of the need for equitable remedies.[64]

Humphreys's more specific suggestions for reform conform to the general suggestions discussed above. If they were enacted, he believed they would defeudalize and make land easier to alienate, or convey. Among his suggestions were the ability of half brothers and grandparents to inherit;[65] the abolition of the *estate tail*, or the legal requirement that inheritance must go to the heirs of the donee's body rather than to the heirs generally;[66] changes in the terms of executory dispositions or deeds that cannot be performed until a later date, thereby delaying the power to alienate or sell;[67] an end to feudal tenures or the system of holding lands in subordination to some social superior;[68] extension of testamentary disposition from land to which a testator is entitled at the making of his will, to all to which he may be entitled at his death;[69] greater protection to the rights of creditors;[70] uniformity of the laws requiring land registration and the extension of their use;[71] codification of the law of real property into language simple enough for the general public to know their rights;[72] a model of the new substantive law of real property on the lines of the law of personal property where there existed no traces of tenure, uses, or trusts;[73] and regulation of the elaborate system, founded by equity, upon the conversion of land into money and the reverse.[74] Humphreys's suggestions were inspired by the continental civil codes working especially well in the Netherlands, a commercialized nation free from feudalism.[75]

Regarding the rights of marriage, which involved curtesy, dower, and the wife's separate estate, Humphreys stated that they "require much correction"[76] and on "principles wholly different from those which at present regulate them."[77] *Curtesy* was, at common law, a life estate of the husband in the real property his wife owned during marriage, provided they had children capable of inheriting that estate. *Dower* was, at common law, the legal right the wife acquired at marriage in the real estate of her husband. It equaled only one-third of the value of the lands he owned during marriage. Humphreys also observed that "the harsh law, which gives *absolutely* to the husband all the wife's personal estate, of whatever magnitude, which she may become *possessed* of during the marriage, cries feelingly for correction."[78]

Again, equity was not the institution to which Humphreys looked for a remedy:

The palliatives introduced by courts of equity, the limited opportunities they possess of exercising their jurisdiction, their subtle refinements to drag the property within it, the fluctuation of their doctrines on the subject and the consequent uncertainty they occasion, combine to create an evil nearly as great as what they seek to redress.[79]

Consonant with this criticism of equity, Humphreys suggested that the following article be enacted into law:[80]

Any settlement under the preceding article [which allowed interspousal agreements, either before or after marriage respecting their landed property] may be made upon, or the land of any person, or the profits thereof, may be given to, the wife, for her exclusive and inalienable enjoyment, during the actual or proposed marriage; or, where a stranger is the donor, during any future marriage.[81]

Humphreys intended that this article, if passed, "supersedes the necessity of trustees for protecting the wife in what she actually enjoys at present in equity in her own name, and might do equally so at law, by rendering her a *feme sole* [single woman] as to her separate rights."[82]

The fictional fine was used as a device whenever someone intended to dispose of lands that were not part of a wife's separate estate. To avoid the necessity of using this fiction, Humphreys proposed that the legislature consider the following article:

The wife may, during the marriage, dispose of or release her lands, or her interest . . . [in any settlement by her husband or a third person as allowed by Humphreys's proposed plan] either by deed, with the written consent of her husband, or by will; but, if by deed, the same must be acknowledged by her, as her free act, before a judge of one of his Majesty's courts of record . . . or before the clerk of the peace of the county where she shall reside; which officer shall secretly examine here thereon; and a certificate of such examination shall be endorsed on the instrument so acknowledged, and shall be signed by such officer; and such certificate may be afterwards registered, pursuant to the regulations . . . [in title proposed by Humphreys on registration], with the clerk of the peace of the county where any land affected by the instrument in question lies.[83]

Although Humphreys's suggestions, which later became part of New York law,[84] were steps toward the freer alienability, or transfer, of land, toward defeudalization, and ultimately leading to the Married Women's Property Acts, they were not motivated by feminism. In fact his text exhibits some blatant indifference to the rights of women. For example, one of the articles he proposed for his recommended system of reform provided that: "The husband is entitled to the wife's land during their intermarriage; unless any disposition to the contrary be made. . . . "[85] Although he did provide for the ability to make such "dispositions to the contrary" by private agreement between husband and wife or with third persons, the burden, Humphreys suggested, should be on the private person to contract to the contrary. If no such contract were made, the husband would retain his old feudal life interests. Humphreys, who hated feudalism, tolerated this feudal vestige on the spurious grounds that "any benefit arising from a change would be too questionable to warrant the interfering with it."[86] Another feudal vestige he tolerated was the unequal treatment of widows and widowers. He proposed that:

If the husband survive the wife, he is entitled as follows: viz, if she leave issue, to a moiety of the profits of whatever land she may die possessed of, during his life, if any such issue shall so long continue; if she leave no issue, or if such issue shall afterwards fail, then to the land itself, during his life.[87]

In contrast, he also provided that:

If the wife survive the husband, she is entitled to the following proportions of the profits of whatever land he may die possessed of: viz. if he leave issue, then to one-third part of such profits, during her life, if any such issue shall so long continue: if he leave no issue, or if such issue shall afterwards fail, then to a moiety of such profits during her life; to commence respectively from her husband's death, or from the failure of such issue; as the case may be.[88]

In Humphreys's comments following these proposed articles, he stated: "I prefer leaving the land in the hands of the persons most interested in its good management; and this maxim has guided me in framing these two articles."[89] This indifference to female equality was again demonstrated in his comments in support of the article quoted above, which was designed to supersede the conveyance of land by way of a fine, or the compromise of a fictitious suit. Humphreys contended that the article "gives uniformity to every discription of disposition by married women, and places a guard, which is now wanting, against their feebleness, where their power of appointment is exercisable *by deed*."[90]

One could question whether Humphreys's belief that females were feeble people not interested in the good management of property contradicts his stated goals to abolish feudalism and correct the defects he saw in the law of marital property. One could further question whether his presumption was not even more offensive than the reasoning that had given rise to the feudal law of marital property, which was to keep land in the hands of warriors.

Humphreys also proposed to abolish the passive or technical trust.[91] A *passive trust* is distinguished from an an active one in that the trustee has no active duty to perform. It was a device used merely to ensure a married woman, before the Married Women's Property Acts, an estate separate from her husband rather than to make use of the skills and judgment of a trustee. A proposed article of Humphreys's provided:

No use, trust, or confidence shall be declared of any land or of any charge upon the same, for the mere and direct benefit of any third persons, and all assurances declaring any such use, trust, or confidence shall... be utterly void.[92]

Another article provided:

All dispositions of or respecting land, shall be made to the alienee, and not to any other person to the use of or in trust for man; and all estates and interests in land shall be deemed legal right, cognizable in the courts of law.[93]

If the above articles had been enacted along with the article allowing third persons to give land to a married woman, the practical effect would have been that married women could own land with more control over it than under the prior trust system of preserving married women's estates separate from their husbands. Humphreys did not intend to abolish the active trust.[94] Consequently if his plan had been enacted into law, a trust could have been established for the benefit of a married woman as long as the trustee would be one entrusted with the "actual disposition, management, or receipt, of lands, or the rents and profits thereof, or any interest in or charge upon the same...."[95] Someone could, therefore, set up the trust for active, and therefore be legal, purposes according to Humphreys's proposed plan.

Humphreys's ideas for law reform influenced the committee to revise the New York State property statutes. His attack on the use and trust was one of the reasons why the Married Women's Property Acts became a necessity. A close look at the effect of the New York Revised Statutes makes this clear.

Notes

1. R. POUND, THE FORMATIVE ERA OF AMERICAN LAW 42 (1938) [hereinafter cited as FORMATIVE ERA].

2. *Id.* at 43.

3. *Accord,* W. BUTLER, THE REVISION OF THE STATUTES OF THE STATE OF NEW YORK AND THE REVISERS 20-21 (1889); S. PRALL, THE AGITATION FOR LAW REFORM DURING THE PURITAN REVOLUTION 1640-1660, at 67, 145-48 (1966). Note also that James Carter, the man who was most active in the campaign to defeat the civil code of David Dudley Field, was commissioned to do so by the Association of the Bar of the City of New York.

4. *See, e.g.,* 2 H. BROUGHAM, SPEECHES 287-88 (1938); H. STANTON, SKETCHES OF REFORMS AND REFORMERS OF GREAT BRITAIN AND IRELAND 87, 95 (1849).

5. 6 J. BENTHAM, THE WORKS OF JEREMY BENTHAM 146 (J. Bowring ed. 1843).

6. 3 *id.* at 155-210.

7. 1 *id.* at 235.

8. *Id.*

9. 3 *id.* at 232.

10. *Id.*

11. *Id.*

12. *Id.*

13. *Id.* at 206; 4 *id.* at 460.

14. 3 *id.* at 206; 4 *id.* at 460-61.

15. 5 *id.* at 235; 4 *id.* at 459.

16. 3 *id.* at 206.

17. 5 *id.* at 235.

18. 3 *id.* at 205-10.

19. *Id.* at 205.

20. *Id.*

21. *Id.*

22. *Id.*

23. *Id.* at 210.

24. *Id.*

25. *Id.*

26. *Id.*

27. *Id.*

28. Bloomfield, *William Sampson and the Codifiers: The Roots of American Legal Reform, 1820-1830*, 11 AM. J. LEGAL HIST. 234, 236 (1967) [hereinafter cited as *The Codifiers*].

29. *Id.* at 237.

30. *Id.* at 238.

31. *See, e.g.,* W. SAMPSON, DISCOURSE AND CORRESPONDENCE WITH VARIOUS LEARNED JURISTS UPON THE HISTORY OF THE LAW (1826); W. SAMPSON, DISCOURSE AND REPORT FROM NEW YORK COMMISSIONERS (1826); W. SAMPSON, AN ANNIVERSARY DISCOURSE DELIVERED BEFORE THE HISTORICAL SOCIETY OF NEW YORK (1823) [hereinafter cited as ANNIVERSARY DISCOURSE].

32. *See, e.g.,* The Case of the Journeymen Cordwainers of the City of New York, 1 Yate's Sel. Cas. 81, 142 (N.Y. 1811).

33. *See, e.g.,* ANNIVERSARY DISCOURSE *passim*; W. SAMPSON, MEMOIRS OF WILLIAM SAMPSON 311 (1817). Sampson states that the American Revolution had reduced the theories of the great philosophers of England, France, and other countries into practice.

34. *See* note 31 *supra.*

35. ANNIVERSARY DISCOURSE 17.

36. *Id.*

37. *Id.*

38. *See id.* at 54.

39. *Id..*

40. *Id.* at 54-56.

41. *See id.* at 59.

42. *Id.* at 57, 61.

43. *Id.* at 54-55.

44. *Id.* at 67.

45. *Id.* at 17.

46. *Id.* at 53.

47. *Id.* at 57.

48. *Id.* at 16, 52.

49. *Id.* at 56.

50. *Id.* at 57.

51. *Id.*

52. *Id.* at 63.

53. *Id.* at 64.

54. *See The Codifiers* 243 and materials cited therein.

55. *Id.* at 243.

56. *Id.* at 248, 251; C. WARREN, A HISTORY OF THE AMERICAN BAR 523-25 (1911).

57. J. HUMPHREYS, OBSERVATIONS ON THE ACTUAL STATE OF THE ENGLISH LAWS OF REAL PROPERTY WITH OUTLINE FOR A SYSTEMATIC REFORM (2d ed. 1827) [hereinafter cited as OBSERVATIONS WITH OUTLINE FOR SYSTEMATIC REFORM].

58. *Id.* at 215-34.
59. *Id.* at 218-19.
60. *Id.* at 220 (emphasis in original).
61. *Id.*
62. *Id.*
63. *Id.* at 229.
64. *Id.* at 223.
65. *Id.* at 221.
66. *Id.* at 222.
67. *Id.*
68. *Id.*
69. *Id.* at 223.
70. *Id.* at 223-24.
71. *Id.* at 224-25.
72. *Id.* at 225-28.
73. *Id.* at 228-29.
74. *Id.* at 233-34.
75. *Id.* at 230-34.
76. *Id.* at 222-23.
77. *Id.* at 222.
78. *Id.* at 259 (emphasis in original).
79. *Id.* at 259-60.
80. *Id.* at 262.
81. *Id.* at 258.
82. *Id.* at 262.
83. *Id.* at 258-59.
84. Stevenson, *Influence of Bentham and Humphreys on the New York Property Legislation of 1828*, 1 AM. J. LEGAL HIST. 155 (1957).
85. OBSERVATIONS WITH OUTLINE FOR SYSTEMATIC REFORM 257.
86. *Id.* at 259.
87. *Id.* at 257.
88. *Id.* at 257-58.
89. *Id.* at 261.
90. *Id.* at 263 (emphasis in original).
91. *Id.* at 273.
92. *Id.* at 272-73.
93. *Id.* at 274.
94. *Id.* at 273-75, 347-48.
95. *Id.* at 347.

5 THE MOVEMENT FOR CODIFICATION IN NEW YORK STATE

I.

Roscoe Pound pointed out that great things were expected of legislative lawmaking or codification in the early days of the republic.[1] William Butler, the late nineteenth-century historian of the New York Revised Statutes, believed there was great popular interest in the revision.[2] Butler's opinion substantiates Pound's theory. Pound claimed that there existed a powerful idea of "legislative omnicompetence" created by a belief that the legislators were "peculiarly the representatives of the sovereign people, with all the powers of the sovereign devolved upon them."[3]

Gordon Wood, a specialist in early American history, explained this phenomenon.[4] American preoccupation with the need to replace unwritten common law with written law was a consequence of a new presumption about the nature of law as the command of a sovereign will. If the law is a command, the source of the command must be legitimate. That is, it must come from the very people who were to be governed by the command. At the same time, the only real protection for those subject to the law was to control the content as well as the source of the command; hence the written specification must be controlled. It is, therefore, no surprise that the leading codifier in the common-law world was Jeremy Bentham, a prominent member of the positivist school of jurisprudence. Wood also explained the American fear of judicial discretion: "With no printed indigenous decisions there could be little reliance on local precedents other than those in memory, and although English authorities were cited constantly they appear to have expanded rather than restricted judicial discretion."[5] Americans's fear of this unfettered discretion caused the preference for legislative intervention.[6] They were conscious of the need for equity's mitigating effect on law but "denied the judicial discretion that made equitable interpretations necessary and possible."[7] The only judicial discretion tolerated by a steadfast legislative supremacist might be a type of equity on a statute, that is, an application of the statute by analogy to unprovided-for cases.

Morton J. Horwitz, professor of law at Harvard Law School, agrees that what underlay the demand for codification was the principle that in a republic, a judge should be required to follow the law, and the growing conviction that since much of English common law itself was a product of the whim of judges, judges could not be depended upon merely to apply the existing law.[8] Horwitz, like Wood, saw the postrevolutionary codification movement as ultimately charging that the law was "inherently a product of power and will" and therefore political.[9]

Another reason for the mood of legislative supremacy was the disfavor with which the common law was looked upon after the Revolution. As Pound stated, "[t]he common law, as something English, was under a cloud after our Revolution."[10] Anglophobes looked to Roman law as expressed in French law as an alternative.[11]

Two men hostile to judicial discretion and influenced by the study of French law led the codification movement in New York. They were Edward Livingston and David Dudley Field. Their efforts helped to pave the way for the easy passage of the Married Women's Property Acts.

II. The Contributions of Edward Livingston

Edward Livingston, born in 1764 into a family prominent in New York political and legal life since 1675,[12] was a student of Roman, Spanish, and French law as well as Anglo-American common law.[13] In politics he was a Jeffersonian Republican and a Jacksonian Democrat. As such he became active in New York State and Louisiana and in national politics. In 1794 he was elected to Congress as a Jeffersonian Republican. In 1801 he was appointed by President Thomas Jefferson to be United States district attorney for New York. That same year he was chosen by the State Council of New York as mayor of New York City. In 1804 he moved to New Orleans to practice law. After serving a term in the Louisiana State legislature, he was elected to the United States Senate and served from 1829 to 1831. In 1831 he was appointed secretary of state and in 1833, a minister to France.[14]

One of his favorite political themes was a call for codification. Unsuccessful in achieving codification in New York, he was successful in early nineteenth-century Louisiana, a state whose legal system still is indebted to his work. His philosophy of codification is not only worthy of examination because of his direct efforts in New York, but also because of his influence on future codifiers and law reformers active in that state and the rest of the nation. His ideas form a bridge from Bentham to David Dudley Field, the man who dedicated his life to doing for the rest of new York law what the Revised Statutes would do for property law.[15]

Livingston did not share Bentham's faith in the ability to write a "complete" code. Because he saw the inevitability of a case coming before a court that had not been provided for by the code draftsmen, Livingston developed a sophisticated methodology for handling the "unprovided-for case." This methodology paralleled the continental civil law method of law reform.[16] Livingston explained the role of the judge after the code was enacted. "If the case be a new one, he must decide without law; he must frame his judgment by analogical reasoning from the law in similar cases...."[17] The judges should "decide according to such principles as they believe the legislature would have been guided by had the case been foreseen."[18] Nevertheless, Livingston shared Bentham's hostility for judge-made law. Even if the judge were to be faced by a truly unprovided-for case, there would be no justification for *stare decisis*,[19] or the use of precedent. The purpose for excluding all precedent was two-fold. First, litigants would be protected from all preexisting uncodified law (what Bentham would have characterized as *ex post facto* dog training); second, later litigants would be protected from decisions that were the product of hardened definitions of code articles. Thus each new case was to be started with a fresh examination of the same code article, rather than with a judicial interpretation of the article.

Although Livingston saw the need for some judicial discretion on the rare occasion of the truly unprovided-for case, he shared Bentham's view that law reform was a job for the legislature. However, under Livingston's method, in contrast to Bentham's plan, the judge was to refer to the legislature the law reform prompted by an unprovided-for case. This reference was to be a *suggestion* only. A judge was never to possess lawmaking powers. Nevertheless, Livingston conceded that the unprovided-for case had to be decided and that such decision would be made by a judge. Livingston foresaw the fact that legal method was a process, and the code system required flexibility just as did the common-law method. He stated that "the best code that can be provided is but a framework for its own progress toward perfection."[20]

To ensure that codification indeed progressed toward perfection, Livingston called for a constant revision of the code based on the actual practice of the courts deciding disputes between private litigants. Livingston made this method explicit in an 1823 report to the Louisiana legislature.

The judges are directed to lay at stated times before the General Assembly, a circumstantial account of every case for the decision of which they have thought themselves obliged to recur to the use of the discretion thus given [by Article 21]; while regular reports of the ordinary cases of construction, to be made by a Commission officer, will enable the Legislative Body to explain ambiguities, supply deficiencies and to correct errors that may be discovered in the Laws by the test of experience in their operation. By these means our Code, although imperfect at first, will be progressing towards perfection, and judicial decisions will be means of improving legislation, but will not be laws themselves.[21]

Thus for Livingston judicial opinions would operate as reports to the legislature whenever revision was seen to be necessary by that branch of government whose function it was to apply the law to individual cases. How this procedure would have worked as both a democratic and an efficient method of law reform, one cannot know for certain, for although Livingston's civil code was passed into law in 1825 by the Louisiana legislature, his plan for revision of the code was not.[22]

III. The Contributions of David Dudley Field

David Dudley Field, the great codifier from New York State, was influenced by Roman law,[23] Jeremy Bentham,[24] Edward Livingston,[25] and the success of codification in continental Europe.[26] Unlike the other proponents of codification, Field is reputed to have been little concerned with revolutionalizing substantive law. Rather he was thought to be concerned merely with arranging it into a better form.[27] Perhaps this can be explained by the fact that Field came to the codification movement at a relatively late date. Although the other codifiers worked in the immediate aftermath of the American Revolution, which ultimately advanced the interests of the urban commercial classes, the first draft of Field's civil code did not appear until 1862 and the final draft, not until 1865. By that time the Revised Statutes had already codified New York's substantive law of property. Another possible explanation for Field's reputation for moderatism might be that the Act of April 6, 1857, which appointed commissioners of the code, expressed what Field thought was a very limited duty, that is, "to reduce into a written and systematic code the whole body of the law of this State, or so much and such parts thereof as shall seem to them practicable and expedient. . . ."[28] Despite Field's reputation, he did advocate innovation, not merely codification, of existing law,[29] and Field did in fact make innovations in his model code.[30]

Field shared Bentham, Livingston, and William Sampson's concern with the problem of judicial discretion. In an article in the *American Law Review*, January-February 1866, Field contended: "There are certain propositions which have become maxims of government, one of which is that the legislative and judicial departments should be kept distinct, or, in other words, that the same person should not be both lawgiver and judge."[31] Again in his *Introduction to the Complete Civil Code,*[32] he argued: "The question . . . is between written and unwritten law; that is to say, between law written by the lawgiver, and law not thus written; between law promulgated by that department of the government which alone has the prerogative of making and promulgating the laws, and law not so promulgated."[33] In the same work he contended that if flexibility advocated by the opponents of codification means "that a rule ought to be subject to the discretion of the Judges, the proposition is unsound, for the Judge should not have dispensing power."[34] In a letter to the California bar dated November 28, 1870, Field said that "when the Courts decide, without a code, they have a greater liberty of decision than with it. . . . [S]uch liberty . . . [is] not . . . a good thing. No Judge should have power to decide a cause without a rule to decide it by, else the suitor is subjected to his caprice."[35]

Underlying Field's hostility toward judicial discretion was an acceptance of the positivist view of what law was and a rejection of a romantic view expressed by the historical school of law. Field refused to accept the notion that judges do not make, but only declare, common law. In an address before the Law Academy of Philadelphia on April 5, 1886, Field asked: "Who made this common law, if the judges did not? Your Legislature did not make it."[36] To bolster his arguments, Field quoted John Austin, the positivist who believed law to be a command from a political superior to a political inferior.

Austin said in ridicule of Blackstone: "What hindered him from seeing this was a childish fiction employed by our judges, that judiciary or common law is not made by them, but is a miraculous something made by nobody, existing, I suppose, from eternity, and merely declared from time to time by the judges?"[37] Austin was not the only positivist Field cited in arguments for the acceptance of codification. Field was wont to quote Bentham's famous equation of common law to dog training.[38] Like his predecessors, Field hoped to limit judicial discretion by making the law simple, understandable, and systematically organized—in other words, codified.[39]

By the time Field assumed leadership of the American codification movement, a strong counterattack had developed. His two significant foes were the Association of the Bar of the City of New York and James C. Carter, a prominent New York City attorney who was under the influence of Savigny's Historical School of Jurisprudence, which was based on German Volkish Romanticism.[40] From Field's response to this attack, his theory of law reform through codification is made clear.[41] Field recognized that inherent in the objections to his plan was the belief that it was not possible to provide for all future cases.[42] His answer was that in penal cases, if an individual committed an act not proscribed by the code, he was to go without punishment,[43] since no one should be punished for an *ex post facto* law. If it were a civil matter that was unprovided for, Field, like Livingston, recommended that analogies be made from the general rules of the code.[44] Field proposed an explicit formula for judges who, after the code was passed, were faced with an unprovided-for case.

[I]f there be an existing rule of law omitted from this Code, and not inconsistent with it, that rule will continue to exist in the same form in which it now exists; while if any new rule, now for the first time introduced, should not answer the good ends for which it is intended, which can be known only from experience, it can be amended or abrogated by the same lawgiving department which made it; and if new cases arise, as they will, which have not been foreseen, they may be decided, if decided at all, precisely as they would now be decided, that is to say, by analogy to some rule in the Code, or to some rule omitted from the Code and therefore still existing, or by the dictates of natural justice.[45]

Thus Field foresaw, more realistically than did Bentham, the inevitability of some judicial discretion. Instead of merely decreeing that it shall not exist, Field concentrated his efforts on tempering this discretion by means of the code methodology. Field, as concerned as Bentham with restricting judge-made law, saw a distinction that Bentham did not see between *ex post facto* judicial policymaking and the administration of laws by judicial application of established policies to the circumstances of each case as it arose. Field considered the former to be strictly forbidden[46] and the latter to be legitimate.[47] As an example, Field explained that establishing general rules or policies, such as that a contract is void if it is against public policy, is a job for the legislature, and deciding what is or is not against the policy is a job for the courts.[48] The purpose of allowing this distinction was to provide enough flexibility to keep law as a process simultaneously stable and, therefore, not *ex post facto*, yet progressive enough to meet social and economic changes from generation to generation.[49]

To ensure that progress in the law comes from the legislature, that is, from the general principles embodied in the code, and not from the judiciary, in the form of *stare decisis* or judicial discretion contrary to the principles embodied in the code, Field wrote what would have been sections 6 and 2032 had his civil code been adopted. Section 6 stated that: "In this State there is no common law, in any case, where the law is declared by the five Codes."[50] Section 2032 mandated that: "The rule that statutes in derogation of the common law are to be strictly construed, has no application to this code."[51]

It is clear from Field's own references that he was as influenced by Roman law[52] and by continental jurisprudence[53] as was Livingston. Both men hoped that a code and the method of analogical interpretation would, if enacted, provide the same legislative control over lawmaking as they believed existed in Europe. However, the common-law method was too deeply entrenched in New York by the second half of the nineteenth century for this hope to be realized.[54] Consequently, unlike Livingston's civil code for Louisiana, Field's civil code was never made New York State law. Field's code of civil procedure, however, was enacted in 1848 by the same legislature that passed the first Married Women's Property Act.

Another factor underlying Field's years of struggle for law reform was his generally progressive spirit. He, like Livingston, exhibited an enduring faith in science and the improvability of society. In fact, some of his arguments for codification employed analogies from scientific or technological progress.[55] Because he was part of that tradition which believed in progress, science, and the improvability of society, Field could work for scientific law reforms, international peace, abolition of slavery, and feminism. Thus Field could share James Humphreys's desire to make land as easily and securely alienable, or transferable, as any other item of commerce;[56] but he, unlike Humphreys, was motivated by a profeminist position as well. In his civil code, some of the substantive innovations he suggested concerned the rights of married women. Field's plan began where Humphreys's ended. He wrote provisions that, if they had been enacted, would have "secured" the equal rights of married women with respect to their children and their property. For example, he would have included sections abolishing both *dower* and *curtesy*,[57] the concepts that provided a widow with a life estate of only one-third of her deceased husband's lands and a widower with a life estate of all of his deceased wife's lands as long as a child was born alive.

Field discerned the interrelationship between feudalism and married women's lack of civil capacity. He blamed common law for its retention of "feudal tenures with all their burdensome incidents... land... inalienable without livery of seisin, and wives...[having] only the rights which a barbarous age conceded them."[58] He believed that only through codification could "the closer assimilation of the law of real and personal property, and the changes in the relation of husband and wife, as to property...be effected...wisely and safely...."[59] Seeing the reform of married women's property law as an aspect of commercialization and modernization of law, Field remarked in 1886:

> The careful student of history will find that from the time when the English judges resisted the negotiability of the notes of merchants down to the hour when the last shackle was stricken from the hands of woman in the holding of her own property and taking the fruit of her own labor, the real and healthy growth of the law has proceeded not from the seats of judges, but from the halls of legislative assemblies.[60]

It is clear that Field, like Sampson and Bentham, was a product of the Enlightenment. In the tradition of the earlier codifiers, Field wanted to see the end of the *barbarous age*, a term used by Enlightenment thinkers as a synonym for feudalism. It was to this unenlightened age that Field attributed civil death for women and slavery for blacks. But it was this same age of feudalism in which common law developed. Since common law had failed to represent accurately the social relationships of what Field viewed as the new enlightened age of the nineteenth century, he thought codification was needed. Examples of the success of legislatures, where common law had failed, were the bourgeoisification of married women's legal status, the recognition of bourgeois notions of sound commercial relations already existing among merchants, and the end of feudal distinction between real and movable property. All of these examples illustrate a transformation of law to meet the needs of a commercial society.

The codifiers could never accept the perception of law as merely the uncontrollable unfolding of the Volk spirit. Since to the codifiers law was something that could be tampered with, systematized, made scientific, and thereby improved, they had to fight Carter and his historical notions of jurisprudence. Thus it was not only the feudal content but also the method of law that the codifiers sought to revise. Since married women were to benefit from the revision in the law made by proponents of codification, one must look closer at the prior law of real property and the process of defeudalization through legislative revision of property law.

Notes

1. R. POUND, THE FORMATIVE ERA OF AMERICAN LAW 38 (1938) [hereinafter cited as FORMATIVE ERA]. *But see* Horwitz, *The Conservative Tradition in the Writing of American Legal History*, 17 AM. J. LEGAL HIST. 275, 276 (1973), wherein Horwitz indicts Pound for his hegemony over the content and values of nineteenth-century

legal historiography exemplified by Pound's delight over "the happy and glorious triumph of the common law over . . . the codifiers."

2. W. BUTLER, THE REVISION OF THE STATUTES OF THE STATE OF NEW YORK AND THE REVISERS 38 (1889) [hereinafter cited as REVISION & REVISERS]. *See also, Law of Real Property*, 1 AM. JURIST 58 at 59-61 (1829); *Law Reform in America*, 6 LAW MAGAZINE & REV. 127 at 135, (1831).

3. FORMATIVE ERA 39.

4. *See* G. WOOD, THE CREATION OF THE AMERICAN REPUBLIC 1776-1787, at 292-93 (1969).

5. *Id.* at 297.

6. *Id.* at 298.

7. *Id.* at 301.

8. M. J. HORWITZ, THE TRANSFORMATION OF AMERICAN LAW 1780-1860, at 17-18 (1977).

9. *Id.* at 257.

10. FORMATIVE ERA 40.

11. *Id.*

12. W. HATCHER, EDWARD LIVINGSTON, JEFFERSONIAN REPUBLICAN AND JACKSONIAN DEMOCRAT 2-4 (1940).

13. *Id.* at 4.

14. *Id.* chs. XV and XVI.

15. Address by David Dudley Field, Law Academy of Philadelphia (Apr. 15, 1886), *reprinted in* 3 SPEECHES, ARGUMENTS AND MISCELLANEOUS PAPERS OF DAVID DUDLEY FIELD 245 (T. Coan ed. 1890) [hereinafter cited as FIELD'S PAPERS].

16. *See* E. LIVINGSTON, WORKS ON CRIMINAL JURISPRUDENCE 91-92 (1873) [hereinafter cited as LIVINGSTON'S WORKS]; Franklin, *Concerning the Historic Importance of Edward Livingston*, 11 TUL. L. REV. 160, 180-98 (1937) [hereinafter cited as *Importance of Livingston*]; Morrow, *Louisiana Blueprint: Civilian Codification and Legal Method for State and Nation*, 17 TUL. L. REV. 351, 389-91 (1943) [hereinafter cited as *Louisiana Blueprint*].

17. 1 LIVINGSTON'S WORKS 586.

18. 2 *id.* at 458.

19. *Louisiana Blueprint* 391.

20. 1 LIVINGSTON'S WORKS 173.

21. E. LIVINGSTON, REPORT OF THE COMMISSION ON REVISION OF THE LOUISIANA CODE 10 (1823).

22. Letter from Edward Livingston to Jeremy Bentham (July 1, 1880), *reprinted in* 2 J. BENTHAM, THE WORKS OF JEREMY BENTHAM 51-53 (J. Bowring ed. 1843).

23. *See, e.g., Answer to Mr. James C. Carter*, in 3 FIELD'S PAPERS 417.

24. *See, e.g., id.* at 420. Note Field's reference to Bentham's dog-training analogy.

25. 3 R. POUND, JURISPRUDENCE 709 (1959).

26. *See, eg.,* Address by David Dudley Field, Law Academy of Philadelphia. (Apr. 15, 1886), *reprinted in* 3 FIELD'S PAPERS 257. *See also* Nelson, *The Reform of Common Law Pleading in Massachusetts 1760-1830: Adjudication as a Prelude to Legislation*, 122 U. PA. L. REV. 97 (1973), wherein Nelson suggests that Field was also influenced by a half century of evolution in common-law pleading.

27. H. FIELD, THE LIFE OF DAVID DUDLEY FIELD 73-74 (1898). *But see* Horwitz, *The Rise of Legal Formalism*, 19 AM. J. LEGAL HIST. 251, 262-63 (1975), wherein Horwitz

characterizes the Field Code as "the final exhaustion of the earlier Codification Movement's most radical goal of codifying and thereby transforming substantive law as well" and as "the conversion of substantive legal conflict into exclusively technical debates over procedure...."

28. 1 FIELD'S PAPERS 317.

29. *See e.g., id.* at 312, 326-27, 337. *Cf.* Peckham, *The Association of the Bar*, in 1 HIST. OF THE BENCH AND BAR OF NEW YORK 191, 204 (1897).

30. *See, e.g.,* D. FIELD, PROPOSED CIVIL CODE §§82, 83, 348, 801, 802, 809, 811, 2033 (1865) [hereinafter cited as FIELD'S PROPOSED CODE].

31. 3 FIELD'S PAPERS 239.

32. FIELDS'S PROPOSED CODE.

33. 1 FIELD'S PAPERS 325.

34. *Id.* at 331.

35. *Id.* at 354.

36. 3 *id.* at 250.

37. *Id.* at 250-51.

38. *Id.* at 420.

39. 1 *id.* at 317-23.

40. For the philosophy and arguments of this countermovement, *see* J. Carter, Law—Its Origin and Growth (1907); Address by James C. Carter, Virginia State Bar Association Annual Meeting (July 25, 1889).

41. One of the many places in which Field addressed the issue of objections to his proposed civil code is in the introduction to the 1865 version. FIELD'S PROPOSED CODE.

42. *Id.* at xvi.

43. *Id.* at xvii.

44. *Id.* at xviii.

45. *Id.* at xix.

46. *Id.* at xxii-xxiii.

47. *Id.* at xxiv.

48. *Id.* at xxiv-xxv.

49. *Id.*

50. *Id.* §6.

51. *Id.* §2032.

52. 3 FIELD'S PAPERS 412-19; 1 *id.* at 310.

53. FIELD'S PROPOSED CODE xv, xvi, xxx; 1 FIELD'S PAPERS 310, 326, 346, 358; 3 *id.* at 257.

54. *Importance of Livingston* 169.

55. *See e.g.,* 1 FIELD'S PAPERS 340 (analogy to the development of the railway); 3 *id.* at 251 (analogy to the laying of the first transatlantic cable by his brother Cyris W. Field).

56. *See* 3 *id.* at 265; 1 *id.* at 320-321.

57. 1 *id.* at 320.

58. *Id.* at 335.

59. *Id.* at 337.

60. 2 *id.* at 354.

6 LAW REFORM IN NEW YORK: THE EFFECTIVE DEFEUDALIZATION AND COMMERCIALIZATION OF PROPERTY LAW BY THE REVISED STATUTES OF 1828

In New York State, the legislative-reform movement began during the Revolution. In 1782 entailed estates, or estates in fee tail,[1] which placed limitations on inheritance, were abolished.[2] By the 1820s the reform movement set out to continue the work begun by the revolutionary lawmakers. A commission was set up to revamp the law of future interests,[3] or those interests in property other than present rights of possession. The product of that commission's work was a three-volume modernization of law entitled *The Revised Statutes* and the commisson's members became known as "the Revisers."

Referring to the Revised Statutes of 1827-28, Lawrence Friedman, a recent commentator on American legal history, noted: "This famous enactment could be properly called a code."[4] It exhibited simplification of expression and a correlation of all of the parts to the whole. Moreover there is clear evidence that the Revisers and their code were influenced by the French Civil Code and the civil-law method for dealing with unprovided-for cases.[5]

Henry P. Wheaton, the creator of the first written plan or outline for the entire work,[6] graduated with honors from Brown University at the age of seventeen. Three years later, in 1805, he was admitted to the bar. A year later he translated the French Civil Code into English.[7] As William A. Butler, historian of the revision, pointed out, Wheaton designated the plan a *project*, "a word which his habits of study as a civilian and a publicist suggested to him as best descriptive of such novel and far reaching propositions."[8]

The Revised Statutes were written in the period described by Pound as "the formative era of American law."[9] Pound believed the task of the formative era was "to work out from our inherited legal materials a general body of law for what was to be a politically and economically unified land."[10] The inherited law was

heavily burdened with the formalism of the strict law. Its ideals were those of the relationally organized society of the Middle Ages and so quite out of line with the needs and ideals of men who were opening up the wilderness. It spoke from an era of organization while the colonists represented an oncoming era of individualism.[11]

Characteristic of this period of archaic law was an atmosphere of mystification, even for the legal profession.[12] Clearly, however, disputes arose and required settlement. Most of the reported cases deciding these disputes concerned questions of procedure and property law.[13] Since disputes usually do not have to be settled unless the question is unclear, it might be safe to assume that procedure and property law were the least clear areas of law. It is, therefore, not surprising that procedure and property law became the two focal points of law reform for codification proponents. The man who is credited with codification of procedural law is David Dudley Field. Property law was codified by members of the New York State Revision Commission, who were influenced by Jeremy Bentham, William Sampson, and James Humphreys.[14] Sampson and Bentham gave the Revisers a philosophical framework, and Humphreys provided the advice of a practicing lawyer hampered professionally by an outmoded legal system. The men who were responsible for the actual revision were John Duer, Benjamin F. Butler, and John C. Spencer.

William Allen Butler, historian of the revision and son of one of the Revisers, in 1889 attributed the revision to the "[r]adical changes . . . made in the organic law and in the mode of administering government" that the Constitution of 1821 embodied.[15] The Revision, Butler related, was not intended to be merely a reenactment of the existing law in a consolidated form, but was to be a "new and complete system of original laws . . . made serviceable by fundamental and far reaching changes and by a symmetrical and scientific arrangement."[16] The system aimed to have "the whole written law . . . under appropriate titles, classified in natural order and arranged, as to each of its branches, in a clear and scientific method. . . . "[17]

The Enlightenment influence is clear. Laws should be in accord with nature, that is, science; science is an ordered system, and ordered systems are knowable. Thus the faith of the Revisers was of "redeeming the laws from the uncertainties and obscurities" of English Law.[18] Accordingly, in an address to the legislature on January 4, 1825, the Revisers delivered their statement of purpose

to free our written code from the prolixities, uncertainties, and confusion incident to the style and manner in which it has hitherto been framed, and to apply to the elucidaton of this branch of the noblest of all sciences, those principles of an enlarged philosophy, which now obtain in every other department of knowledge.[19]

The outline of the new system was entitled "General Arrangement" but was endorsed "Project of General Plan of Revision handed in by Mr. Butler, May 11, 1825." The appellation *project* demonstrates the influence on the Revisers of the French codification of civil law after the French Revolution.[20] In fact, Henry Wheaton, the Reviser who had preceded Duer on the committee, had studied civil law at Poitiers in France before he translated the French Civil

Code into English.[21] Further evidence of French influence can be found in Governor De Witt Clinton's 1825 message favoring a code comparable to the postrevolutionary French Civil Code. Clinton spoke for the new commercial classes that required a new legal expression of social relations. He pronounced that

the whole system of our jurisprudence requires revised arrangement and correction. A complete code founded on the salutory principles of society, adapted to the interests of commerce and the useful arts, the state of society and the nature of our governments, and embracing those improvements which are enjoyed by enlightened experience, would be a public blessing. It would free our laws from uncertainty, elevate a liberal and honorable profession and utterly destroy judicial legislation, which is fundamentally at war with the principles of representative government.[22]

Those employed at the task of "judicial legislation" of course fought the codification idea, which threatened their *raison d'être*.[23] Sentiment from the bench and bar hostile to any imitation of French civilian methodology caused the Revisers to declare publicly that their work was not intended to be a codification.[24] Nevertheless the Revisers' goals were identical to those of civilian codifiers—to create a scientific system: modernized, defeudalized, demystified, clear, and certain. Such a system, with its source in the legislature, aimed to free the legal system from judicial discretion.

Real property law, the core of feudal common law, was the substantive area of law most in need of revision. As Butler explained it in 1889:

The lawyers and judges of England united in perpetuating rules and enforcing methods as to the title to land which it became almost impossible to apply with any certainty or safety.[25]

As Lawrence Friedman has written, America was a "nation of amateurs," and conveyancing under the common law to ensure good title was "no job for an amateur."[26] The problem of fettered alienation—a restraint on the conveyance of property—became so acute that those crying for reform were able to outshout conservative common-law jurists.[27] Voices on both sides of the Atlantic carried on the debate. The most influential voices of reform were those of William Sampson, Jeremy Bentham, Lord Brougham, James Humphreys, and Edward Livingston. These men were to devise an attack on the judicial discretion of the courts. To them only codification could ensure legislative rather than judicial lawmaking. As it happened, the New York property legislation of 1828 eased the passage of the Married Women's Property Acts twenty years later.

Charles E. Stevenson, a modern-day historian of the Revision, demonstrated that Jeremy Bentham influenced the Revisers both directly and indirectly. Stevenson persuasively argued in 1957 that at one time or another, Bentham was in communication with the rulers of nearly every civilized country in the world, urging a code of laws for each of them. Although it may well be impossible to trace the influence of Bentham's work on any particular individual, it is certain that his works were read by thinking men in the United States long before his death in 1832. And to any of these readers who might also possess the zeal of a reformer, here as in England, was a tool ready for the work to be done.[28]

Indirectly, Bentham influenced the Revisers, according to Stevenson, through the mediation of Lord Brougham, the statesman and law reformer, and James Humphreys, the practicing conveyancer and law reformer. Bentham's ideas, said Stevenson, are clearly evident in the writings and speeches of these two men. It was Bentham who first developed the idea of codification as a science that could be used to defeudalize and modernize the laws. The philosophy behind it was a pragmatic interest balancing—"the greatest good for the greatest number."

Stevenson pointed out that Lord Brougham, a nineteenth-century statesman of great stature and renown, actually acknowledged Bentham's influence. Brougham once said:

The age of Law Reform and the age of Jeremy Bentham are one and the same. He is the father of all branches of reform... No one before him had ever thought seriously of exposing the defects of our English system of jurisprudence.... He it was who first made the mighty step of trying the whole provisions of our jurisprudence by the test of expediency, fearlessly examining how far each part was connected with the rest; and with a yet more undaunted courage, inquiring how far even its most consistent and symmetrical arrangements were framed according to the principles which should pervade a Code of Laws—their adaptation to the circumstances of society, to the wants of men, and to the promotion of human happiness.[29]

As Bentham influenced Brougham, so did Brougham influence the Revisers. In the Revisers' notes there are references to Lord Brougham's famous six-hour speech made in Parliament on February 7, 1828, calling for law reform.[30]

Humphreys's 1826 book, *Observations on the Actual State of the English Laws of Real Property with Outline of a Code,*[31] pointed out the defects of the law of property and also presented an outline of a code that he thought could remedy these defects. Humphreys's work, which was of two-fold service to the Revisers, not only served as a model to help them complete their work in the allotted time of three and one-half years, but also won them the support of the bar, which was to use the new code.[32] Humphreys was a barrister and conveyancer at the height of his profession. To present the legislature and the bar with a code on a model of such a personage facilitated its acceptance.[33] The Revisers acknowledged their use of Humphreys's work especially in writing the chapter on trusts and the Rule against Perpetuities.[34] In their notes they "cheerfully acknowledged that in the preparation of this chapter [on trusts] we have derived most important aid from his valuable work."[35] They also specifically acknowledged the influence of Brougham on the law regarding the Statute of Uses.[36]

The Revisers aimed to demystify as well as defeudalize.[37] Understanding the cause of the mystification of laws, the Revisers explained that mystification was the inevitable result of the struggle between "two sets of distinct and opposite maxims, different in origin and hostile in principle."[38] One was the feudal rules of the common law expressed in the law of land tenures,[39] and the second was "an elaborate system of expedients, very artificial and ingenious, devised in the course of ages by courts and lawyers, with some aid from the legislators for the express purpose of evading the rules of the Common Law. . . ."[40] The purpose of these expedients was to facilitate the alienation, or conveyance, of estates. Although the conflict was leading to greater alienability, and thus defeudalization, the result of the struggle was an "impenetrable mystery."[41] As the Revisers themselves wrote, "It is the conflict continued through centuries between these hostile systems that has generated that infinity of subtleties and refinements with which this branch of our jurisprudence is overloaded."[42] The fiction of *ejectment*—a lawsuit to get back land taken away wrongfully—and the *fine* and *common recovery*—two other fictions devised to convey land—were a few of these expedients.

The *law of tenures* had its roots in the feudal method of demanding and rendering military service. It was a system of holding land or tenancy in subordination to some superior who was the lord of the tenant who occupied the tenancy. All land ultimately was the dominion of the king, but interests in the land, or *seisin*, were delivered down the feudal social, political, and military hierarchy. In exchange for the right to use the land, each person holding an interest in the land promised to render loyalty and military services to the person above him.

Livery of seisin was the method of land transfer used by this hierarchical system. This was a ceremony that transferred seisin, or the highest interest in land a subject could acquire, in exchange for his military duty, or his homage and fealty. The ceremonial transfer to seisin from the *feoffer* (giver of the fee or tenancy) to the *feoffer* (receiver of the fee or tenancy) was the operative act that created the right of the feoffor to demand from the feofee the performance of feudal services and the corresponding duty of the feoffee to do them. Seisin, then, kept the feudal society together. Each person in the feudal hierarchy had a right-duty relationship with the person next to him. The king was at the top of the hierarchy and ultimately owned all the land in which others held present possessory interests. An important rule of this feudal order was that there must never be a time when the seisin could not be located in someone possessing a present freehold interest. The reason behind the rule was national defense. The feudal duties must always be performed; therefore, someone must always have seisin.

From this necessity the principle of land tenures or incomplete ownership developed. Not surprisingly, however, the combination of incomplete ownership of land and the method of transfer of lands by livery of seisin eventually brought evasionary tactics needed to facilitate the transfer of lands by people who could own the land outright to others who could likewise enjoy a clear title. These evasionary tactics were the "expedients" to which the Revisers referred.

The Revisers believed that "[t]he interests of society require that the power of the owner to fetter the alienation and suspend the ownership of an estate by future limitations should be confined within certain limits."[43] The remedy they offered was to "abolish all technical rules and distinctions, having no relation to the essential nature of property and the means of its beneficial enjoyment, but which, derived from the feudal system, rest solely upon feudal reasons."[44] Their method was to examine each rule of law and "if it is irrational and foolish, or the reasons upon which it is rested are obsolete, abolish it at once."[45] This method they believed would "sweep away an immense mass of useless refinements and distinctions; [would] relieve the law of real property ...from its abstruseness and uncertainty, and render it, as a system, intelligible and consistent."[46]

The Revisers knew the reason for their mission. The American Revolution had been won, and private law had to be adapted to the needs of the economic classes that benefited from the Revolution. They noted that:

In England, the continuance of the landed property in the hands of the aristocracy is the basis upon which the monarchy itself may be said to rest, but, with us, it should never be forgotten that it is the partibility, the frequent division and unchecked alienation of property, that are essential to the health and vigor of our republican institutions.[47]

Thomas Jefferson, the Francophile, understood this need, too. In a letter to James Madison from Paris dated September 6, 1789, Jefferson proclaimed that "the earth belongs in usufruct to the living."[48] *Usufruct* was the civil law right to enjoy property vested in another. By this slogan, Jefferson arguably was calling for an end to the feudal land law that provided for the creation of incomplete trusts by wills with the concomitant right of the testator to give directions for future transfer from the grave. These directions from the nonliving were particularly offensive when they presumed feudal traditions such as *primogeniture*, whereby the first son inherited everything, and land *entails*, which limited succession and were thus needed to ensure primogeniture.

In his letter, Jefferson stated that the question whether one generation of men has a right to bind another was "among the fundamental principles of every government."[49] If the principle that the world belongs in usufruct to the living is accepted by the new government, the question of whether the nation "may abolish the charges and privileges attached on lands, including the whole catalogue—ecclesiastical and feudal"[50] is answered in the affirmative.

Jefferson's use of the word *ecclesiastical* implies an attack on chancery's solution to land law as well as on the feudal common law.

Even the conservative Anglophile James Kent, chancellor of equity and commentator on the law, understood that dynamic. In his *Commentaries on American Law,*[51] he was critical of entails, or the limitation on the transfer of property to enumerated classes of descendants, usually to the firstborn son. Agreeing with the Revisers that entails ought to be abolished, Kent maintained:

Entailments are recommended in monarchial governments, as a protection to the power and influence of the landed aristocracy; but such a policy has no application to republican establishments, where wealth does not form a permanent distinction, and under which every individual of every family has his equal rights, and is equally invited, by the genius of the institutions, to depend upon his own merit and exertions. Every family, stripped of artifical supports, is obliged in this country, to repose upon the virtue of its descendants for the perpetuity of its fame.[52]

An intolerable fiction that had to be wiped out by postrevolutionary legislation was the fiction of ejectment.[53] According to the Revisers' Report to the Legislature in 1828, they proposed utterly to destroy and abolish the fictional action of ejectment,[54] but the action of the fine and common recovery was only to be modified.[55] However, the assembly was more radical than were the Revisers. It not only approved the abolition of the action of ejectment, but also passed a resolution directing the Revisers to abolish fines and recoveries. The legislature then passed the law abolishing

all writs of rights, writs of dower, writs of entry and writs of assize, all fines and common recoveries, and all other real actions known to the Common Law, not enumerated and retained in this Chapter; and all writs and other process heretofore used in real action, which are not specifically retained in this chapter, shall be and they are hereby abolished.[56]

The Revisers, as shown above, were influenced by the movement for law reform through legislation. Although some defeudalization was accomplished by equity and fictions of common-law judges, their desire was for cognizability, demystification, systematization, and a science of law that would make conveyancing safe for a nation of amateurs. Before the Revised Statutes, the feudal rule of seisin could be avoided in equity only through the *use* or *trust*, methods whereby one person got legal ownership of land and another person got to use the land. The use or trust was developed in equity to facilitate conveyancing, but it resulted in further complications, or as the Revisers termed it, "impenetrable mystery." Because of hostility toward judicial prerogative and out of a desire to simplify land law, the use and trust became objects of attack. Equity's negation of feudalism only augmented the confusion and mystification. Moreover, equity was administered by the hated prerogative court of chancery. Consequently the Revisers set out to usurp the task of defeudalization from chancery and place it in the hands of the legislature. As they put it: "[T]he law and practice of the Ecclesiastical Courts have ... been hidden mysteries."[57]

One of the reforms of the Revisers was to abolish the rule in *Shelley's Case*[58] and thereby end the necessity of going to chancery to avoid the rule. They also sought to negate uses and trusts.[59] The Revisers discouraged the creation of trusts in land because they could be used to hinder free alienation. Trusts were allowed by the Revised Satutes only for a few, specific purposes where the dangers of land being tied up were slight and the need great, for example, trusts for the benefit of a minor.[60]

In their notes,[61] the Revisers acknowledged the influence of Lord Brougham. They made references to Brougham's speech, which called for the restoration of the Statute of Uses.[62] By this statute, all equitable estates created by *feoffment* (gift of inheritable land) to use and by bargain and sale were executed into legal estates. Its purpose was to restore to common law courts, which had increasingly lost litigants to chancery, jurisdiction over real property, however, statute could be avoided by creating a use on a use or by creating an active trust.[63] A use on a use circumvented the statute because only the first use was executed into a legal estate. The active trust was an exception to the rule. Such trusts required the trustee to perform affirmative management duties with respect to the property. Therefore they were not executed by the statute.

The Revisers were also influenced by Humphreys.[64] They acknowledged his aid in their published notes when they revised the rule requiring one dealing with a trustee to look to the application of the monies paid to the trustee;[65] when they placed limitations on the use and effect of powers of appointment, which had been used to defeat the legal rights of creditors;[66] when they eliminated the need for the word *heirs* in a deed to convey a fee;[67] and when they established a rule about disbursing rents and profits in cases involving a suspension of land ownership.[68]

After the Statute of Uses, landowners had increased power to control the use of land from the grave.[69] This, to the dismay of Jefferson and the Revisers, created a fetter on free alienation by tying up the use of land for centuries into the future. By the late seventeenth century, however, this power was mitigated by the Rule Against Perpetuities pronounced in the *Duke of Norfolk's Case*.[70] This rule made void any contingent interest created in a transferee, which, viewed from the moment of its creation, was not certain to vest within the life of a person living at the time the interest was created, plus twenty-one years.

Although this English rule did aid free alienation, Humphreys offered an improvement that the Revisers took into consideration. Humphreys suggested elimination of the twenty-one years in gross at the end of the period.[71] The Revisers, who wanted to keep the land market open and mobile, tightened the English Rule Against Perpetuities by placing a more severe limit on the time that land could be tied up within a family. Under the old rule, *future interests*, or those interests in land in which the privilege of possession is in the future rather than the present, were deemed void only for "remoteness of vesting." In contrast, the Revisers made future interest void if they merely "suspended" the "power of alienation" unduly.[72]

It is clear, against their background, that the Revised Statutes defeudalized, commercialized,[73] and simplified[74] the law of real property. However, it is significant that they made more complex the law of married women's property since trusts, or the device that had been used to create a separate estate for married women, were made more uncertain. Moreover married women, like all other New Yorkers, could no longer levy a fine, that is, transfer land by fictionally acknowledging the right of the transferee to the property.

The Revisers defeudalized social relations among men but left intergender social relations feudal. Given the incompleteness of this reform, the Married Women's Property Acts were to be demanded. Nonetheless, it took the legislature another twenty years to complete the defeudalization by extending the process to married women. In the meantime the ideological struggle for hegemony over the instrumentality of law reform continued. Advocates of judicial hegemony cried for the restoration of the trust. Legislative supremacists wanted to abolish chancery as well as the trust over which it had jurisdiction. Because the law of married women's property was enmeshed in this struggle, it is important to examine the struggle in the years from 1828 to 1848 with care. Such examination will help to explain the passage of the Married Women's Property Acts and the feminist movement this passage inspired.

Notes

1. Estate in fee tail, sometimes called an entailed estate or simply entail, is defined as:

> A fee abridged or limited to the issue, or certain classes of issue, instead of descending to all the heirs ... but sometimes it is ... used ... to signify a succession of life-estates.
>
> BLACK'S LAW DICTIONARY 624 (4th ed. 1951).

2. N.Y. E P T L § 6-1.2 (McKinney 1782).
3. Future interests are defined as:

> Interests in land or other things in which the privilege of possession or of enjoyment is future and not present.

> BLACK'S LAW DICTIONARY 806 (4th ed. 1951).

4. L. FRIEDMAN, A HISTORY OF AMERICAN LAW 211 (1973) [hereinafter cited as HIST. AM. LAW]. Nineteenth-century commentators would agree with such characterization. *See, e.g., Law Reforms and Law Reformers*, 3 AM. L. REGISTER 513

at 521 (1864), in which the author makes a distinction between codification and a mere consolidation of statutes. The Revised Statutes of 1830, the author contended, went further than consolidation and "undertook the entire codification of some branches of the law, especially concerning real estate."

5. *See e.g., Law of Real Property*, 1 AM. JURIST 58 at 78-79 (1829), wherein the contemporary author, after recognizing Humphreys's great influence over the New York Revised Statutes, showed how Humprehys replaced Blackstone's Canons of Descent with the rules of descent of the civil law. Humphreys was reputed to be a student of the systems of nations other than English, which accounted for his radical approach to reform. *Id.* at 60.

Accord, J. PARKES, NEW YORK COURT OF CHANCERY AND REAL PROPERTY LAW lxxxiii (1830) [hereinafter cited as PARKES].

See Written and Unwritten Systems of Laws, 9 AM. JURIST 5 (1833), for a discussion by a contemporary author of the limitations of the common-law method and the advantages of the Roman-law method of analogizing from code articles. The author believed that an understanding of the nature of a true code could be gained only by looking at the civil law of continental countries and not merely from English law. The civil-law or code method was characterized as a science instead of a mosaic of independent fragments that described common law, according to the author. *Id.* at 11. About this "scientific" code method, the author stated:

> The code therefore widely confines itself to the general principle, and leaves to the speculation of the sages of the law, to the practice of the courts, and above all to time and experience of society, to fill up the jurisprudence.

Id. at 21.

6. W. BUTLER, THE REVISION OF THE STATUTES OF THE STATE OF NEW YORK AND THE REVISERS 18 (1889) [hereinafter cited as REVISION & REVISERS]. Wheaton became a reporter for the United States Supreme Court and was the author of a famous text on international law. *See* HIST. AM. LAW 283, 287.

7. J. MARKE, VIGNETTES OF LEGAL HISTORY 56-57 (1965).

8. REVISION & REVISERS 19.

9. R. POUND, THE FORMATIVE ERA OF AMERICAN LAW (1938) *passim* [hereinafter cited as FORMATIVE ERA].

10. *Id.* at 8.

11. *Id.* at 6.

12. *Id.* at 8.

13. *Id.* at 9-10.

14. *See* Stevenson, *Influence of Bentham and Humphreys on the New York Property Legislation of 1828*, 1 AM. J. LEGAL HIST. 155 (1957) [hereinafter cited as *Influence of Bentham & Humphreys in N.Y.*].

15. REVISION & REVISERS 5-6.

16. *Id.* at 9-10.

17. *Id.* at 10.

18. *Id.*

19. Quoted *id.* at 11.

20. *Id.* at 18-19.

21. 20 DICTIONARY OF AMERICAN BIOGRAPHY 39-42 (1936).

22. Quoted in REVISION & REVISERS 21.

23. *Id.* at 20-22.

24. *See* Report to the Legislature quoted *id.* at 22. It is interesting to note that the 1826 edition of Humphreys's book was OBSERVATIONS ON THE ACTUAL STATE OF ENGLISH REAL PROPERTY WITH OUTLINE OF A CODE, and the 1827 edition was entitled OBSERVATIONS ON THE ACTUAL STATE OF THE ENGLISH LAWS OF REAL PROPERTY WITH OUTLINE FOR A SYSTEMATIC REFORM. One can only speculate on why he found it necessary to alter the title.

25. REVISION & REVISERS 33.

26. HIST. AM. LAW 210.

27. REVISION & REVISERS 33-34. *Accord, Law of Real Property, supra* note 5, at 60; *Law Reform in America* 6 LAW MAGAZINE & REV. 127 at 135 (1831).

28. *Influence of Bentham & Humphreys in N.Y.* 159.

29. 2 H. BROUGHAM, SPPECHES 287-88 (1838) cited *id.* at 158.

30. *See* REVISERS' NOTES 3 N.Y. REV. STAT. 580 (1836) [hereinafter cited as REVISERS' NOTES]. Although these notes were published in the 1836 edition, they were written in connection with the 1828 edition.

31. J. HUMPREHYS, OBSERVATIONS ON THE ACTUAL STATE OF THE ENGLISH LAWS OF REAL PROPERTY WITH OUTLINE OF A CODE (1826).

32. *See Influence of Bentham & Humphreys in N.Y.* 161.

33. *Id.* at 165.

34. A *perpetuity* is defined as:

Such a limitation of property as renders it unalienable beyond the period allowed by law.

BLACK'S LAW DICTIONARY 1299 (4th ed. 1951). The rule against perpetuity is defined as a

principle that no interest in property is good unless it must vest, if at all, not later than 21 years, plus period of gestation, after some life or lives in being at time of creation of interest.

BLACK'S LAW DICTIONARY 1498 (4th ed. 1951).

35. REVISERS' NOTES 587.

36. *Id.* at 584.

37. REVISION & REVISERS 34.

38. Quoted *id.* at 35.

39. *Id.*

40. Quoted *id.*

41. These are the words of contemporary commentator quoted *id.* at 34.

42. Quoted *id.* at 35. The struggle between hostile systems referred to by the Revisers was the struggle between feudal tenures and free alienation. It began in England in 1066 when William the Conqueror laid the foundations of feudal land law. For a thorough explanation of this development of property law, see T. BERGIN & P. HASKELL, PREFACE TO ESTATES IN LAND AND FUTURE INTERESTS (1966).

43. Quoted in REVISION & REVISERS 35.
44. Quoted *id*. at 35-36.
45. Quoted *id*. at 36.
46. Quoted *id*.
47. Quoted *id*.
48. Letter from Thomas Jefferson to James Madison (Sept. 6, 1789) *reprinted in* 15 PAPERS OF THOMAS JEFFERSON 392 (Boyd ed. 1958).
49. *Id*.
50. *Id*. at 396.
51. J. KENT, COMMENTARIES ON AMERICAN LAW (2d ed. 1832).
52. 4 *id*. at 20.
53. Ejectment is defined as:

[an] action . . . which lay for the recovery of possession of land, and for damages for the unlawful detention of its possession.

BLACK'S LAW DICTIONARY 607 (4th ed. 1951). This fiction, premised upon dishonesty, dates from the early fourteenth century. It was invented to conform to the rule that someone must always be seized of every parcel of land while simultaneously acting to facilitate alienation. If one party claimed a parcel of land of which another was in possession, instead of the two parties impleading, or suing, each other, as in any other action to recover money or to try title to moveable property, they were forced to set up two fictitious parties. John Doe, one fictitious party, pretended to be the real plaintiff, and Richard Roe, the other fictitious party, the real defendant. John Doe then alleged that the land Richard Roe had was his, because he had a valid lease given by one of the real parties, and that he came on the premises where he was met by Richard Roe who had a lease by the other real party. Roe, Doe had to claim, ousted him. Roe was then deemed to be the "causal ejector" and feoffee.

54. REVISION & REVISERS 44.
55. *Id*.
56. N.Y. REV. STAT., ch. 4, §24 (1828).
57. The reason why the law and practice of the ecclesiastical courts was so mysterious was not sinister. Rather, equity law was complex because of the piecemeal manner in which it developed. Only slowly could feudal rules be negated by equity. The result was a confusing mass of rules and devices to avoid these rules. The struggle took shape in the sixteenth century. For a thorough explanation of the development of the trust, see BERGIN & HASKELL, *supra* note 42, at 61-122.
58. 1 Rep 88(b) (1581). *See* REVISION & REVISERS 48-49.
59. REVISERS' NOTES 587; *Accord*, REVISION & REVISERS 56.
60. HIST. AM. LAW 211, 222.
61. REVISERS' NOTES 587.
62. 27 Hen. 8, c. 10 (1536).
63. An *active trust* is:

One which imposes upon the trustee the duty of taking active measures in the execution of the trust, as . . . distinguished from a "passive" or "dry" trust. BLACK'S LAW DICTIONARY 1680 (4th ed. 1951).

64. *Influence of Bentham & Humphreys in N.Y.* 166.

65. REVISERS' NOTES 586.

66. *Id.* at 589.

67. *Id.* at 601.

68. *Id.* at 578.

69. BERGIN & HASKELL 119.

70. 3 Ch. Cas. 1 (1682).

71. REVISERS' NOTES 572.

72. HIST. AM. LAW 211.

73. For a contemporary viewpoint agreeing with this generality, *see Written and Unwritten Systems of Laws*, 9 AM. JURIST 5 (1833). The author viewed codification in New York, the Roman Republic, and postrevolutionary France as an instrument of commerce and the feudal common law as an outgrowth of the customs and usages of "ferocious barbarians" unsuited to an urban society of "polished merchants and cultimated philosophers." *Id.* at 28 and 36.

74. For a contemporary viewpoint agreeing with this generality, *see* PARKES at lxxiii.

> The simplicity and improvement of the laws of Real Property [in New York] greatly diminish the sources of equity litigation; and feudal tenures do not supply the copious streams of business which flow into the English courts of Chancery.

Parkes also found the transfer of property facilitated. *id.* at xiii.

7 LAW REFORM AND MARRIED WOMEN'S SEPARATE ESTATE: THE EFFECT OF THE LEGISLATIVE-REFORM MOVEMENT ON THE PRIOR LAW OF MARRIED WOMEN—THE INCOMPLETE REFORM

I.

The passage of the New York Married Women's Property Act of 1848 was a result of many factors. The question is: why was it passed in New York State in 1848? A simple answer is that it was passed because women agitated for it. But such an answer begs the question, leaving more fundamental questions unanswered. Why did women agitate for such act in 1848 in New York State? Why did an all male legislature respond affirmatively? These questions cannot be understood apart from the history of the statutory changes in property law that occurred in New York in the 1820s and 1830s. These changes simultaneously weakened equity, the historic safeguarder of the property of wealthy women, and defeudalized or bourgeoisified the law of real property, thereby expanding the number of potential property owners of both sexes.

Although an expansion of the legal rights of married women was not among the outstanding goals of the movement to reform property law, such expansion was, nevertheless, a product of the law-reform movement's ramifications. One important goal of the law-reform movement was to limit the application of the *trust*, whereby one person had an equitable ownership in property and another person had legal title to the property. This, of course, was to have serious implications for the class of women who depended on the trust to hold property separate from their husbands. Since the New York State Revised Statutes of 1836 severely limited the application of the trust, the debate between 1836 and 1848 was whether to fill the void left by the Revised Statutes' limitations on the trust by a new statute that could accomplish the same goal in a more direct way or whether to restore the trust to its old position of viability. The proponents of thorough law reform through legislation advocated the former alternative, while the opponents of the Married Women's Property Acts opted for the latter alternative. Before examining the nature of the debate, it is important to understand what the Revised Statutes had done to the trust.

II. Uses and Trusts Under the Revised Statutes of 1836

The second half of the Revised Statutes of 1836 concerned the acquisition, enjoyment, and transmission of real and personal property. Chapter one, title two, article two, concerned the law of uses and trusts. Section 45, the first section to article two, abolished all *uses*—whereby one person held legal ownership to property while another person used it—except as authorized by the Revised Statutes and deemed every estate in land a right unless otherwise provided by the statute.[1] Complementing this abolition of uses and trusts was section 46, a modern version of the old English Statute of Uses,[2] which provided that: "Every estate which is now held as an use, executed under any former statute of this state, is confirmed as a legal estate."[3] It was also complemented by section 47, which gave actual legal possession of lands to those who had held the property in trust.[4]

These provisions demonstrate one very important weakness in Mary Beard's analysis of the role of equity that had led her to conclude that married women had had the right to own property and that the early feminists had denied this fact for political advantages that could be gained from polemics about civil death or perhaps because they did not know the rights of women in equity jurisprudence. On the contrary, however, married women's estate in equity after these statutes were passed was not sufficiently secure to justify Beard's theory that women who agitated for the legal right to own property were motivated by a lack of knowledge of equity's ability to keep them from being a subject class. The effect of these provisions was to make equitable estates legal. That is, the prior equitable owner or beneficiary of the use or trust was to become the legal owner and the prior legal owner or trustee was to have no interest. However, since the legal estate of a married woman in 1836 belonged to her husband, if her equitable estate were to be executed into a legal estate, she would lose her equitable or beneficial ownership without gaining a corresponding legal estate. Thus the reform of 1836 with respect to a married woman was an incomplete reform and would remain such until she gained a corresponding right to own property at law. If this state of affairs motivated feminists, their agitation was more than mere polemics. Moreover their motivation was not lack of knowledge of a right, but rather was knowledge that they had recently lost a right.

The "except when otherwise provided" clause of section 45 referred to sections 48, 50, and 55. Section 48 recognized the validity of active trusts.[5] Sections 50[6] and 55[7] provided for the creation of express trusts for purposes such as selling land for the benefit of creditors and legatees and to administer actively the rents and profits of lands for another's use during the other's lifetime.

The statutes were revised again in 1846 but the article on uses and trusts was substantially the same as the 1836 law.[8] This is also true of the proposed Field code provisions, which were not made into law.[9]

In the notes that followed the 1836 edition,[10] the Revisers justified their radical treatment of the trust by declaring that:

In England, the necessity of such reform was confessed during the last session of its parliament, by the leading statesmen of every party; and in consequence of the success of Mr. Brougham's motion, founded on his celebrated speech, commissioners have been appointed, to whom, with other subjects, the trusts of inquiring into the state of the laws of real property, and reporting suitable changes and improvements, has been specially committed.[11]

They also expressed an admiration for the demystified continental civil law, which had influenced their work.

If we direct our attention to the laws of other nations and countries, we shall find, perhaps to our surprise, that so far as they relate to real property, they are in a measure free from the objections to which our system is liable. In the civil law, the regulations concerning the enjoyment, alienation and transmission of real estate, comparatively speaking, are neither numerous, nor difficult to be understood, and in the Code Napoleon they form a very small and perfectly intelligible portion of that immortal work. It is not extravagant to say that the French law of real estate, may be sufficiently understood by a few days of diligent study.[12]

The Revisers also explained the reasons for abolishing the trusts, depsite the fact that trusts had so long been used to mitigate feudalism. Expressing concern for both the rights of creditors in a commercial society and the need for demystification, the Revisers maintained:

...[U]ses were attended with many inconveniences, and led to great abuses. They tended to defraud creditors who had no remedy against the equitable estate and purchasers, whose conveyances or leases from the equitable owner, the trustee, could always avoid. They enable the trustee, by conveying, or submitting to a disseisin, and by other means, to defeat the rights of the beneficial owner; and a frequent resort to equity became necessary, to compel him to perform the trust. And, in our judgment, above all, by separating the legal and equitable estate, and introducing two classes of rights over the same lands, governed by different rules, and subject to different jurisdictions they rendered titles perplexed and obscure, and multiplied litigation.[13]

This commentary by those who wanted to abolish the trust further weakens Beard's analysis. Not only were equitable devices complex and mystifying, but equitable ownership with legal ownership in the trustee was not always satisfactory. The fact is made manifest by the Revisers' concern with the trustee's ability to defeat the rights of the beneficiary, that is, to use the property other than in her best interests. Moeover the separate jurisdictions of law and equity, each with separate rules and procedures, made land transfer and debtor-creditor relations needlessly complex. Thus to defeudalize, commercialize, and simplify the legal system, it was seen as wise to suggest that only one jurisdiction prevail. That one jurisdiction was not to be equity.[14]

Influenced by Lord Brougham's speech, the Revisers aimed to restore substantially the Statute of Uses while adding statutory substitutes to maintain the beneficial aspects of the use or trust. As they stated in their notes:

It is to remove these serious inconveniences... that the Revisers propose the entire abolition of uses, whilst by the new provisions which they have suggested, all the benefits admitted to flow from the present system, are retained and increased. By making a grant without the actual delivery of possession or livery of seisin, effectual to pass every estate and interest in lands, ... the utility of conveyances deriving their effect from the statute of uses, is superseded, and a cheap intelligible and universal form of transferring titles is substituted in their place. The new modifications of property which uses have sanctioned, are preserved by repealing the rules of the common law, by which they were prohibited and permitting every estate to be created by grant, which can be created by devise. And this is the effect of the provisions in relation to expectant estates, contained in the first Article of this Title.[15]

The Revisers' decision to abolish only formal trusts and to allow the active trust was influenced by James Humphreys.[16] Formal trusts were abolished, according to the Revisers' notes, because

it is plainly needless to retain them. They separate the legal and equitable estate, for no purpose that the law ought to sanction. They answer no end whatever but to facilitate fraud; to render titles more complicated, and to increase the business of chancery.[17]

On the other hand

active trusts, as a late writer [Mr. Humphreys], has properly termed them, are recognized in every system of law, and their utility, under proper restrictions, is undeniable. They seem, indeed, indispensable to the proper enjoyment and management of property. The Revisers, therefore, propose to retain them, only limiting their continuance,... and defining the purposes for which they may be created.[18]

As these references indicate, the formal trust was abolished for sound commercial reasons such as decreasing fraud and increasing the marketability of land. Also an important consideration was the desire to limit the business of chancery, the court that administered equity law, by simplifying the law of property to negate the prior need to resort to chancery. Taking a comparative law approach, the Revisers decided to retain the active trust, which could be used for those who were indeed incapable of managing their own property.

They distinguished the active trust from the formal trust, which they claimed existed "for no purpose that the law ought to sanction." Perhaps they overlooked the purpose of keeping a married woman's property separate from her husband.

III. Reaction to the Treatment of the Trust by the Revised Statutes

With regard to the abolition of the formal trust, the Revisers faced some opposition. Chancellor Kent believed the trust provisions could not work. In his famous and widely read *Commentaries on American Law*, he contended that the desire to "preserve and perpetuate family influence and property" was "very prevalent with mankind" and was "deeply seated in the affections."[19] "We cannot hope," he argued, to "check the enterprising spirit of gain, the pride of families, the anxieties of parents, the importunities of luxury, the fixedness of habits, the subtleties of intellect."[20] By these words, Kent was referring to affections fathers had for their daughters and the desires of these fathers to perpetuate their families' influence and control over property, rather than see the families' property in the hands of their daughters' husbands, who would, but for the trusts, have owned their wives' property bestowed upon them by their fathers through gifts or wills. Skeptical of law reform through legislation, he predicted widespread evasion: the "fairest and proudest models of legislation that can be matured in the closet" could not prevail against the "usages of a civilized people."[21]

In the law journals of the day, the debate raged. The *American Jurist* ran a series entitled "Codification and Reform of the Law."[22] The July 1839 issue condemned the abolition of the use as a dangerous example of "hasty legislation"[23] and "ill-considered reform."[24] The article accused the Revisers of being

dismayed by the intricate learning of uses and trusts, and feeling themselves unprepared to meet the arduous task of encountering its "refinements, distinctions and abstruseness," they vainly resolved to make an effort to sweep away the mass altogether, to make the system intelligible and consistent.[25]

The pros and cons of the Revisers' attack on the trust, as well as on feudal tenures, was carried on in many more journals between 1836 and 1848.[26] This widespread publicity is evidence that the legal community was well aware of the controversy, as were the members of the legislature.

By the time the married women's property bills were before the legislature, arguments had crystalized. The reports from the Committee on the Judiciary on the petitions to extend and protect the rights of property of married women demonstrates that the fate of those petitions was intermingled with the movement for law reform previously discussed. A report in favor of the acts came out of committee on April 12, 1842. Although the committee was too constrained by other priorities to frame the act at that time, they were unanimously agreed to favor a more liberal extension of the rights of married women. Their biases against feudal common law and in favor of the legislative-reform movement are demonstrated in their statement regarding the feasibility of passing such an act. Referring to the committee's concern for the delicacy of the institution of marriage, which would be affected by such legislation, the report stated:

Consistently with this principle of prudence they yet think that something of a safe and salutory character could be done and ought to be done, to engraft at least partially upon the hard and stubborn trunk of the common law the more liberal principle in relation to this subject of which a successful precedent has long been held out to as in most of the codes of other countries founded on the civil law.[27]

Two years later another report came out of this same committee. In contrast to the former one, the report of February 26, 1844, is illustrative of the arguments against the act. But similar to the former report, this report also places the debate over the Married Women's Property Act into the context of the broader debate over law reform. In fact, the issue was placed in this context by petitioners who asked the legislature to revise the law of married women's property. The petitioners, hostile to the trust, asked that an act be introduced that would secure the property and protect the rights of married women without reference to any express trust created for the benefit of the wife.[28] The petitioners were hostile to the common law as well. In their petitions, they denounced the husband's entitlement to his wife's property.[29]

The remedy sought by the petitioners was that property, both real and personal, belonging to any women before marriage or that may thereafter be transferred, conveyed, or vested in any married woman by deed, gift, bequest, or devise shall be held and deemed to be her own separate estate and subject to her own conduct and disposal in the same manner and as effectually as if she were a single woman.[30] Reasons were provided by the petitioners to support their request.

The law which deprives the wife of her own property, making her wholly dependent on her husband for support, is liable to destroy the very elements of domestic harmony and happiness, to diminish the self-respect of woman, and thereby the respect of her fellow beings, prevents the improvement of married women, and begets a spirit of meanness and duplicity which is unfavorable alike to the happiness and best interests of both parties.[31]

It is interesting to see how the committee answered these complaints. First, they presented the argument of historicism. The committee report argued that the law had "formed a part of the common law for centures"[32] and has "stood the test of time."[33] Then, they argued in favor of judicial lawmaking and against legislative innovations.

One of the greatest evils of the day is excessive legislation and continued change of our statutory regulations. So long as legislation is confined to a correction of ascertained and known defects or evils, so far it is legitimate and useful, but beyond that, it is dangerous and may be mischievous. "*Stare Decisis*" is a maxim, the importance of which is known to and appreciated by everyone at all familiar with judicial decisions, and to "abide by the law as written," should be a maxim of equal force with legislators, until a manifest evil is shown to exist, and a clear and plain remedy for that evil is pointed out.[34]

Here is a reversal of the codifiers' argument. The uncertainties of the law are not caused by *stare decisis* (let the decision stand) as the codifiers would argue, but according to this committee report arise "from the frequent attempts to remedy by legislation."[35] To support this assertion, the committee made a comparison between the state of society in countries where feudal common law existed and the state of society where the codified postrevolutionary civil law governed the rights of married women. The hostility toward France and the French Civil Code shows clearly through this comparison. The committee's reporter concluded that:

[I]n the European states, and particularly France, the effect of these laws upon the morals of the community is very apparent, and if the spirit of innovation, which is now so rife in the land, is allowed to prevail, and that code of laws which is now in operation in but a small part of our territory, shall prevail throughout the states it will be found that like causes produce like effects, and we shall rival France and some of the other continental nations in the laxity of our morals.[36]

The fear of the codification movement, which admittedly took the French Civil Code as a model, is apparent in that argument. Also apparent is a fear that the proposed legislation would damage the institution of marriage and create loose morals. Speaking again of France, the reporter contended:

Husband and wife having their separate property, . . . have also their separate amours and intrigues; each interfering as little with the other in this matter, as they do in their pecuniary matters. A lover separate from the husband becomes almost a necessary appendage to the wife; and this laxity of morals, beginning as it does from this cause, is not confined to the circle within which it has its origin, but it extends by its example through all classes.

The want of chastity in the female is not considered a deadly offense, . . . and why is this? It is because infidelity to the marriage vow is tolerated at least, if not encouraged by the laws, destroying in part and unity of the married state.[37]

Although the reporter was hostile to law reform through legislation, he was receptive to law reform by equity. He stated that the committee believed "experience has shown that no evil can result from giving to the wife the benefit of property intended for her use through the intervention of a trust."[38] The reporter argued that the trust did not interefere with morality and chastity as would a married women's property act.

It is believed that the management of property for the benefit of the wife, through the intervention of a trustee, will be less likely to produce collision between husband and wife than the direct management of it by the wife, aside from the fact that the direction and control of the property being regulated by the terms of the trust, it is impossible that the interests of the husband and wife can run counter to each other in respect to their property.[39]

This reasoning is patently false. On the contrary, the trust was used by fathers who wanted to give their property to their daughters rather than their sons-in-law, whom the fathers often distrusted. As A. V. Dicey, the Vinerian professor of English law at Oxford from 1882-1909, demonstrated, the husband, contrary to the report's rosy picture, was "the enemy against whose exorbitant common-law rights the Court of Chancery waged constant war."[40] Dicey recalled the stages through which the Court of Chancery had completely achieved its victory over the enemy husband by the eve of the nineteenth century.[41] The first stage of this ingenious judicial legislation was the decision that property given to a trustee for the separate use of a woman, whether before or after marriage, is her separate property. Separate property meant separate from her husband. The next step occurred when property was given to or settled upon a woman for her separate use, but no trustee was appointed by the donor. The Court of Chancery, under such circumstances, made the husband into the trustee and bound him to treat it in terms of the "trust," that is, as her separate property. In the next stage of judicial creativity, the Court of Chancery developed the idea that a trustee must deal with the property of a married woman in accordance with her directions. This gave the woman powers analogous to a right of alienation, that is, a right to convey property. Unless the marriage settlement, will, or grant put a restraint on anticipation, the married woman had the power to give away or sell her separate property, to leave it to whomever she wished by will, and to charge it, or obligate it, with her contracts.

Meanwhile the Revised Statutes had obviated the work of chancery. The committee that reviewed the petition requesting an "act for the more effectual protection of the rights of property of married women" concluded that it was the Revised Statutes that created the necessity for the legislature to protect married women's property more effectively. Noting the gaps in the law created by the Revised Statutes, the reporter pointed out that no longer could real property be secured to the separate use of the wife by an antenuptial settlement or by settlement made after marriage by a third person making the husband a trustee.[42] The committee believed that: "in the attempt to codify and simplify the law of uses and trusts, this class of trust estates was inadvertently omitted by the Revisers and by the Legislature."[43]

Thus the critics of the French Civil Code were also those who opposed the Revisers' treatment of uses and trusts and the petition for a Married Women's Property Act. The committee advised the House that the Act for the More

Effectual Protection of the Rights of Property of Married Women ought not be passed into law.[44] Instead, they offered a substitute bill entitled an Act in Relation to Uses and Trusts.[45] They hoped that:

> With an alteration of the law, by permitting trusts in real estate to be created for the sole benefit of feme covert, females and their friends have it in their power, whenever prudence may dictate it, to secure the property of the wife in the safest possible manner, without at all endangering the happiness of her for whose benefit it was deisgned.[46]

Nevertheless their recommendations were not destined to prevail. Two years later the Constitution of 1846 abolished chancery, the court that created trusts as a method of law reform, and four years after this report the first New York Married Women's Property Act was passed to fill the void in the law of married women's property caused by the limitations placed on uses and trusts by the Revised Statutes and the abolition of chancery.[47]

Notes

1. Uses and trusts, except as authorized and modified, in the Article, are abolished; and every estate and interest in lands, shall be deemed a legal right, cognizable as such in the courts of law, except when otherwise provided in this Chapter.

   N.Y. REV. STAT., ch. 1, §45 (1836).

2. 27 Hen. 8, c. 10 (1536).
3. N.Y. REV. STAT., ch. 1, §46 (1836).
4. Every person, who, by virtue of any grant, assignment or devise, now is, or hereafter shall be entitled to the actual possession of lands, and the receipt of the rents and profits thereof, in law or in equity, shall be deemed to have a legal estate therein, of the same quality and duration, and subject to the same conditions as his beneficial interest.

   N.Y. REV. STAT., ch. 1, §47 (1836).

5. The last preceding section shall not divest the estate of any trustees, in any existing trust, where the title of such trustees, is not merely nominal, but is connected with some power of actual disposition or management, in relation to the lands which are the subject of the trust.

   N.Y. REV. STAT., ch. 1, §48 (1836).

6. The preceding sections in this article shall not extend to trusts, arising or resulting by implication of law, nor be construed to prevent or affect the creation of such express trusts, as are hereinafter authorized and defined.

N.Y. REV. STAT., ch. 1, §50 (1836).

7. Express trusts may be created, for any or either of the following purposes:
1. To sell lands for the benefits of the creditors;
2. To sell, mortgage or lease lands, for the benefit of legatees, or for the purpose of satisfying any charge thereon;
3. To receive the rents and profits of lands, and apply them to the use of any person, during the life of such person, or for any shorter term, subject to the rules prescribed in the first Article of this Title;
4. To receive the rents and profits of lands, and to accumulate the same, for the purposes and within the limits prescribed in the first Article of this Title.

N.Y. REV. STAT., ch. 1, §55 (1836).

8. *Compare* N.Y. REV. STAT., pt. 2, ch. 1, tit. 2 (1846) *with* N.Y.REV. STAT., ch. 1, §§45-58, 50, 55 (1836).
9. *See* FIELD'S PROPOSED CODE tit. IV (1865).
10. Some of these notes were written in connection with the 1828 revision.
11. REVISERS' NOTES 3 N.Y. REV. STAT. 580 (1836).
12. *Id.*
13. *Id.* at 582.
14. By the 1846 New York State Constitution, chancery was abolished. *See* discussion *infra* regarding the merger of law and equity into one jurisdiction.
15. REVISERS' NOTES, *supra* note 11, at 580.
16. *See* references to Humphreys made by the Revisers *id.* at 583.
17. *Id.*
18. *Id.* Implied trusts, too, were not abolished. They were retained to prevent fraud. Provisions on dower were similar to Humphreys's outline. N.Y. REV. STAT., pt. 2, tit. 3 (1836).
19. 4 J. KENT, COMMENTARIES ON AMERICAN LAW 19 (2d ed. 1832).
20. *Id.* at 313.
21. *Id.*
22. *Codification and Reform of the Law*—No.7, 21 AM. JURIST 352-53 (1839).
23. *Id.* at 353.
24. *Id.* at 357.
25. *Id.* at 369.
26. *See, e.g., Recent Revisions & C. of Statute Laws—New York*, 18 AM. JURIST 244 (1837); *Codification and Reform of the Law*—No. 7, 21 AM. JURIST 352 (1839); *Codification and Reform of the Law*—No. 8, 22 AM. JURIST 282 (1840); Telkampf, *On Codification, or the Systematizing of the Law*, 26 AM. JURIST 113 (1841); Telkampf, *On Codification or Systematizing of the Law: Objections Against Codification Answered*, 27 AM. JURIST 283 (1842); *Trusts for Separate Use*, N.Y. Legal Observer, Nov. 26, 1842, at 113, col. 1; *Separate Estate of Married Women*, 3 AM. L. MAGAZINE (1844); *Accumulation from Property Settled to Separate Use*, N.Y. Legal Observer, March 1844, at 3, col. 1; *The Law of Real Property as Affected by the Revised Statutes of the State of New York*, 4 AM. L. MAGAZINE 310 (1844-45); *The Law of Real*

Property as Affected by the Revised Statutes of the State of New York, 5 AM. L. MAGAZINE 50 (1845); *Uses and Trusts as Affected by the Revised Statutes of the State of New York*, 6 AM. L. MAGAZINE 268 (1845).

27. N.Y. ASSEM. DOC. No. 189, at 2 (April 12, 1842).

28. N.Y. ASSEM. DOC. No. 96, at 1 (Feb. 26, 1844) [hereinafter cited as DOC. No. 96].

29. *Id.* at 2.

30. *Id.* at 3.

31. Cited *id.* at 3.

32. *Id.* at 2.

33. *Id.*

34. *Id.* at 2.

35. *Id.*

36. *Id.* at 8.

37. *Id.* at 9.

38. DOC. No. 96, at 10.

39. *Id.*

40. A. DICEY, LECTURER ON THE RELATION BETWEEN LAW AND PUBLIC OPINION IN ENGLAND DURING THE NINETEENTH CENTURY 376 (rev. ed. 1962).

41. *Id.* at 376-79.

42. DOC. No. 96, at 10.

43. *Id.*

44. *Id.* at 11.

45. *Id.*

46. *Id.* at 10.

47. N.Y. SEN. J., March 29, 1848, at 443; N.Y. ASSEM. J., April 6, 1848, at 1129.

8 A PROPOSED MARRIED WOMEN'S PROPERTY ACT: A REACTION TO THE LAW-REFORM MOVEMENT'S INCOMPLETE REFORM

Judge Thomas Herttell introduced a bill into the New York State Assembly for the protection and preservation of the rights and property of married women in April 1837,[1] over a decade before the first Married Women's Property Act was passed and the Senaca Falls Women's Rights Convention was held. Since his proposed bill and the arguments he advanced in support of it were motiviated by both feminism and a commitment to filling the gaps left by the Revised Statutes with regard to the property of married women, his efforts are worthy of close examination despite the fact that his bill was never enacted into law. His work is also important because his arguments were printed into a widely read pamphlet that inspired female activists to petition the legislature for an act to more effectively protect married women's property.

The first section of the Herttell bill provided that a married woman could hold legal title, as if single, to any property, both real and personal. Like the Married Women's Property Act of 1848, a married woman under the proposed Herttell bill would have been entitled to hold legal title to any property acquired by "inheritance, gift, bequest or devise."[2] Unlike the 1848 act, however, the Herttell bill would have given legal title to a married woman of that property "which she may acquire by her own industry and management."[3] This included "rents, issues, or profits of real estate."[4] Arguably, a married woman would have been entitled to the wages she earned as well as to the money made on money acquired by gift or inheritance.

Wages and earnings were not protected by the 1848 act.[5] Therefore, the Herttell bill would have granted more rights to women themselves than the bill that was actually enacted into law in 1848. This is an indication of a profeminist inclination in Herttell, absent in the drafter of the latter act. The 1848 act in reality protected the property of the married woman's father rather than that which a married woman herself acquired.

The Herttell bill also would have obliterated the distinction between dower and curtesy, medieval concepts that had provided a widow with a life estate of only one-third of the lands of her deceased husband and a widower with a life estate in all of his deceased wife's lands as long as a child was born alive. This distinction, as noted above, was of no import to Humphreys. Section two of Herttell's proposed bill provided

[t]hat on the demise of the wife during the lifetime of her husband, he shall be entitled to such portion of the property owned and possessed by his wife at the time of her demise, in like manner and to the same or like extent, as by the laws of this state the widow is entitled to have and possess of the property possessed by her husband at the time of his demise.[6]

The provision tends to indicate that Herttell was more a feminist than were the advocates of married women's property legislation of the following decade.

A close examination of the provisions of his proposed bill further illustrates Herttell's feminist motivations. Section three demonstrated his belief that the husband was the enemy against whom the wife needed the protection of the legal system. It provided that it would be "unlawful"[7] for a married woman to convey her real or personal property to her husband unless by order of a chancellor or vice chancellor. Such a judicial officer, moreover, must be "satisfied on due proof"[8] that the wife was acting voluntarily and that the purposes for the transfer "appear to be proper, just and necessary, and beneficial to the wife."[9]

Section five, providing that a married woman would lawfully dispose of her estate by will "in a like manner . . . as other persons are by law authorized to do,"[10] implicitly recognized that women were competent adults. Section four of the bill was redundant in light of section one (except for the provision of a right to convey). It restated the concept that a married woman should hold legal title to all property, deed, gift, bequest, devise, or earnings. However, this section would have introduced into the bill the concept of married women's *separate estate*, a term of art derived from equity law. The property, Herttell proposed, should be "deemed to be her own separate estate . . . subject to her own control and disposal, in like manner and as effectively as if she were *feme sole* [a single woman]."[11]

Despite Herttell's introduction of this phrase from equity, it is clear that he intended more than a codification of the status quo, that is, more than a codification of equity. His remarks in the New York State Assembly on May 20, 1836, in support of his resolution concerning the rights and property of married women demonstrated a feminist motivation. Again Herttell vilified the husband, hoping for the law to "protect the rights and property of married women from injury and waste by means of the improvident, prodigal, intemperate and dissolute habits and practices of their husbands."[12] Such an approach was surely calculated to appeal to any father in the legislature.

Herttell was motivated by a type of feminism that was founded on an analogy to black slavery. He decried the law giving married women's property to the husband as "unjust in principle, oppressive in its operation, and demoralizing in its results."[13] Characterizing married women as "like African captives . . . sold . . . to a master,"[14] he added that "[b]y depriving the wife of her property, and vesting it in her husband . . . she becomes in a manner, a pauper, dependent ever for subsistence solely on her husband."[15] Herttell asked, "what human being is more unjustly treated—more injured, abused, and unhappy or more to be commiserated than a wife and a mother, when subjected to the evils above mentioned?"[16] Herttell was also concerned about the evils incident to a woman's marriage to a fortune hunter. Changes in the law, he predicted, would have many beneficial results. A wife, for example, would be "respected as the equal of a good husband,"[17] and gross societal evils such as pauperism, ignorance, and crime would be cured.[18]

In addition to Herttell's emphasis on what might be termed *feminism* or *equal rights* for women, he was also clearly motivated by Anglophobia. His argument was directed against the Anglophile conservative American judiciary that Herttell believed was keeping the law feudal despite the American Revolution and the newly instituted government. He characterized the law giving a married woman's property to her husband as "a law which originated in the dark ages, in a foreign country, in which an absolute and despotic king, and an intolerant and persecuting clergy, ruled a people oppressed, demoralized and degraded, by an unhallowed combination of political and ecclesiastical tyranny...."[19] Herttell believed the legislature should demolish the judiciary[20] for permitting laws sanctioning the "anomalous and inconsistent spectacle of having established a constitution and government based on the sovereign power of the people and the principle of equal rights, and then adopting laws which originated many ages since under a monarchical government, and were intended and calculated to sustain it...."[21] This "anomalous and inconsistent spectacle," Herttell suggested, was the source of "all, or most of the evils which elicit the loud, frequent and well grounded complaints which are now so generally heard against our whole judiciary system...."[22]

Herttell, like the codifiers, was interested in legal defeudalization. To this end he argued that:

The whole fabric of our present judiciary must be demolished, and all the rotten rubbish of obsolete, antiquated, and complex principles, forms and proceedings of feudal times, which have been incautiously retained in, or incorporated with, our judiciary system, and by which it has become inadequate to its intended purpose, must be swept away....[23]

After the old judicial power based on English feudal law was abolished, Herttell hoped that a new system

more simple, prompt and less expensive—more propitious to be furtherance of justice—more consistent with the object of our free government—more congenial with the spirit and provisions of our constitution, and more in harmony with the equal rights and liberties of the people, [could] be fully reared and accomplished.[24]

Judge Thomas Herttell's arguments in the assembly in support of his 1837 bill were published as a pamphlet in 1839.[25] Passing through several editions, apparently it was widely read. It helped prepare the public and the legislators for the passage of the Married Women's Property Act of 1848 and also inspired women reformers such as Ernestine Rose and Elizabeth Cady Stanton to petition the legislature for action. His arguments therefore are worthy of a close examination. Like those in his speech the year before, the arguments in this pamphlet demonstrate a feminist sympathy. Again he presented the case for married women through arguments analogizing their position to that of an African slave.[26] Like most nineteenth-century feminists, Herttell was influenced by the Enlightenment and its natural rights philosophy. Arguing that there was a natural right to own property and that married women were human beings who should not be denied the same rights enjoyed by males and unmarried females,[27] New York State's denial of this right to married women, he concluded, was contrary to both natural law and the New York State Constitution.[28]

What is most interesting about Herttell's speech, however, is neither his feminism nor his Enlightenment outlook. Rather it is the affinity of his thought to thoughts of those interested in law reform. As such, the speech clearly indicates why the Married Women's Property Acts were passed with so little resistance. Like the law reformers, Herttell was hostile to the reception of British common law because it was feudal and inappropriate for a commercial economy.[29] In fact the Herttell bill was partly drafted by John C. Spencer, one of the Revisers of the Statutes.[30]

Herttell's arguments demonstrate that the Married Women's Property Acts were necessitated by the incomplete revolution that occurred in revising the statutes. He contended that parts of the Revised Statutes that received from English common law the rule taking property of a married woman and vesting it in her husband were unconstitutional.[31] The Revised Statutes, although a great step toward defeudalization and modernization of the law of property, did not go far enough toward making the law concerning married women conform to the needs of a commercial society. Herttell pinpointed the reason.

The Revisers started with the intention of prescribing and defining the trust and powers relative to *personal* as well as *real* eastate. Yet there is not to be found in our Statute book a *solitary provision by virtue of which a trust can be legally created for personal property.*[32]

This meant, according to Herttell, that money, bonds, notes, and other personal property all had to go to the husband. Only fathers with landed wealth, not fathers with commercial wealth, could give or bequeath property to a daughter in trust.

This was not the only shortcoming of the Revisers' treatment of the trust that troubled Herttell. He also pointed out that the right of a female after marriage, to execute a *trust* and *power created before marriage*, is so very questionable, that it is seldom hazarded and never attempted by any well informed and discreet parent, to secure property by such means, to a daughter and her children, with a view to protect it from loss or waste through the misfortune of a good, or the misconduct of a bad husband.[33]

Moreover, even when the trust of real property for the use of a married woman was secure, the result remained unsatisfactory to Hertell's critical analysis. The married woman beneficiary, he pointed out, "can have neither pins, needles, hose, linen, nor any other article but such as the trustee shall be satisfied are requisite and necessary, and which he must buy and furnish for the wife of another man."[34] Herttell assumed that "no father could wish a daughter to be placed in such an unpleasant predicament; nor would any husband, good or bad, nor any wife, be satisfied with such an arrangement."[35] Asking "and what *interests*, are more *separate* and distinct than when one of the married parties takes all [both power and property], and leaves the other nothing, but the *legal obligation* to submit without a murmur," Herttell rejected any concept of the husband and wife as two with one interest.[36] The unwholesome state of affairs, he argued, worked against instead of for the domestic harmony sought by those opposed to granting married women the right to own porperty.[37] Thus Herttell astutely recognized that to gain support for an act that was to render changes in family law, it was helpful to argue that the changes would reinforce rather than weaken traditional notions of good intrafamily relationships.

The women who petitioned the legislature in the years intervening between the Herttell bill and the 1848 bill used arguments similar to Hertell's. In their petition, the women stated: "The law which deprives the wife of her own property, making her wholly dependent on her husband for support, is liable to destroy the very elements of domestic harmony and happiness...."[38]

Whether a husband and wife usually had divergent interests may or may not be true. The cases that litigated disputes involving the question of married women's property are evidence of the actual impact the statute was to have. These cases demonstrate that the situation was more complex than merely a struggle between a good woman and a "prodigal" husband. In fact most of the cases construing the acts arose from disputes in which the husband and wife had similar interests in a struggle against third-party creditors of one or both spouses. Before examining the practical effects of the statute through an analysis of specific cases, a closer look at the role of women who agitated in favor of the act is essential. Arguments in favor of the passage of a married woman's act demonstrate both their affinity for Herttell's feminism and for the law-reform movement's concern with the political need for defeudalization and modernization of the private law of property. In the final analysis, it was the alliance with defeudalization rather than the feminist arguments that ensured passage of this bill with so little resistance.

Nevertheless it was a feminist victory and it was this silent victory that launched the later noisy campaign for women's suffrage.

Notes

1. N.Y.ASSEM. J., Apr. 24, 1837, at 121.
2. T. HERTTELL, THE CONDITION, INFLUENCE, RIGHTS AND APPEAL OF WOMEN 272 (3rd ed. 1845), wherein the bill was reprinted [hereinafter cited as APPEAL OF WOMEN].
3. *Id.*
4. *Id.*.
5. 1848 N.Y. LAWS ch. 200.
6. APPEAL OF WOMEN 272.
7. *Id.*
8. *Id.*
9. *Id.* at 273.
10. *Id.*
11. *Id.*
12. *Id.* at 265.
13. *Id.* at 266.
14. *Id.* at 267.
15. *Id.*
16. *Id.* at 268.
17. *Id.* at 270.
18. *Id.* at 271.
19. *Id.* at 266.
20. *Id.* at 269.
21. *Id.* at 268.
22. *Id.*
23. *Id.* at 269. These words anticipated the work of the 1846 Constitutional Convention, the merger of law and equity, and the Field Code of modern procedure.
24. *Id.*
25. T. HERTTELL, THE RIGHT OF MARRIED WOMEN TO HOLD AND CONTRACT PROPERTY SUSTAINED BY THE CONSTITUTION OF THE STATE OF NEW YORK (1839).
26. *Id.* at 8-9, 44-45.
27. *Id.* at 15-16, 18-19, 22-23, 29.
28. *Id.*
29. *See, id.* at 7, 8, 15, 57.
30. *Id.* at 5.
31. *Id.* at 8, 14.
32. *Id* at 10-11 (emphasis in original).
33. *Id.* at 11 (emphasis in original).
34. *Id.* at 13.
35. *Id.*
36. *Id.* at 67.
37. *Id.* at 67, 71.
38. N.Y. ASSEM. DOC. NO. 96, at 3 (Feb. 26, 1844).

9 THE NEW YORK STATE CONSTITUTIONAL CONVENTION OF 1846 AND THE FIRST NEW YORK MARRIED WOMEN'S PROPERTY ACT

I. The Convention of 1846

Some of the most prominent members of the nineteenth-century women's rights movement believed that the spirit of the 1846 New York State Constitutional Convention and the newly enacted constitution facilitated passage of the Married Women's Property Acts two years later.[1] Similarly, David Dudley Field attributed to the convention a mandate to him and the other code commissioners to undertake the "work of codification which was contemplated by the constitution of 1846...."[2] Indeed, the Constitution of 1846 carried three provisions aimed at law reform by legislation. The twelfth section of article one provided that: "All Feudal tenures of every description, with all their incidents are declared to be abolished...."[3] The seventeenth section of the first article provided that:

> The Legislature, at its first session after the adption of this constitution shall appoint three Commissioners whose duty it shall be to reduce into a written and systematic Code the whole body of the law of this State, or so much and such parts thereof as to the said Commissioners shall seem practicable....[4]

The twenty-fourth section of the sixth article further provided that:

> The Legislature, at its first session after the adoption of this constitution, shall provide for the appointment of three Commissioners, whose duty it shall be to revise, reform, simplify and abridge the rules and practice, pleadings, forms and proceedings of the courts of record of this State....[5]

Since both the Married Women's Property Act and the movement for codification, two efforts to modernize and defeudalize the laws, gained impetus from this constitutional convention, it is worth closer examination. To begin, the Constitution of 1846 abolished the Court of Chancery by failing to provide for its existence in article VI (the judiciary article) and also merged law and equity in article VI, section three. Before the convention, chancery had protected married women's property through the device of the trust; had functioned as a major force in defeudalization of substantive property law; and had begun the development of commercial law for merchants, a group whose interests were inadequately provided for at common law. Thus the effects of the convention were two-fold. The convention reflected a democratic spirit that called for an expanded franchise, and, in abolishing chancery and merging law and equity, it created yet another gap in law reform by equity that was subsequently to be filled by the codification of equity principles into the Married Women's Property Acts.

Significantly, the 1846 Constitutional Convention thoroughly debated the subject of married women's property rights. The convention opened Monday, June 1, 1846, and by Wednesday, June 10, a resolution was proffered by John Bowdish, a thirty-eight-year-old married merchant and farmer representing Montgomery County, on behalf of his colleague John Nellis, a forty-nine-year-old married lawyer and farmer also from Montgomery County. This resolution provided:

Resolved, That a committee be appointed to consider and report on the expediency of giving to females the right to hold and transfer, after marriage, all property real and personal, acquired by them before or by gift, devise or bequest after marriage, and of making them and their property liable for their debts contracted before or after marriage, and in case of the inability of the husband, liable for the support and maintenance of their families.[6]

The resolution was referred to the Committee on Rights and Privileges of the Citizen with Bowdish's consent. Fifteen days later, John Wood, a sixty-two-year-old married farmer from Rockland County, submitted a more comprehensive resolution that, as adopted, read:

Resolved, That the committee on rights and privileges of citizens of this state enquire into the propriety and expediency of securing to married women by Constitutional provision, the right and power to control and manage their real and personal estate or property they may have at the time of their marriage, or which they may afterwards be entitled to by descent, devise, bequest, contract, gift, or any other proceeding which may entitle them to the right of the property, to empower them to make bargains and contracts for the same, to bind them by such contracts or agreements, relating thereto, and that the said property be liable for the debts individually contracted by them, and also for their support and the support and maintenance of their children, and that they may by last will and testament devise and bequeath the same, and that laws may be passed by the legislature for the descent of such property in cases of intestacy, and also to secure to the husband the same interests in his wife's estate and property, that his wife would by law be entitled to in his under similar circumstances, and that a married woman may before or after death of her husband, enforce a contract or agreement made with her during marriage, for her support and maintenance.[7]

On Friday, October 2, the issue of married women's property was raised again. Ira Harris, a forty-three-year-old lawyer representing Albany County, moved instructions to the committee to report on the following section of the Tallmadge Report.

All property of the wife owned by her at the time of her marriage and that acquired by her afterwards by gift, devise or descent or otherwise than from her husband, shall be her separate property. Laws shall be passed providing for the registry of the wife's separate property and more clearly defining rights thereto; as well as to property held by her with her husband.[8]

Harris, a widower, wanted section fourteen passed because he anticipated that "it would be productive to domestic happiness,"[9] but his reasoning triggered a debate. Harris's opponent was Charles O'Conor, a forty-two-year-old lawyer representing New York County. Although never married himself, O'Conor argued that the section, if passed, "would be productive of domestic unhappiness."[10] The Tallmadge Report, of which section fourteen was a part, was a report on the "rights of man." O'Conor's view of the rights of man excluded the rights of women.[11] He seemed to be dehumanizing women, for he distinguished between the rights of women and the rights of man. In his retort to Harris he advocated that the convention "devote a little [time] to the rights of men as well as the rights of women."[12]

After O'Conor's attack, Ansel Bascom moved to amend by substituting the following for the section proposed by Harris:

The contract of marriage shall not be held to vest in either of the contracting parties, the property of the other or to create a liability upon either to discharge the debts or obligations of the other.[13]

Bascom, the delegate from Seneca County, was a thirty-two-year-old married lawyer. He insisted upon the right of a man and wife to contract freely with regard to their property. A condition precedent to such freedom of contract was the necessity of ending the "violent construction that the law put upon the marriage contract, making it entirely different and more comprehensive than the contract itself."[14] Bascom, perhaps in an effort to placate O'Conor, declared that his "amendment aims to secure the rights of men too."[15] He argued that the "reason for the violent construction that the law puts upon the marriage contract, by which the property of the wife is vested in the husband, is founded upon the liability of the husband to pay her debts contracted before marriage...."[16] If the amendment were passed, men would be relieved of this constructive liability to offset the wife's new gain.[17]

After Bascom proposed his amendment, Conrad Swackhamer, a delegate from Kings County, delivered a long oration advocating the rights of women. Swackhamer, a thirty-one-year-old married mechanic, clearly influenced by Romanism and the Enlightenment, insisted that the oppression of women was a consequence of the fact that "we were just emerging from a system of feudalism, oppressive to woman and degrading to man."[18] After referring to the matrimonial condition in this country as "a false and barbarous system transported from other countries,"[19] he argued that the marriage contract made the wife's "bondage . . . as complete as that of the southern slave."[20] Contrasting this sorry state of affairs to the status of Roman matrons after the Punic Wars, Swackhamer declared:

It was then that the women of Rome took a position in society before unknown to their sex. It was during this period that their oppressors seemed to have discovered that they had souls, and that they possessed intelligence and power; for then they began to consult them respecting matters of state, and admit them to the councils of the nation.[21]

Implied in his remarks was a preference for the civil-law treatment of married women's property and status over the English feudal common-law treatment. Similar implications can be drawn from the remarks of George W. Patterson, a married farmer representing Chautauqua County. Patterson urged joint ownership of marital property,[22] for such were the property relations of married couples under a community property concept in jurisdictions that derived their civil law from Germanic law. Patterson, however, believed that reform of the laws of martial property was a job for the legislature rather than for a constitutional convention. Arphaxed Loomis, a forty-eight-year-old married lawyer from Herkimer County, joined in agreement with Patterson, stating that, "this was a subject of too much difficulty and delicacy to be put in so permanent a form as a constitutional provision."[23] This position was consistent with a Romanist conception of a constitution as a brief document consisting only of general principles.

On October fifth, the rights of married women were again debated. This was the day that the Committee of Revision gave their report on what was to be the revised constitution. As proposed, section seven read as follows:

All the property of the wife, owned by her at the time of her marriage, and that acquired by her afterwards, by gift, devise, descent, or otherwise than from her husband, shall be her separate property. Laws shall be passed providing for the registry of the wife's separate property, and more clearly defining her rights thereto as well as to property held by her with her husband.[24]

In reality, this was the Harris proposal, which was again attacked by O'Conor, who regarded this section as "more important than any which had been adopted—perhaps than all the rest of the constitution."[25] This unmarried delegate argued that "[i]f there was anything in our institutions that ought not to be touched by the stern hand of the *reformer*, it was the sacred ordinance of marriage and the relations arising out of it."[26] Unlike Swackhamer, O'Conor praised English common law with its feudal Christian precept of the unity of husband and wife, finding it eminently suited to the American experience. He was pleased that the revolutions that had changed government here and in England left the law of married women untouched.[27] O'Conor feared that if the law of married women "were changed and man and wife converted as it were into mere partners... a most essential injury would result to the endearing relations of married life."[28] His argument was that:

A wife with a separate estate secured to her independent disposal and management, might be a sole trader; she might rival her husband in trade or become the partner of his rival. Diverse and opposing interests would be likely to grow out of such relations; controversies would arise, husband and wife would become armed against each other to the utter destruction of the sentiments which they should entertain towards each other, and to the utter subversion of true felicity in married life.[29]

Weaknesses in the factual basis of O'Conor's argument might be explained by his lack of marital experience. In actuality, the financial interests of two members of the same household were almost always one and the same whether or not the husband had control over the wife's property. This fact was manifested by the cases litigated after the Married Women's Property Acts were passed. Contrary to O'Conor's prognosis, the husband and wife were almost invariably on the same side of the lawsuit, and parties adverse to them were most often their debtors, creditors, or employers.

O'Conor was interested in preserving existing social relations, or "manners," as he called them. He understood the social ramifications of the proposal, acknowledging that "[a] law like that proposed was unnecessary"[30] for the woman from the wealthy classes. Such a woman's father provided for special marriage settlements. O'Conor, however, was gratified that such settlements "affected not the humble cottage, nor any great portion of society."[31] O'Conor also understood that the proposal would deviate from British common law and move New York family law in the direction of continental civil law. He implored the convention to "look at the state of society in the nations of continental Europe, governed by the civil law, where the estate of the wife was kept separate, and to compare it with the beautiful and divine simplicity of the marriage relation in England and this state...."[32] "After such comparison," he asked, "would any man say that a change from these to those was desirable?"[33] He importuned "all who held the married state in respect, to pause and deliberate before they fixed permanently in the fundamental law, this new and dangerous principle."[34]

O'Conor was answered by Robert H. Morris, a delegate from New York. Morris, a forty-two-year-old married lawyer, had served as mayor and recorder of New York, and he was able to relate to the convention many cases that had come to his attention while in public service. Appealing to fathers at the convention, he told of females who brought property to their husbands only to be beggared by the profligacy of the men whose duty it was to have sustained and comforted them,[35] of wives who had worked day and night with the needle, and had not only supported husband and family, but had laid up something against a wet day—but whose earnings had been seized and squandered by a dissolute husband—where friends and relatives under his promises of reformation had come forward and furnished a house for the family; but when promises were broken, and the house stripped of everything by the creditors of the debauchee of a husband, and his family, turned into the street.[36]

Experience working with the New York police taught Morris of the

existence of an organized system of fortune hunting in Europe under which heiresses here were made the victims of a partition among "nice young men" having in view solely the property to be acquired by marriage under our law.[37]

Morris contended that the Harris proposal, if passed, would strengthen rather than diminish family harmony. He rejected the concept "that the harmony of a family consisted in the man's 'pocketing all the cash.'"[38] Like O'Conor, Morris knew that some few women had the benefit of private settlements for separate property. Rather than restrict such settlements, in contrast to O'Conor, he wanted this right extended. He asked: "[W]hy could not this provision which every prudent man made for his children, be made general—so that the children of the ignorant or the careless may have the benefit of it?"[39]

"[A]s a father, anxious to secure to his own the benefit of the little that he might leave to them,"[40] Harris spoke in defense of his proposal, urging, as Morris had done, that the proposition be made the general rule. Harris, too, recognized that the debate concerned a "comparison between the civil and the common law,"[41] remarking that many had "alluded to the condition of the married state in countries were the civil law is in operation, and where the common law prevailed."[42] Attempting to mitigate this point of contention, Harris argued that the proposition would merely allow more fathers to do directly what a few fathers presently were doing indirectly. Nevertheless, he demonstrated little reverence for the common-law system that necessitated the use of such complicated and unevenly accessible legal devices. Married women in the United States, he maintained, achieved what benefits they had despite, rather than because of, the common law, whose principles "originated in a dark and barbarous age."[43]

Despite these efforts, the Harris proposal was rejected by a vote of fifty-nine to fifty.[44] Throughout the debate, opponents of the Harris proposal claimed that any change in the law of married women was for the legislature to effect rather than for a constitutional convention engaged in drafting a fundamental law.[45]

II. The Passage of the 1848 New York Married Women's Property Act

Two years after the convention narrowly defeated the Harris proposal, the legislature overwhelmingly passed an act to protect married women's property. It is interesting that the arguments were quite similar to those made at the convention. Opponents in the legislature invoked arguments for the maintenance of domestic tranquility and Anglo-American common law. France, French women, and French civil law became focal points of their attack. These arguments were countered by attacks on the irrational, feudal common law with its barbarous treatment of women. Even the personal views of marriage and the personal goals to protect the property of daughters advanced by the legislators were analogous to the views of the members of the convention.

The story of its passage was told by George Geddes in a letter to Matilda Gage reprinted in *The History of Woman Suffrage*.[46] Geddes, a state senator in 1848, claimed to have "very distinct recollections of the whole history of this very radical measure."[47] Judge Fine of St. Lawrence, who was the bill's originator, Geddes recalled, was troubled by the legal options available to him and his wife. Not himself sharing the interests of the fortune hunters as described at the convention by Morris, Fine had tried in vain to keep the property of his wife distinct from his own. Judge Fine was described by his colleague Geddes as a "stately man...of...conservative tendencies."[48] Clearly he was not one to promote the laxity of morals predicted by delegate O'Conor.

Geddes himself supported the bill for the same reasons Harris supported a constitutional provision. Like Harris, he had a young daughter to whom he wanted to leave his property. He had availed himself of a trust instrument, as fathers had so long done before him. Nevertheless he was not satisfied that the trust would adequately protect his daughter. Given the facts that trusts were in a tenuous legal position since the Revised Statutes of 1836, and that chancery and chancery judgeships were abolished in 1846, Geddes's concern was well justified.

In his letter, Geddes recalled an opponent to the bill in the Senate. Like delegate O'Connor, this man was never married. According to Geddes, he was "a lawyer well-read in the old books, and versed in the adjudications which had determined that husband and wife were but one person, and the husband that person."[49] Also like O'Connor, that senator, according to the Geddes account, "expressed great fears in regard to meddling with this well-settled condition of domestic happiness" and, therefore, "made long... arguments to show the ruin this law [would] work."[50] Unlike delegate O'Connor, however, this senator voted for the bill in its final decision, indicating the wide support for defeudalizing property law despite inevitable ramifications in family law.

The bill passed the assembly with even greater ease than it passed the Senate. Speaker of the House Hadley personally saw to it that the bill passed. As Speaker, he had the power to override the usual legislative procedures. According to Geddes, Hadley thought the bill a good one that ought to pass. He never sent the bill to a committee of the whole but rather sent it directly to a select committee for it to be reported complete.

Geddes also recalled that he knew of no debates that preceded the Act of 1848. This is further evidence that there was little opposition to this radical reform. Geddes attributed this lack of opposition to the fact that "[g]reat measures often occupy the thoughts of men and women long before they take substantial form and become things of life."[51]

Notes

1. E. STANTON, S. ANTHONY & M. GAGE, THE HISTORY OF WOMAN SUFFRAGE 63 (1881-1922) [hereinafter cited as HISTORY OF WOMAN SUFFRAGE] (see the editorial comments). Elizabeth Cady Stanton, Susan B. Anthony, and Matilda Gage were renowned nineteenth-century feminist activists.

2. 1 D. FIELD, SPEECHES, ARGUMENTS AND MISCELLANEOUS PAPERS OF DAVID DUDLEY FIELD 245 (T. Coan ed. 1890). In fact the 1846 Constitutional Convention was controlled by law reform and codification advocates. A nineteenth-century commentator observed:

> In 1846 . . . an opportunity arrived for which law reformers had anxiously waited. A convention was summoned by a vast majority of the people to revise the constitution of the state. That convention was controlled by men who, if not fully sympathizing with Mr. Field's views, were yet resolved to leave no obstacle in the way of their adoption by the legislature. While a decisive majority refused to blend the administration of law and equity into one system by a provision of the fundamental law, an equally decisive majority refused to deprive the legislature of the power to do so. . . .

Law Reforms and Law Reformers, 3 AM. L. REGISTER 513, 523 (1864).

3. N.Y. CONST. art. I, §12 (1846).
4. N.Y. CONST. art. I, §17 (1846).
5. N.Y. CONST. art. VI, §24 (1846).
6. G. BISHOP & W. ATTREE, REPORT OF THE DEBATES AND PROCEDURES OF THE CONVENTION FOR THE REVISION OF THE CONSTITUTION OF THE STATE OF NEW YORK 1846, at 80 (1846) [hereinafter cited as BISHOP & ATTREE]; S. CROSWELL & R. SUTTON, DEBATES & PROCEEDINGS IN THE NEW YORK STATE CONVENTION FOR THE REVISION OF THE CONSTITUTION 55 (1846) [hereinafter cited as CROSWELL & SUTTON].
7. BISHOP & ATTREE 156; CROSWELL & SUTTON 116-17.
8. BISHOP & ATTREE 1038; CROSWELL & SUTTON 794.
9. CROSWELL & SUTTON 794.
10. *Id.* The Tallmadge Report, of which §14 was a part, was a report on the rights of man.
11. BISHOP & ATTREE 1038.
12. CROSWELL & SUTTON 794.
13. *Id.*
14. BISHOP & ATTREE 1039; CROSWELL & SUTTON 795.
15. BISHOP & ATTREE 1039; CROSWELL & SUTTON 795.
16. BISHOP & ATTREE 1039; CROSWELL & SUTTON 795.

17. *See* BISHOP & ATTREE 1029; CROSWELL & SUTTON 795.
18. BISHOP & ATTREE 1039.
19. *Id.* at 1041.
20. *Id.* at 1040.
21. *Id.* at 1039.
22. BISHOP & ATTREE 1042; CROSWELL & SUTTON 795.
23. BISHOP & ATTREE 1042; CROSWELL & SUTTON 795.
24. BISHOP & ATTREE 1056; CROSWELL & SUTTON 811.
25. BISHOP & ATTREE 1057.
26. *Id.* (emphasis in original)
27. *Id.*
28. *Id.*
29. *Id.*
30. *Id.* at 1058.
31. *Id.*
32. *Id.*
33. *Id.*
34. *Id.* at 1057.
35. *Id.* at 1059.
36. *Id.*
37. *Id.*
38. *Id.* at 1058-59.
39. *Id.* at 1059; CROSWELL & SUTTON 812.
40. CROSWELL & SUTTON 812.
41. BISHOP & ATTREE 1059.
42. *Id.*
43. *Id.* at 1060; CROSWELL & SUTTON 812.
44. BISHOP & ATTREE 1060; CROSWELL & SUTTON 813.
45. BISHOP & ATTREE 1059 (remarks of Brown). *Cf. id.* at 1042 (remarks of Patterson); *id.* at 1057 (remarks of O'Connor).
46. 1 HISTORY OF WOMAN SUFFRAGE (1881-1922).
47. *Id.* at 64.
48. *Id.*
49. *Id.* at 65.
50. *Id.*
51. *Id.*

10 LAW REFORM IN NEW YORK: THE VICTORY OF LAW REFORM THROUGH LEGISLATION—THE ABOLITION OF CHANCERY AND THE MERGER OF LAW AND EQUITY

By 1848 equity's treatment of married women would be codified into the Married Women's Property Acts and married women's status would be defeudalized too. Also by 1848 the rigid feudal common-law procedural forms would be modernized by the Field Code, decreasing the necessity of Aristotelian equity. Therefore, by the midnineteenth century, equity could in effect be abolished as a separate jurisdiction through the merger of law and equity into a uniform system of courts. With chancery abolished, the 1848 Married Women's Property Act was needed merely to maintain the status quo. It is only within the setting of these reforms that the passage of the Married Women's Property Acts, virtually without agitation and without opposition, can be understood.

Because married women's property before enactment of the Married Women's Acts was protected by the Court of Chancery, it is important to understand the fate of chancery itself on the eve of the passage of the acts. Chancery, in the first half of the nineteenth century, as explained previously, was unpopular with law reformers who were legislative supremacists. There was much opposition to judicial control over law reform, control exercised for centuries by English chancellors. There was likewise opposition to the Council of Revision composed of judges and the governor. This council was viewed as yet another judicial interference with the prerogatives of the legislature. Moreover, the division of the judicial system into two jurisdictions with two sets of procedures was destined to be transformed into a single, modern procedural system. Since chancery courts protected married women's property, and since chancery was abolished by the 1846 constitution when no provision was made for it in article VI (the judiciary article), the status of the concept of married women's separate property became tenuous. Because of this close relationship between the law of married women's property and chancery, it is important to become familiar with the history of the New York movement to reform procedural law as well as that to reform substantive law.

The distinction between law and equity was unknown in New Netherland where civil law prevailed.[1] Neither, according to the revisers of New York's property statutes, did feudal tenures exist while the colony was under the Dutch government.[2] The need for a separate tribunal to correct the defects of this feudal common law began to be felt when increasing commercial wealth and land speculation brought conveyancing of property into greater use, giving rise to more frequent controversies concerning trusts (their creation and execution) and similar subjects of equity jurisprudence that the law courts lacked jurisdiction to entertain.[3]

The constitutional and political situation that set the stage for the passage of the Married Women's Property Acts demonstrated the struggle between judicial and legislative hegemony over lawmaking. If the forces for legislative lawmaking were to triumph, they had to destroy and replace chancery as the modernizer of law. Therefore, the legislative reform movement could not stop with substantive revisions. Of necessity it had to revise procedural law. The procedural reform movement called for a merger of law and equity, a merger that ultimately abolished chancery.

Far from remaining abstract, the struggle narrowed to personalities. The villain became James Kent, chancellor from 1814 to 1823 and author of the widely read text *Commentaries on American Law*.[4] To Kent there were two great problems for early republican law: the relationship of English common law to the law of the new republic and the relations among the judiciary, the legislature, and the executive.[5] Kent's solution was to receive English law into New York. He maintained that since innovations were dangerous, he would follow the English chancellors' conceptions of equity.[6] Kent, incident to his functions as chancellor, enjoyed powers far beyond those of his British counterparts. The chancellor of New York enjoyed the unique power to sit in the court of last resort. Although he could not vote, Kent could argue in support of his own judgment below. Another unique power derived from his seat on the Council of Revision, which had been established by the 1777 Constitution. The council could veto legislation. These powers reinforced his reputation as a villain and complicated the struggle against chancery. His opponents characterized him as a counterrevolutionary Anglophile on a "throne of equity." The whole idea of a chancellor, they argued, was associated with kingship.[7]

The movement to merge law and equity was carried on at constitutional conventions. The first of these constitutional conventions met at Albany on August 28, 1821. The Democrats dominated this meeting.[8] The main points of attack, according to one historian's reading of the debates of the convention, were the primacy of the judicial establishment, with its abnormal political power as vetoer of legislation through the Council of Revision, and the qualified electoral franchise erected on a basis of landed interests.[9] These institutions were atavisms of the prerevolutionary British experience, which Kent cherished.[10] The hostility towards things British focused on the chancellor and resulted in a call to abolish chancery and merge equity into law courts. Many proposals were made at this convention to transfer the entire equity powers of the chancellor to the Supreme Court.[11] Although these suggestions were not carried,[12] the powers of the judges were somewhat circumscribed by the new constitution, which destroyed the Council of Revision. Furthermore, although the office of chancellor was not abolished, Kent's career as chancellor was. His term of office, due to expire in a few months when he reached the mandatory retirement age of sixty, was not extended. Moreover, the constitution did authorize the legislature to vest equity powers in common-law judges.[13] This was the first substantial step in the movement to merge law and equity. Since it demonstrated the feasibility of the merger, it was to be an important step. The second step was taken in 1823. That year an act was passed authorizing the circuit judges to hold courts of equity.[14] Although it was quickly repealed,[15] restoring power to the chancellor, the circuit judges were allowed to act as vice chancellors within their circuits. This situation continued until the next convention to revise the constitution was held in 1846.

In the years between the two constitutional conventions, the movement for reform continued to grow. Some of the motivations for reform have been recorded in the law journals of the 1830s. In 1837 the *American Jurist* published an article suggesting reform in remedial law.[16] The reason for reform was to ensure that "citizens, who are subject to the law, . . . have the power, 'to obtain right and justice freely, and without being obliged to purchase it . . .'"[17] This article, clearly advocating a cognizable legal system, demonstrated the obstacle to knowability created by the distinctions between law and equity.[18] Under the old system, litigants had to choose the right forum the first time or be subjected to the double costs in time and money of starting over in the proper court. That is, each litigant was compelled to decide at great peril whether common-law forums offered him an adequate remedy.

The case with which the author chose to demonstrate this recurring problem of nineteenth-century practitioners was taken from a contemporary textbook that cited this case as a warning to those who were to practice law. The real case, which had made its way into the textbook, had been handled by an experienced practitioner, thus demonstrating that laymen were not the only ones confused by prereformed property law. The lawyer was described by the textbook as "very eminent for his legal attainments, sound opinions and great practice."[19] The eminent barrister advised his client that there was no remedy whatever against a married woman who, having a substantial separate estate, had joined with her husband in a promissory note for £2,500 for a debt of her husband. The attorney had based his opinion on the common-law principle that the contract of a married woman was absolutely void. He failed to advise the creditor of any remedy in equity against her separate estate. The client later consulted an equity counselor. This second lawyer gave the client little better advice. He advised the creditor only of his equitable remedy despite the fact that after the death of the husband, the wife had promised to pay, and, therefore, she could have been arrested and sued at law. A bill in chancery was finally filed. However, because of the delays involved in separating the jurisdictions of law and equity, a great part of the property had been dissipated, and the wife had escaped to France with the remaining funds. The creditor never recovered his loan.

Thus debtor-creditor relationships, which were an integral part of the new commercial society, demanded both an end to common-law rules regarding the contract of married women and the merger of law and equity. It is no surprise that the same constitutional convention that debated rights of married women also reorganized the judiciary. It is also consistent that the same legislature that passed a Married Women's Property Act also passed an act to abolish the feudal common-law forms of actions and pleadings and the distinction between legal and equitable remedies in favor of a uniform course of proceedings in all cases.[20]

Again in 1838 the *American Jurist* published an article illustrating the reasons why reform was needed. In a debate with the opponents of merger,[21] the author maintained that one of the most compelling reasons for merger was that:

Our laws are no longer the same; the labors of the real property commissioners, based on the theoretical principles of Bentham, Humphreys, and other writers, have already produced a complete revolution in that branch of our laws, in which the conflicts between the equity and common-law jurisdictions have been ever most conspicuous.[22]

Thus it can be seen that the author believed the Revised Statutes, having defeudalized common law with regard to property law, had succeeded in removing the need for equity, the jurisdiction acknowledged to have made the initial inroads against feudal common law. "Is it to be supposed, that organic changes in the laws themselves will not render equally imperative a corresponding change in the jurisdictions, which are their organs?" the author asked those objecting to the merger.[23] He answered the rhetorical question himself.

Unless these two reforms go hand in hand together, it is obvious that the attempt to put new wine into old bottles; to accommodate rules founded on modern civilization, to the barbarous jurisdiction of the middle ages, will be attended with the most pernicious effects. . . . [24]

The author's hope was to ensure that lawmaking would become a science, "the science of forensic legislation."[25] The work of Jeremy Bentham, John Austin, and James Humphreys as jurists was analogized by the author to that of the natural scientist Herschel.[26]

The 1846 Constitution provided direction to the legislature to appoint commissioners to revise, simplify, and abridge the practice, form, and proceedings in all of the courts of justice of the state.[27] In response to the steps taken at the convention, David Dudley Field published, in January 1847, a treatise entitled *What Shall Be Done with the Practice of the Courts? Shall It Be Wholly Reformed? Questions Addressed to Lawyers.*[28] A memorial followed, signed by lawyers of the state, urging the legislature to abolish the old forms of action and to provide for a uniform method of proceeding in all cases, whether of legal or equitable cognizance. A commission on practice and pleading was appointed that was to become known as the Field Commission.[29] The code of civil procedure, which was written and enacted into law, known as the Field Code, abolished all distinction between actions at law and suits in equity as it provided one simplified form of action for the protection of private rights and the redress of private wrongs. Yet as one modern legal historian, Morton J. Horwitz, explained, the merger of law and equity by the Field Code was not merely a "rationalization" of civil procedure, but rather marked the "final and compete emasculation of Equity as an independent source of legal standards."[30]

Hence the movement for scientific law reform through legislation, begun under the inspiration of Bentham, Austin, and Humphreys, was to be continued by David Dudley Field who was commissioned to draft the new code of unified procedure. Field worked in conjunction with a committee of New York State senators. Among the senators who served on the committee was Henry B. Stanton, husband and colleague of Elizabeth Cady Stanton, one of the women who petitioned the legislature to defeudalize and modernize the law of married women's property.[31] Thus in yet another way the women's movement became linked to the movement for law reform through legislation.[32]

Notes

1. Redfield, *English Colonial Polity and Judicial Administration 1664-1776*, in 1 HISTORY OF THE BENCH AND BAR OF NEW YORK 35, 69 (1897) [hereinafter cited as *English Colonial Polity*].

2. REVISERS' NOTES 3 REV. STAT. 565 (1836); *cf.* 1 E. STANTON, S. ANTHONY, & M. GAGE, THE HISTORY OF WOMAN SUFFRAGE 63-64 (1889). (The feminist editors claimed that the Dutch aristocracy favored the passage of the Married Women's Property Acts); R. MORRIS, STUDIES IN THE HISTORY OF AMERICAN LAW WITH SPECIAL REFERENCE TO THE SEVENTEENTH AND EIGHTEENTH CENTURIES 176-77 (1930). Morris stated that the influence of "Roman-Dutch law... resulted in the extension of the contractual power to married women on a scale more lavish than that which obtained in any... other colonial jurisdiction...."

3. *English Colonial Polity* 69.

4. *See* L. FRIEDMAN, A HISTORY OF AMERICAN LAW 290 (1973). Friedman pointed

out that Kent's COMMENTARIES, because of its great popularity, went through twelve editions over more than forty years.

5. Fowler, *Constitutional and Related Aspects from 1801 to the Constitution of 1894*, in 1 HISTORY OF THE BENCH AND BAR OF NEW YORK 123, 126 (1897). Robert Ludlow Fowler worked with David Dudley Field and was well qualified to tell the story of the merger of law and equity [hereinafter cited as *Constitutional Aspects 1801-1894*].

6. *See, e.g.*, Kent's references in a judicial opinion written by him, Manning v. Executors of Manning, 1 Johns. ch. 527 at 530. (1815).

7. *Constitutional Aspects 1801-1894*, at 127.

8. *Id.* at 130.

9. *Id.* at 131.

10. *See* J. HORTON, JAMES KENT, A STUDY IN CONSERVATISM 1763-1847 (1939).

11. *Constitutional Aspects 1801-1894*, at 133.

12. *Id.* at 133.

13. *Id.* at 134.

14. Act of April 17, 1823, ch. 182, 1823 N.Y. Laws 208.

15. *Constitutional Aspects 1801-1894*, at 133-34.

16. *Reform in Remedial Law*, 17 AM. JURIST 253 (1937).

17. *Id.* at 296.

18. *Id.* at 297.

19. Cited *id.* at 298.

20. Act of April 12, 1848, ch. 379, 1848 N.Y. Laws 32.

21. Johnes, *On the Leading Arguments Urged in England for a Continuation of the Separation of Law and Equity Jurisdictions*, 20 AM. JURIST 111 (1838).

22. *Id.* at 114.

23. *Id.*

24. *Id.*

25. *Id.*

26. *Id.* at 114-15.

27. N. Y. CONST. art. 6, § 24 (1846).

28. *Constitutional Aspects 1801-1894*, at 163. The essay referred to is reprinted in 1 D. FIELD, SPEECHES, ARGUMENTS AND MISCELLANEOUS PAPERS OF DAVID DUDLEY FIELD 226 (T. Coan ed. 1890).

29. *See Law Reform and Law Reformers*, 3 AM. L. REGISTER 513 at 524-25 (1864), for a discussion of how David Dudley Field was almost excluded from membership on the commission by his political enemies and for a discussion of the Whig makeup of the 1848 New York legislature, which facilitated the commission's great influence with that body.

30. Horwitz, *The Rise of Legal Formalism*, 19 AM. J. LEGAL HIST. 251, 263 (1975).

31. H. STANTON, RANDOM RECOLLECTIONS 171 (3rd ed. 1887).

32. It is also interesting to note that Thomas Grimké, brother of abolitionists and feminists Sarah and Angelina Grimké, was also involved with both feminism and the codification movement. His ideas are not discussed in this work because they were more influential in South Carolina than in New York State. *See* P. MILLER, THE LEGAL MIND IN AMERICA 147 (1962).

11 THE ROLE OF WOMEN IN THE STRUGGLE FOR LAW REFORM THROUGH LEGISLATION AS AGENTS FOR THEIR OWN INTERESTS

I.

Three women were agents of the movement for law reform by legislation. These three women saw that change was coming and were able to hasten the adaptation of the legal system to already changed political, economic, and social systems. The women so involved were Ernestine Powtowski Rose, Elizabeth Cady Stanton, and Paulina Wright Davis.[1]

Ernestine Rose was born in Piotrkow, Poland, in 1810.[2] At the age of sixteen, she had her first encounter with the law. It concerned her property rights. Her mother had recently died, leaving her an inheritance. Her father had contracted away this inheritance to a man he had chosen to be her husband. Ernestine had no intention of performing her part of this "contract" and was angered when the man refused to return her dowry. Although the daughter of a rabbi, who under Jewish custom played the role of a judge, Ernestine took her case to a civil court. The sixteen-year-old girl argued her own case and won.

When she was seventeen, Ernestine had her next legal and economic struggle. In 1827, having left her father's house and moved to Berlin, she quickly learned that a Polish Jew could remain in Germany only for a limited time, meanwhile being forbidden to engage in any trade or business. In Germany at this time, the lawmaker was the king. Ernestine, after petitioning the king, was granted an audience and pled her own case. Unable to have the law struck down on its face, she was successful in having its effects mitigated as it applied to her. The king decreed that she would be able to stay in Germany as long as she wished and would be able to carry on a trade or business. Subsequently she manufactured perfume to support herself.

She came to America in 1836 with her newly acquired husband, William Rose. He was a jeweler and silversmith whom she met while involved in the Owenite movement in London. That was the year Judge Thomas Herttell, assemblyman from New York City, introduced into the Assembly of the State of New York his progressive resolution.

Herttell had hoped to elicit public attention by his resolution and by introducing a bill the following year. He was not successful in drawing the attention of many married women. Nevertheless his activism did attract Ernestine Rose's attention and the attention of wealthy Dutch fathers of married daughters.[3] Rose, however, was no more successful in winning support for the bill than was Judge Herttell. In a letter to Susan B. Anthony,[4] she admitted that it was only after much trouble that she obtained five signatures on a petition to the New York legislature to secure for married women the right to hold real estate in their own names. Both the women and the men to whom she spoke on her tour for signatures expressed the convictions that the relations between the sexes should not be altered. In Rose's words: "Some of the ladies said the gentlemen would laugh at them; others that they had rights enough; and the men said that the women had too many rights already."[5]

Paulina Wright Davis's recollection of their disappointed efforts as petitioners substantiates that of Rose. In a pamphlet[6] she wrote in 1871, Davis admitted: "In 1836, Mrs. Ernestine L. Rose ... began lecturing ... She also, in the same year, sent to the legislature of New York a petition with five names [which cost her weary miles of walking, and hours of talking], asking for the property rights of married women."[7] Nevertheless Rose continued sending petitions. Moreover she addressed the legislature in person on five occasions between the defeat of Herttell's bill and the passage of the first New York Married Women's Property Act in 1848.[8] This reluctance of common people to sign such petitions tends to support the conclusion that the contemporary public shared the fear of changes in family law that were expressed by the legislative committee in their report rejecting the petitioners' request for the passage of a married women's property act.

Elizabeth Cady Stanton, daughter of a judge and wife of a lawyer, was also a feminist social reformer. As such, she was predisposed to become an agent for the legislative movement to adjust property to the realities of a commercial society. Stanton recounted much of her story in her autobiography, *Eighty Years and More: Reminiscences 1815-1897*[9] and in the pages of *The History of Woman Suffrage,* [10] the six-volume work of which she was an editor. Her interest in reforming laws dealing with women, she claimed, stemmed from experiences of her childhood.[11] From an early age, she both read the laws in regard to women and sat in on client interviews conducted by her father, whose law office adjoined the house in which the family lived.[12] From such experience, Stanton gained an understanding of the relationship between feudalism and married women's status. In her autobiography she wrote:

In our Scotch neighborhood many men still retained the old feudal ideas of women and property. Fathers, at their death, would will the bulk of their property to the eldest son, with the proviso that the mother was to have a home with him. Hence it was not unusual for the mother, who had brought all the property into the family to be made an unhappy dependent on the bounty of an uncongenial daughter-in-law and a dissipated son.[13]

Other evidence shows that Elizabeth Cady Stanton understood the relationship between women's emancipation and the law-reform movement. Her papers demonstrate a solid grasp of the nature and goals of the movement. As the law-reform movement had called for demystification and a knowable legal system, so, too, did Stanton want women to comprehend the law. Moreover she called women's attention to the need for the feminist movement to be framed in context of these reforms.

Stanton's father, Judge Cady, was the first one to explain to her how judge-made laws could be reformed through legislation. He told his young daughter, who was hostile to the current legal system, "when you are grown up you must go down to Albany and talk to the legislators... [I]f you can persuade them to pass new laws, the old ones will be a dead letter."[14] Elizabeth Stanton claimed that this became the object of her life.[15] In fact knowledge of the law and how to reform it was a goal she advocated for all women. In "Our Young Girls,"[16] one of Stanton's most popular lectures, she argued:

... [I]f the elevating purifying influence of women is needed anywhere, it is in our courts of justice, especially in those cases involving the interests of her own sex....

Would not the study of Blackstone's and Kent's Commentaries enlarge their minds and be of more practical benefit than the magazine of fashion... or hours everyday devoted to the needle?[17]

In Stanton's work entitled "Why Legislature Should Make Precedents,"[18] this feminist showed an astute knowledge of the power of legislatures to change law rapidly, totally, and with impressive efficiency. As the legislature had the sheer raw power to disenfranchise, by a single act, the women of New Jersey who had had the right to vote for several years after that state's constitution was passed, she called for legislatures to use that same swift and complete power to enfranchise women.[19]

As she recalled in her autobiography, Stanton was a friend of Lord Brougham, whom she met during her famous visit to London to attend the World Antislavery Convention in 1840.[20] Lord Brougham, whose call for the defeudalization of English property law influenced the law-reform movement in New York State, was also an abolitionist and a radical feminist.[21] His feminism, one aspect of an integrated approach to reform,[22] was useful to Stanton. In a letter to the New York Suffrage Association, she quoted Brougham as saying: "The laws for women, in both state and church, are a disgrace to the civilization of the Nineteenth Century."[23] Brougham inspired other feminists as well as Stanton. Lucretia Mott praised his call for a total reconstruction of the whole marriage system," since "any attempt to amend it would prove useless."[24] According to Brougham's plan, this reform should be accomplished by the legislature, since neither equity nor common law had proved sufficient in the past.

> ...The great charter, in establishing the supremacy of law over prerogative, provides only for justice between man and man; for woman nothing is left but common law, accumulations and modifications of original heathenism, which no amount of filtration through ecclesiastical courts could change into Christian laws. They are declared unworthy of Christian people by great jurists; still they remain unchanged.[25]

Elizabeth Cady Stanton was one of the women who planned the first women's rights convention at Seneca Falls, New York, in 1848. She was also one of the very few women who knew of, and struggled for, passage of the early Married Women's Property Acts both before the legislature and among the delegates to the 1846 Constitutional Convention.[26] While she was accomplishing all of this, her husband, Henry Brewster Stanton, was with her. He accompanied her on her trip to the World Antislavery Convention in London. There he met British reformers who were added to the list of the many American reformers who were already his colleagues.[27] The writings of Henry Stanton are a valuable tool in accurately reconstructing the true relationship among law reform, feminism, and abolitionism.

In 1849, the year after the first New York Married Women's Property Act was passed, *Sketches of Reforms and Reformers of Great Britain and Ireland*,[28] by Henry B. Stanton, was published. Most likely, its author had worked on the book during the very year his wife was petitioning the legislature for an act to protect married women's property and was planning the first women's rights convention. Presumably, Elizabeth Stanton was cognizant of her husband's work and was also acquainted with the reformers about whom he wrote. Therefore, it is important to note that Henry Stanton devoted several chapters of his work to the movement for law reform and law reformers. To Jeremy Bentham and Lord Brougham, Henry Stanton devoted entire chapters. He referred to Bentham as "one of the most remarkable men that has appeared in our age" and as "the father of modern law reform."[29] The author's admiring description of Bentham's work demonstrated intimate knowledge of it. Stanton credited Bentham for influencing Brougham[30] as well as the revisers and codifiers of America.[31] Lord Brougham's life and work, particularly his struggle against both feudal common law and equity, were also greatly admired by Henry Stanton. Of Brougham, Stanton noted: "As an advocate and a jurist, many of his speeches at the bar and opinions on the bench will live long after the... court of chancery cease to oppress and vex mankind."[32] Brougham advocated the interests of the manufacturing and commercial classes. Henry Stanton, aware of this,[33] praised Brougham's seven-hour speech on law reform made to Parliament in 1828—a speech that

Stanton believed "sketched the absurdities and abuses of every branch of the common law, and detailed the amendments he proposed in its principles and administration."[34]

Henry Stanton was similarly interested in the great English law reformers of whom he wrote. In 1840, during the trip to England, he attended a session of Parliament to hear Brougham.[35] While on that same journey he went to Edinburgh, where he had an interview with Lord Francis Jeffrey.[36] Stanton recalled that Jeffrey

took an interest in law reform and asked me a good many questions about the New York Revised Statutes and their authors, which I reciprocated by inquiring into the habits and studies of the strange codifier Jeremy Bentham . . . who always seemed to me to be in the law what Dr. Franklin was in science, Dr. Johnson in literature and Dr. Greeley in journalism.[37]

Elizabeth Stanton shared her husband's admiration of law reformers. Her autobiography speaks with great respect of Lord Brougham and her meeting with him. Moreover her public speeches arguing that women should know the law, an idea long advanced by the advocates of codification and law reform, serve as further evidence supporting the theory that as a feminist, Elizabeth Cady Stanton was a conscious agent of the law-reform movement.

II.

Elizabeth Cady Stanton understood the significance of the 1848 act. In her autobiography, she related the influence the Married Women's Property Acts had on the women's rights movement.

The same year of the [Seneca Falls] Convention, the Married Women's Property Bill, which had given rise to some discussion on women's rights in New York, had passed the legislature. This encouraged action on the part of women, as the reflection naturally arose that, if the men who make the laws were ready for some onward step, surely the women themselves should express some interest in the legislation.[38]

Ernestine Rose's recollection supports Stanton's analysis. Despite meager response to her petition, Rose continued her efforts. The result, as she retold it in her letter to the editors of the *History of Woman Suffrage*, was that: "no sooner did it become legal than all the women said, 'Oh! that is right! We ought always to have had that.'"[39] Thus the law's passage convinced women who formerly thought they "had rights enough" to believe that perhaps they did not.[40] That is, there is some evidence that the women who were reluctant to help Ernestine Rose, Paulina Davis, and Elizabeth Stanton to aid the law's passage were inspired by that very law into activisim, an activism manifested in the Seneca Falls Convention, which in turn hastened the suffrage movement. Similarly the 1848 act encouraged women to demand amendments to this law that were to secure even more legal rights for women. This interpretation is substantiated by a letter of Ernestine Rose. Writing for the *Boston Investigator*, April 11, 1860,[41] she claimed that the 1848 and 1849 Married Women's Property Acts were "a beginning and an important step, for it proved that a law had to be altered, and that some others might need it just as much."[42] This was a step that helped to launch the nineteenth-century movement. Because of it, Rose explained, in the same letter, "[t]he field of labor then grew wider, and... commenced our conventions."[43]

The 1848 act was amended in 1849, 1860, 1862, 1884, and 1896. In the years after the 1848 act, women's rights conventions became almost an annual event. The *Declaration of Rights and Sentiments*[44] of the Seneca Falls Convention shows the concern for married women's legal status and their right to hold property. The document, written three months after the act passed the legislature, was partly inspired by it. Its bill of particulars contained grievances such as:

He has made her, if married, in the eye of the law, civilly dead. He has taken from her all rights in property, even to the wages she earns.

He has made her, morally, an irresponsible being, as she can commit many crimes with impunity, provided they be done in the presence of her husband. In the covenant of marriage, she is compelled to promise obedience to her husband, he becoming, to all intents and purposes, her master—the law giving him power to deprive her of her liberty, and to administer chastisement. He has so framed the laws of divorce, as to what shall be the proper causes, and in case of separation, to whom the guardianship of the children shall be given, as to be wholly regardless of the happiness of women—the law, in all cases, going upon the false supposition of the supremacy of man, and giving all power into his hands.[45]

These grievances are an interesting combination of already acquired and yet to be acquired rights. By 1848 New York women had the right to own property, but the status of other disabilities incident to the doctrine of unity remained uncertain. Yet Elizabeth Cady Stanton found it helpful that "the demands made at the convention were not entirely new."[46] The *Declaration* shows women were still concerned with civil death and with the right to property. The right to contract, sue, and be sued were not specifically granted by the 1848 act, nor were wages secure. Under the common-law doctrine of a husband's rights to his wife's services, property acquired in payment of services became the property of the husband. The 1848 statute specifically dealt with property received by gift, grant, devise, or bequest, leaving the question of a married woman's right to her own wages an unsettled question.

In 1853 a women's rights state convention was held in Rochester, New York. The convention resolved to present to the legislature certain questions:

Why should not woman's work be paid for according to the quality of the work done, and not the sex of the worker?

Why should not wives, equally with husbands, be entitled to their own earnings?

Why should not widows, equally with widowers, become by law the legal guardians ... of their own children?

On what just ground do the laws make a distinction between men and women, in the regard to the ownership of property, inheritance, and the administration of estates?[47]

Speaking at the convention, Ernestine Rose raised the questin of married women's lack of civil capacity. Matilda Gage, another speaker, raised other legal issues not changed by the 1848 or 1849 acts.[48] A close student of James Kent and Joseph Story, Gage pointed out to the convention that:

A wife has no management in the joint earnings of herself and her husband; they are entirely under control of the husband, who is obliged to furnish the wife merely the common necessaries of life; all that she receives beyond these is looked upon by the law as a favor, and not held as her right. .... A widow is allowed the use merely of one-third of the real estate left at the husband's death; and when her minor children have grown up she must surrender the personal property, even to the family Bible, and the pictures of her dear children.[49]

In 1854 another New York State convention was held in Albany, the state capital. Among the resolutions presented by Reverend Antoinette L. Brown was one that called for an end to the "preposterous fiction of law, that in the eye of the law the husband and wife are one person, that person being the husband."[50] Another resolution called for revision of the 1848 and 1849 acts to

enable married women to conduct business, to form contracts, to sue and be sued in their own names—to receive and hold the gains of their industry, and be liable for their own debts so far as their interests are separate from those of their husbands—to become joint owners in the joint earnings of the partnership, so far as these interests are identified—to bear witness for or against their husbands, and generally to be held responsible for their own deeds.[51]

Also resolved was:

That as acquiring property by all just and laudable means, and the holding and devising of the same is a human right, women married and single are entitled to this right, and all the usages or laws which withhold it from them are manifestly unjust.[52]

These resolutions show that some property issues were still unresolved by the legislature. Feminists knew that women needed protection of their property rights to fit the needs of free women in the new commercial society and not merely the rights of fathers to keep their estates from falling into the hands of irresponsible sons-in-law. The evidence is clear and convincing that feminists wanted a complete destruction of the feudal doctrine of unity and all its incidents.[53] In 1854 Elizabeth Cady Stanton delivered a declaration to the legislature of New York, adopted by the State Women's Rights Convention held at Albany. It is a document useful to demonstrate what women still wanted after the laws of 1848 and 1849. Stanton, in her address before the legislature, like Brown in her resolutions before the Convention of 1854, remained concerned with the matter of civil death.[54] This fiction was not wiped out by implication from the 1848 and 1849 acts, which permitted women to hold and convey separate property. Thus Stanton asked for civil identity, including the right to sue, be sued, testify against her husband, obtain credit, make contracts, and carry on a trade.[55]

The status and condition of working women also troubled Stanton. She argued that "the wife who is so fortunate as to have inherited property, . . . by the new law in this state . . . is no longer a legal nonentity."[56] This result obtained because the 1848 and 1849 acts, "if fairly construed, will overturn the whole code relating to women and property. The right to property implies the right to buy and sell, to will and bequeath, and herein is the dawning of a civil existence."[57] However, Stanton deplored the fact that the laboring woman had no right to the wages she earned since her services were the property of her husband.[58]

Even with the system of inheritance, Stanton was prepared to do battle. She castigated the inequity of the doctrine of the widow's share in only one-third of the real property and one-half of the personal property of her husband, even when she put in a whole life of effort.[59] She also pleaded passionately for the widow's right to guardianship of her children[60] and for suffrage for women of every marital status.[61] Her argument for the elective franchise shows the relationship of the reform in property law to the women's rights movement it preceded. These reforms furnished excellent arguments for demands for the suffrage. Recognizing the political usefulness, Stanton could shrewdly raise the question:

What is property without the right to protect that property by law? It is mockery to say a certain estate is mine, if, without my consent, you have the right to tax me when and how you please, while I have no voice in making the tax-gatherer, the legislator or the law. The right to property will, of necessity, compel us in due time to the exercise of our right to the elective franchise, and then naturally follows the right to hold office.[62]

Notes

1. 3 E. JAMES, NOTABLE AMERICAN WOMEN 1607-1950, at 195 (3d ed. 1974). *See also* E. STANTON, EIGHTY YEARS AND MORE: REMINISCENCES 1815-1897, at 143-54 (Schocken paper ed. 1971) [hereinafter cited as E. STANTON'S REMINISCENCES].

2. *See* Y. SUHL, ERNESTINE ROSE AND THE BATTLE FOR HUMAN RIGHTS (1959).

3. *Id.* at 57-65. It likewise attracted Elizabeth Cady Stanton's attention. As Stanton's biographer put it:

> In the fall of 1842, Henry Stanton went to Boston to open a law office. Elizabeth stayed on with her family until he was established and spend most of the winter with them in Albany. Here she met many lawyers and legislators and became very much interested in the married women's property bill which Judge Herttell had been persistent in introducing in the legislature since 1836. From him she learned something of the opposition such measures encounter. Women, he explained, because of their ignorance, were not asking for the bill, but, its advocates were the wealthy Dutch aristocracy who hated to see their property pass into the hands of dissolute sons-in-law.

A. LUTZ, CREATED EQUAL 37 (1940).

4. Letter from Ernestine Rose to Susan B. Anthony (Jan. 9, 1877), *reprinted in* 1 E. STANTON, S. ANTHONY, & M. GAGE, THE HISTORY OF WOMAN SUFFRAGE 98-100 (1881-1922) [hereinafter cited as HISTORY OF WOMAN SUFFRAGE].

5. *Id.* at 99.

6. P. DAVIS, A HISTORY OF THE NATIONAL WOMAN'S RIGHTS MOVEMENT (1871).

7. *Id.* at 10-11.

8. Letter from Ernestine Rose, *supra* note 4, at 99.

9. E. STANTON'S REMINISCENCES.

10. HISTORY OF WOMAN SUFFRAGE.

11. E. STANTON'S REMINISCENCES 31.

12. *Id.*

13. *Id.*

14. *Id.* at 32.

15. *Id.* at 32-33.

16. Address by Elizabeth Cady Stanton. (A copy is among the Elizabeth Cady Stanton Papers in the Vassar College Library.)

17. *Id.*

18. E. Stanton, Why Legislatures Should Make Precedents. (A copy is among the Elizabeth Cady Stanton Papers in the Vassar College Library.)

19. *Id.*

20. E. STANTON'S REMINISCENCES 89.

21. *Id.* at 89, 217-18.

22. There is substantial evidence for the inference that Brougham's interest in women's rights antedated feminism as an active political reform movement. Brougham basically wanted a rational, modernized approach to law and the social relations expressed by law. Brougham's early interest in women was more accurately an interest in facilitating conveyances. That is, Brougham was opposed to the fictions of fine and common recovery, methods of transferring land by fictionally acknowledging the right of the transferee to the property. He despised the fact that at common law a man and his wife could not convey an estate of the wife without a fine or recovery. *See* excerpts from Brougham's famous speech, which influenced the Revisers of the New York State Statutes cited in *Law of Real Property*, 1 AM. JURIST 58 at 71-72 (1829). *See also* J.

Parkes, New York Court of Chancery and Real Property Law lxxvii (1830). Brougham was not only hostile to legal fictions, he was also an untiring enemy of chancery. *See Law Reforms and Law Reformers*, 3 Am. L. Register 513 at 519 (1864).

23. Letter from Elizabeth Stanton to the New York Suffrage Association. (A copy is among the Elizabeth Cady Stanton Papers in the Vassar College Library.) A similar use of Brougham's quote was made by Stanton in a letter to the suffrage convention held in Washington, D.C., in 1898. (A copy of this is among the Elizabeth Cady Stanton Papers in the Vassar College Library.)

24. E. Stanton's Reminiscences 217. This speech was quoted in a letter by Lucretia Mott, which was reprinted in Stanton's autobiography to demonstrate Mott's radicalism. *Id.* at 217-18.

25. *Id.*

26. *Id.* at 143-54. According to Elizabeth Stanton's own recollections, she did not enter the movement for married women's property until 1840. At that time she, Ernestine Rose, and Paulina Wright Davis began a petition campaign that kept up until the bill was passed in 1848. However, she conceded that the women's petitions were only a part of the forces that combined to ensure the passage of this significant bill. She also acknowledged the influence of the governor, the jurists, the Dutch aristocratic fathers, and the forces behind the Constitutional Convention of 1846. Note that Stanton recalled conversations with Bascom while he was a delegate to the constitutional convention advocating the rights of married women. *Id.* at 144-45.

27. *Id.* at 71-91.

28. H. Stanton, Sketches of Reforms and Reformers of Geat Britain and Ireland (1849).

29. *Id.* at 87.

30. *Id.* at 95.

31. *Id.* at 97.

32. *Id.* at 176. Henry Stanton had a great disdain for equity and the court of chancery as a solution to the problemof law reform.

33. *Id.* at 179.

34. *Id.* at 181.

35. E. Stanton's Reminiscences 106.

36. *Id.*

37. *Id.* at 106-07.

38. E. Stanton's Reminiscences 150.

39. History of Woman Suffrage 99.

40. *Id.*

41. Letter from Ernestine Rose to the Editor of the Boston Investigator, in the Boston Investigator, April 11, 1860, at 401, col. 4.

42. *Id.*

43. *Id.*

44. Seneca Falls Women's Rights Convention of 1848, *Declaration of Rights and Sentiments, reprinted in* History of Woman Suffrage 70-73.

45. *Id.*

46. E. Stanton's Reminiscences 150.

47. History of Woman Suffrage 577-78.

48. *Id.* at 579.

49. *Id.*

50. *Id.* at 593-94.

51. *Id.* at 594.

52. *Id.*

53. Although the principal concern of this work is the struggle for the achievement of rights at private law, naturally nineteenth-century feminists also wanted political equality in the Enlightenment sense as expressed by Garrisonian antislavery. However, it may be a fiction to distinguish between private and public rights. Marshall, in *Marbury* v. *Madison*, 1 Cranch. 137, 2 L.Ed. 60 (1803), took for the judiciary the power to decide questions of public law from the constitutional grant of power to decide merely questions of private law, that is, questions arising "in Law and Equity" (U.S. Const. art. III, §2). Public law is often a reflection of private law. Behind "equality of laws" is there not the threatened violence of social power? Are not the socially powerful the people of property?

Protalis, upon submitting the *Project* for the French Civil Code, noted the interaction of private and public law:

> Every revolution is a conquest.... The private relations of men among themselves are no longer a concern; only the political and general aim is noticed....
>
> If attention is fixed on the civil laws, it is less to make them more sage or more just, than to make them more favorable to those to whom it is necessary to give a liking for the regime which it is intended to establish....
>
> [G]ood civil laws ... if they do not establish the government, they maintain it.
>
> Cited by Franklin, *The Eighteenth Brumaire in Louisiana*, 16 Tul. L. Rev. 514 at 514-15 (1942).

Portalis also knew the relation between defeudalization of private law, including the common-law status of married women, and the establishment and maintenance of a new political state.

> The marital authority is not respected, because it is by giving very great freedom to women, that there is success in introducing new forms and new manners in the commerce of life. There is the need of overthrowing the whole system of successions, because it is expedient to create a new order of citizens by a new order of proprietors.
>
> Cited *id.* at 515.

Abigail Adams, wife of John Adams, knew of this relationship, too. She was asking for private rights for women when she requested that her husband and the drafters of what she expected to be a civil code "remember the ladies." John Adams's rejection of her request was couched in terms of fears of extending the Revolution to any greater number of people—a political fear. *See* Familiar Letters of John Adams and His Wife Abigail Adams, During the Revolution 149-55 (1970).

Cf. Franklin, *The Eighteenth Brumaire in Louisiana, supra,* for a more detailed discussion of the revolutionary potential of a socially provocative system of private law.

54. Address by Elizabeth Stanton to the legislature of New York, adopted by the State Women's Rights Convention, Albany, New York (Feb. 14, 1854) (Copy on file among the Elizabeth Cady Stanton papers in the Vassar College Library).

55. *Id.* at 9-10.

56. *Id.* at 11.

57. *Id.*

58. *Id.* at 9-10, 18-19.

59. *Id.* at 12-14.

60. *Id.* at 14-16.

61. *Id.* at 11.

62. *Id.*

The Construction of the New York Married Women's Property Acts

He has made her, if married, in the eye of the law, civilly dead. He has taken from her all right in property, even to the wages she earns.

DECLARATION OF RIGHTS AND
SENTIMENTS,
Seneca Falls Convention (1848)

Hard cases make bad law.

Judicial Maxim

INTRODUCTION TO PART TWO

I.

William Blackstone, in the 1765 edition of his *Commentaries on the Laws of England*,[1] described what he purported to be the legal status of married women at common law.[2] It was this portrayal of married women's legal status separate and apart from married women's status in equity, under borough customs, and under other sources of law, that was used as the focal point of nineteenth-century feminist reforms. A comparative analysis of the text of Blackstone with the *Declaration of Rights and Sentiments*[3] of the Seneca Falls Convention of 1848 and the marriage contract[4] of the feminist reformer Lucy Stone (which was publicly printed as a political protest) demonstrate Blackstone's influence on the polemics of nineteenth-century feminism.

Central to Blackstone's interpretation of married women's status was the doctrine of unity. "By marriage," Blackstone pronounced, "the husband and wife are one person in law, that is, the very being or legal existence of the woman is suspended during marriage."[5] To the authors of the *Declaration of Rights and Sentiments*, this doctrine of unity meant that married women, "in the eye of the law, [were] civilly dead."[6] Although Blackstone did not refer to the effects of the doctrine as "civil death," he would have been hard pressed to deny that when by marriage the two became "one," the one was the husband. In fact he admitted that the suspension of a woman's legal existence during marriage "at least" meant her legal existence was "incorporated and consolidated into that of the husband."[7]

Lucy Stone's proposed marriage contract quoted Blackstone as it protested "against the whole system by which 'the legal existence of the wife is suspended during marriage' so that, in most States, she neither has a legal part in the choice of her residence, nor can she make a will, nor sue or be sued in her own name, nor inherit property."[8]

Blackstone had pointed out the ramifications of the doctrine of unity to which Lucy Stone was referring. Due to this incorporation or consolidation of the wife's legal identity into that of her husband, Blackstone explained, she was legally deemed to be acting under the "wing, protection, and cover"[9] of her husband in all her legal relationships. "For this reason," Blackstone continued, "a man cannot grant anything to his wife, or enter into covenant with her: for the grant would be to suppose her separate existence; and to covenant with her, would be only to covenant with himself."[10] Furthermore, Blackstone reasoned, "[i]f the wife be injured in her person or her property, she can bring no action for redress without her husband's concurrence, and in his name, as well as her own: neither can she be sued, without making the husband a defendant."[11] Such legal ramifications of the doctrine of unity were undoubtedly what Stone meant by her protest "against the whole system."

In addition to civil disabilities, the doctrine of unity gave rise to some criminal disabilities. Because the doctrine of unity meant the subordination of the wife to the husband,[12] a presumption existed that if a woman committed a crime in the presence of her husband, that she did it under his influence. As Blackstone pointed out, "in some felonies, and other inferior crimes, committed by her, through constraint of her husband, the law excuses her."[13] Incident to this doctrine, the husband was legally allowed to "give his wife moderate correction."[14] As Blackstone explained, since the husband "is to answer for her misbehavior, the law thought it reasonable to entrust him with this power of restraining her, by domestic chastisement, in the same moderation that a man is allowed to correct his servants or children."[15]

The *Declaration of Rights and Sentiments* specifically protested against this incident of the doctrine of unity. Its authors expressed outrage that the law had made woman "morally, an irresponsible being" who could "commit many crimes with impunity, provided they be done in the presence of her husband."[16] The analogy Blackstone had made between a husband and wife and a man and his servant was also strongly rejected by the *Declaration*, which sought to point out to the world that "to all intents and purposes, [a wife's husband was] her master—the law giving him power to deprive her of her liberty, and to administer chastisement."[17] Likewise Lucy Stone protested "against the laws which give the husband...the custody of the wife's person."[18] Furthermore Stone suggested that "where domestic difficulties arise, ...difficulties should be submitted to the equitable adjustment of arbitrators mutually chosen."[19]

Another incident to the doctrine of unity was its corollary, the doctrine of necessaries. As Blackstone pointed out, "[t]he husband is bound to provide his wife with necessaries by law."[20] In exchange for necessaries, the wife was obligated to render services to her husband. Here the analogy of wife to servant or child is again clear. The *Declaration* denounced the fact that man had "taken from [woman] all the right in property, even to the wages she earns."[21] Stone made a similar protest. She characterized as unjust the laws that give the husband "[t]he absolute right to the product of her industry."[22] The laws that gave a husband "[t]he sole ownership of her personal and use of real estate"[23] were also rejected by Stone.

II.

This examination of Blackstone's influence on early feminist documents demonstrates one of the primary goals of the nineteenth-century women's rights movement—the complete eradication of the common-law disabilities of married women. It was not, however, a task that the courts of New York made lighter. Initial decisions restrictively construed the statutes. In fact it was more than a century after the first New York Married Women's Property Act was passed and the first women's rights convention was held that a New York court used, albeit unconsciously, the methodological principles proposed by Edward Livingston and David Dudley Field to expand the 1848 act by analogy to give it its full meaning or content. The case of *People* v. *Morton*[24] recognized that the Married Women's Property Acts could be read to have effected a radical change in intergender relations. The court in *Morton* applied the act of 1848 by analogy to a 1954 criminal case by which a court finally recognized the potential of the act to bring the demise of Blackstone's portrayal of married women's status.

Before *Morton* can be fully discussed, a century of litigation must be synthesized. A useful way to do this is to investigate how the acts were construed and how judicial construction was affected by further legislation that, in turn, was construed and amended. It has been suggested that the judiciary may have deliberately sabotaged the reforming intent of the legislature.[25] But as pointed out above, Professor Johnston, in his law school curriculum critique, correctly concluded that, "on the basis of our limited knowledge . . . [and] without a great deal more evidence than is presently available . . . we are unjustified in concluding that such was the general pattern."[26]

The first New York Married Women's Property Act did little more than codify equitable rights wealthy daughters had enjoyed for centuries. Only gradually were these rights extended to women of the commercial middle, and working classes. The middle-class woman needed the rights to contract, sue, and be sued in order to be regarded as emancipated competent adults. Although the working-class wife needed the same rights, more specifically she needed the right to the proceeds of her own services. The following chapters provide the evidence Johnston found lacking by synthesizing a century of legal process by which these classes of women achieved their legal rights. In so doing, Professor Johnston's cautious avoidance of over generalization about the role of courts and legislatures is vindicated and the truth of the judicial maxim that hard cases make bad law is demonstrated.

Notes

1. 1 W. BLACKSTONE, COMMENTARIES ON THE LAWS OF ENGLAND (1st ed. 1765) [hereinafter cited as BLACKSTONE].

2. *Id.* at 430-33.

3. *Declaration of Sentiments and Resolutions, Seneca Falls Convention* (1848), *reprinted in* A. KRADITOR, UP FROM THE PEDESTAL 184 (1968) [hereinafter cited as UP FROM THE PEDESTAL].

4. Blackwell & Stone, *Marriage Document* (1855), *reprinted in* UP FROM THE PEDESTAL 149-50.

5. BLACKSTONE 430.

6. UP FROM THE PEDESTAL 185.

7. BLACKSTONE 430.

8. UP FROM THE PEDESTAL 150. The quotation was apparently so well known by the audience Stone attempted to reach that it required only quotation marks and no citation.

9. BLACKSTONE 430.

10. *Id.*

11. *Id.* at 431.

12. As Blackstone expressed it:

But, though our law in general considers man and wife as one person, yet there are some instances in which she is separately considered; as inferior to him, and acting by his compulsion.

BLACKSTONE 432.

13. *Id.*

14. *Id.*

15. *Id.*

16. UP FROM THE PEDESTAL 185.

17. *Id.*

18. *Id.* at 149.

19. *Id.* at 150.

20. BLACKSTONE 430.

21. UP FROM THE PEDESTAL 185.

22. *Id.* at 150.

23. *Id.*

24. 284 App. Div 413, 132 N.Y.S. 2d 302 (1954), *aff'd,* 308 N.Y. 96, 123 N.E.2d 790 (1954). *See generally* Franklin, *Contribution to an Explication of the Activity of the Warren Majority of the Supreme Court,* 24 BUFFALO L. REV. (1957); Franklin, *The Ninth Amendment as Civil Law Method,* 39 TUL. L. REV. 635 (1966); Landis, *Statutes and the Sources of Law,* 2 HARV. J. LEGIS. 7 (1965); Marrow, *Louisiana Blueprint: Civilian Codification and Legal Method for State and Nation,* 17 TUL. L. REV. 537 (1943), for three descriptions by modern legal scholars on how statutes might be treated as sources of principles and expanded by analogy by courts.

25. *See generally* Warren, *Husband's Right to Wife's Services,* 38 HARV. L. REV. 421 (1925); G. CLARK, CASES AND PROBLEMS ON DOMESTIC RELATIONS 322 (1965).

26. Johnston, *Sex and Property,* 47 N.Y.U.L. REV. 1069 (1972).

12 THE MARRIED WOMEN'S PROPERTY ACTS AND THE PROPERTIED WOMAN: DEBTORS AND CREDITORS IN A COMMERCIAL SOCIETY

Central to Blackstone's portrayal of the status of married women was the doctrine of legal unity of husband and wife. The legal personalities of the husband and wife became merged by marriage according to the common law of England. Feminists realized that when the two became one, the "one" was the husband. A woman's "civil death," as an incident of marriage, became the focal point of their attack.

As Blackstone had pointed out, it was from this fictional unity that all of the disabilities of married women followed. Among these restrictions were the right to contract and the right to sue and be sued. Once the 1848 act was passed granting married women the legal right to own property, the courts had the option of either strict interpretation of the statute, that is, allowing married women only the rights set forth in the exact language of the statute, or liberal construction, which might view the statute as the embodiment of general principles that could be applied by analogy to other cases. The courts opted for strict construction with regard to the doctrine of unity, probably because of social pressures not to make radical innovations in the institution of marriage or in intergender relations. However, with regard to the right to contract, the courts, for two reasons, were more liberal. One reason was the needs of creditors in a commercial economy; the other was the availability of an equitable principle that antedated the act and could be used as precedent.

Just as the Court of Chancery had tried to make it possible for a married woman to hold property separately from her husband, so did it develop principles by which a married woman was allowed to exert rights over this property analogous to those exercised over one's property by either a man or an unmarried woman. Thus although courts of equity could not confer upon a married woman the power to make a contract that bound her personally, they were able to give her the power to make a contract, for example, to incur a debt on the credit of separate property that belonged to her at the time the debt was incurred, and it rendered such separate property liable to satisfy the debt.

A. V. Dicey, an English scholar of the role of judicial legislation as affected by public opinion, demonstrated in 1905 that this equitable doctrine had two curious consequences for creditors.[1] One consequence was that the contract, in equity, of a married woman intending to bind her separate property did not bind any property she did not possess at the precise moment when she made the contract or incurred the debt. A second consequence was that the contract of a married woman, if made when she possessed no separate property, in no way bound any separate property or any property she might subsequently obtain. Thus incident to the first consequence, if a married woman owning separate property at the time she incurred a debt spent this property before the debt was repaid, she was not liable for the debt. Moreover if she acquired more separate property after the original property was spent, this second property was not chargeable with her debt. Because of the second consequence, if a married woman, knowing she was soon to receive a gift from her father for her separate use, incurred a debt by contract before the gift was received, although intending to repay the loan out of the gift, it was not in equity chargeable with the debt.

Such technicalities resulted in losses to honest creditors who were not schooled in the technicalities of equity law. Certainly the Married Women's Property Acts could have saved creditors from losses incurred due to technicalities of equitable rules that had evolved as a compromise out of the clash between the common-law fiction of unity and the equitable doctrine of separate property. However, that would have been tantamount to admitting that a radical change had been effected in established intergender relationships. Consequently courts, reluctant to so revolutionize the law of domestic relations, chose to read the equity rules into the new statutes. It was much more palatable, rather than admitting that husband and wife were two people, to believe that the legislature was merely giving to every married woman the same right as propertied women had for centuries enjoyed in equity. Moreover the language of the statutes, couched in equity terminology, added support to constructions, holding that the legislature intended nothing more than to codify equity law.

Interestingly, this judicial fear of facilitating innovations in family law might have had little basis in reality. Litigants before the courts were seldom husband and wife as adverse parties, and the issues that had to be settled seldom involved the marital relationship. Nevertheless courts often wrote into their opinions dicta, that is, gratuitous remarks, to the effect that the Married Women's Property Acts did not destroy the common-law unity of husband and wife. Only very gradually, through the interplay of judicial discretion and further legislation, were the consequences for creditors that Dicey pointed out, and the disabilities denounced by the *Declaration of Sentiments*, to disappear totally.

The first case that came before the New York Court of Appeals was *Vanderheyden and Wife* v. *Mallory and Hunter*.[2] Although it reached the Court of Appeals in November of 1848, seven months after the passage of the first New York Married Women's Property Act, it was not affected by the statute since the dispute arose before the act was passed. In fact the litigation was begun before chancery was abolished by the 1846 New York Constitution. Because it reached the Court of Appeals as an appeal from chancery, it was decided under equitable doctrines and was not influenced by the new statute.

The facts of this case demonstrate the plight of creditors under a legal system bifurcated between law and equity. Respondents Mallory and Hunter were successful plaintiffs in the court below. At the trial, they had alleged that between April 30, 1835, and December 6, 1837, the defendant's wife was a *femme sole* (single woman). She had become indebted to the plaintiffs in the sum of more than $2,000. They had extended this credit only because they knew she was entitled to a large amount of property of her late first husband. On December 6, 1837, the debtor, defendant Mrs. Vanderheyden, married defendant Mr. Vanderheyden. When the defendants did not pay the debt after Mr. Vanderheyden was declared a bankrupt, the plaintiffs instituted a suit at law to collect the debt. Naturally, the bankruptcy was a bar (a barrier) to the suit. Thereupon, the plaintiff creditors took their case to chancery.

At the time the plaintiffs' account was accruing against the defendant wife, she owned the property that had been bequeathed to her by her late husband. It had been paid to her by the executor of her first husband's estate in bank stocks worth over $2,000. The plaintiffs alleged that she owned these shares while their demand was accruing, and that after marriage, with the advice and consent of her husband, transferred these shares to a third person, for the purpose of having them transferred back to her for her sole and separate use. They urged the court to order Mrs. Vanderheyden to pay the demand out of this separate property on the theory that a married woman, in terms of her separate property, is deemed a *feme sole*, and therefore her engagements, or obligations, although they do not bind her personally, do bind her separate property. They argued that the stocks sought were transferred to her sole and separate use on the advice of her husband shortly before his bankruptcy and were thus kept from the husband's creditors.

By his discharge in bankruptcy, Mr. Vanderheyden became forever exonerated from personal liability for the debt, and no suit at law could be brought against his wife during her husband's life. Therefore, the plaintiffs pointed out the consequence of denying the prayer of the bill, or otherwise holding that they stated no claim for which relief could be given. Mr. Vanderheyden would be able to make use of his bankruptcy discharge not only to rid himself of his own and his wife's debts but would also be circumventing justice by what they facetiously characterized as the creation of a new species of subrogation that would allow Mr. Vanderheyden to take the place of his wife's creditors in respect to her separate property and, instead of having it applied to pay debts that were contracted on the credit of it, quietly enjoy it himself.

Subrogation is the substitution of another person in the place of the creditor to whose rights the other person succeeds in relation to the debt. It gives to the substitute person all the rights, priorities, remedies, liens, and securities of the creditor for whom the other person is substituted. By this theory then, the plaintiffs were sarcastically arguing that for the court to decide against them would be tantamount to sanctioning the right of a bankrupt husband to assume the interests of his wife's creditors by "subrogation" when he, in fact, was in an obvious conflict of interest with such creditors. The plaintiffs also argued that the wife's debts did not become the husband's by marriage and, therefore, the discharge from his debts should not release the debts against her.

The defendants, as appellants, argued against these allegations. They contended that the debt in question was not contracted under circumstances giving the creditors a right to proceed against the separate property of Mrs. Vanderheyden, nor had anything been done by her since that gave such right. Rather, they argued that the debt was contractd by Mrs. Vanderheyden as a *feme sole*. Furthermore the plaintiffs had not alleged that the bank stock in question was an inducement to the credit given her. On the contrary, the plaintiffs only alleged that they relied upon money they expected she would receive from the estate of her former husband and not upon the bank stock, which she then owned.

The defendants saw a principle different from that offered by the plaintiffs as controlling the facts of this case. They suggested that the only ground upon which the separate estate of a *femme covert* (married woman) can be reached in equity is that of appointment, that is, some act on her part clearly evincing an intention to charge the very property proceeded against. No appointment was made here, they pointed out, since the time Mrs. Vanderheyden had become a married woman.

Despite the existence of a just debt, the Court of Appeals was persuaded by the defendants' arguments. The problem was to ascertain what circumstances, in the absence of any positive expression of an intention particularly to charge, or obligate, her separate estate, should be deemed sufficient to create such a charge on that estate and what would merely create a general debt. The court noted that the bill contained no allegation that Mrs. Vanderheyden, after her marriage to Mr. Vanderheyden, did any act or made any engagement with or promise to the plaintiffs in reference to their debt against her that actually referred to her separate estate. Therefore, the court reasoned, the claim of an appointment in equity by her for payment of the debt out of her separate estate could not be sustained as within any principle established in equity. The actual funds with which she did promise to pay, that is, the amount she was entitled to get from the estate of her former husband, was not alleged ever to have come into her hands since all that came into her hands was bank stock. Consequently the court concluded that since there was no evidence that she ever, either before or since her marriage, made any contract with the plaintiffs indicating any intention to affect by it the actual property she now held to her separate use, that is, the bank stock, there existed no ground to authorize a court to subject her separate property to the payment of the instant debt.[3]

This case is a good illustration of the problem of creditors before the Married Women's Property Acts. At law a married woman could not bind herself in contract, but neither could she in equity. Equity only gave her the power to make a contract for debt on the credit of her separate property that belonged to her at the time when the debt was incurred, which would render such separate property liable to satisfy the debt. Any money acquired after that agreement or that was of a different fund from the very money agreed upon to pay the debt was not in equity chargeable to the particular debt. Thus due to the fact that the late husband's estate was converted into stock by the executor, the money chargeable never came into her hands. Because she was not personally liable, she could not be forced to pay the debt out of funds other than the ones originally charged.

The defendants, Mr. and Mrs. Vanderheyden, also argued that the discharge in bankruptcy of the husband operated as an extinguishment of the debt against the wife, at least during coverture, or marriage, because the wife's debt was made the husband's debt by the act of marriage. The court agreed.

It is extremely clear, that by law the wife, or her separate property, are not liable for the debts which she owed *dum sola....* I do not see how anything less than an act of the legislature can change the law.[4]

Such an act had not been passed before this case. Consequently the case was decided according to the state of the law before the Married Women's Property Acts. It is, therefore, not surprising that the commercial classes saw a need to reform the law of married women through "an act of the legislature."

Yale v. *Dederer and Wife*[5] was an action brought a decade after the 1848-49 acts to charge the separate estate of Mrs. Dederer, a married woman, with the payment of a promissory note she had signed along with her husband. The trial judge found that there was insufficient evidence to establish the fact that certain cows purchased by the defendants by means of a promissory note to the plaintiff were for the benefit of Mrs. Dederer, or that they went to enhance her separate estate, or that the profits from the cows went for her benefit. Nevertheless the trial judge directed judgment charging her separate estate with payment of the note and authorized the sale of her land in default of a sufficiency of personal estate to pay the debt. Mr. and Mrs. Dederer appealed.

Mr. Dederer, like Mr. Vanderheyden, was insolvent. He was the one who contracted to buy the cows from plaintiff Yale. The plaintiff, however, consented to sell the cows only if Mrs. Dederer, who had a separate estate of several farms, would agree to sign the note with Mr. Dederer as surety for him. Mrs. Dederer argued on appeal that a married woman cannot contract general debts and that when a married woman is a mere surety, equity will not enforce against her separate estate a promise void at law.

The dispute before the court did not involve the fundamental relationship between the sexes about which Herttell had spoken with such eloquence, and which had frightened some opponents of the acts to protect married women's property. Rather the husband and wife had a similar interest, that is, to keep the farm and avoid the debt. The issue for decision was: To what extent, if any, did the acts of 1848 and 1849 change the prior rules requiring a married woman who owned a separate estate to charge that particular estate before a creditor was assured of repayment? The Court of Appeals gave a strict construction to the Married Women's Property Acts and held that the statute did not remove the incapacity that prevented her from contracting debts. That is, her promissory note and other personal engagement were held void as they had been so held by the rules of common law.[6] The reason the court gave to support its holding was reminiscent of Blackstone's famous statement of married women's status at common law.

This legal incapacity is a far higher protection to married women than the wisest scheme of legislation can be, and we should hardly expect to find it removed in a statute intended for "the more effectual protection of her rights."[7]

Once the court chose to give the act strict construction, the question became one similar to the troublesome concept raised by the *Vanderheyden* case. Can and does a married woman charge her separate estate by signing a promissory note not specifying that the money was for the benefit of that separate estate, but merely as surety for her husband? Yale, like Vanderheyden's creditors, failed to collect his money because Mrs. Dederer made only a general engagement to pay money and note specific engagement to pay money out of the particular fund comprising her separate estate. Judgment was reversed and a new trial ordered. At the new trial, Yale would be required to prove the wife's intent to charge her separate estate, for the court held that:

[A]lthough the legal disability to contract remains as at common law, a married woman may, as indicental to the perfect right of property and power of disposition which she takes under this statute, charge her estate for the purposes and to the extent which the rule in equity has heretofore sanctioned in reference to separate estates.[8]

The judgment was reversed upon the ground that the mere signing of a note by a married woman, not in fact for the benefit of her estate, but as surety for another, and not declaring in that note that the loan is to be for her benefit, or an intent to charge her estate, did not operate as a charge upon the estate. Thus the rule, after the Court of Appeals had construed the 1848 and 1849 acts in *Yale*, was that to charge the separate estate of a married woman, the intention to do so must be declared in the very contract that is the foundation of the charge, or the consideration must be obtained for the direct benefit of the estate itself.

It can hardly be said that creditors were in a better position after the first two Married Women's Property Acts than before. The rule remained a complex trap for the unwary. Gradually the law evolved to the point where married women were in the same position as single women and all men, but this slow development left many innocent but mystified creditors as victims of the conservative attitude toward change in the area of family law. The following cases are exemplative of this generalization.

The case of *Sherman* v. *Elder*[9] also involved a debtor-creditor, rather than husband-wife, dispute. A woman, married in 1850, was engaged in business as a grocer, owning the fixtures of her shop and the stock in trade. Upon her marriage, it was agreed that the business should be continued in her name and that her husband should give his services in the business, having his living serve as his compensation. The husband, like Mr. Dederer, was a bankrupt. As time went on, he bought and sold in the name of his wife to improve the business. But the business finally proved a bad one and the husband confessed a judgment for the price of the goods he had bought to replenish the store and for which he had given a note in the name of his wife. Execution on that judgment was levied upon all the stock in trade of the wife's store and sold, by the sheriff, in a forced sale.

The wife argued that the fixtures, shelves, beer pump, cans, weights, demi-johns, clocks, decanters, and so on, which were used in the business at the time of the marriage, were her separate property and should not have been sold by the sheriff. The Court of Appeals agreed with her. The chattels in question were held to be her separate property because they were distinguishable from the stock in trade, goods, and groceries that were the subject of traffic and that were mingled with goods purchased for sale after the marriage and made a part of the trading or business capital as the business was carried on after marriage.

Where strict construction of the statute saved the wife from her husband's creditors in *Yale* v. *Dederer*, a similar result was accomplished through liberal construction of the same acts by the same court just four years later. The court concluded that:

By the act of 1848, as amended in 1849 . . . , the goods and property which belonged to [a woman] at the time of her marriage, were not subject to the disposal of her husband or liable for his debts, but "continued her sole and separate property as if she were a single female." These acts demand a liberal construction to carry into effect the beneficial intent of the legislature.[10]

The contrast between the approaches taken by the court in *Yale* on the one hand, and *Sherman* on the other, illustrate the difficulty one has in making any broad generalizations about tendencies of courts to transform liberal statutes into conservative constructions.

The next case construing the Married Women's Property Acts again involved debtor-creditor relations. *Knapp* v. *Smith*[11] reached the Court of Appeals in 1863, the year after *Sherman* v. *Elder*. The action was brought by a married woman. This woman, married in 1845, was also the wife of an insolvent. Her husband became insolvent in 1851. He had made an assignment of his property in trust for the payment of his debts and continued insolvent to the time of the action. In 1853 John Smith conveyed a farm in fee to the plaintiff, and she gave him a mortgage for the purchase price of $1,200. About the same time, the plaintiff purchased eight cows and one mare from the assignees of her husband in exchange for a note for $300. The colt and heifers for which the suit was brought were acquired partly as the offspring of the mare and cows purchased with the loan money and partly as a gift to the plaintiff by a person other than her husband. The plaintiff wife was suing her husband's creditors to recover the chattel.

At the trial, the referee found that the husband carried on the farm; the family was supported from the products of the farm; the farm was carried on in the name of the plaintiff by her husband as her agent; the interest on the mortgage had been paid from the products of the farm and the note given for the cows had been paid from proceeds of the sale of some of them; the plaintiff wife was the owner of the seized chattel and therefore, as a matter of law, the plaintiff was entitled to recover.

The defendants appealed, presenting the Court of Appeals with a different question. In the absence of fraud, where a debtor-husband is working on his wife's farm as her agent, is the property free from his creditors? The court liberally construed the statute, reasoning that:

The object of the statutes of 1848 and 1849 was to divest the title of the husband *jure mariti* during coverture, and to enable the wife to take the absolute title, as though she were unmarried.[12]

Once again a husband and wife, with mutual interests, prevailed against a creditor who was owed a just debt.

In 1865 *Buckley* v. *Wells*[13] was before the Court of Appeals. In that case a wife sued a sheriff who had seized her separate property to pay her husband's debts. The plaintiff wife, married in 1835, received money in 1849 from her mother's will. Consistent with the pattern of previous litigation, her husband was insolvent. In 1850 she started a business in which the husband worked for board and clothes. There was no question of fraud since he conducted the business as agent for the plaintiff and had made that fact known to those from whom he borrowed money and to the public at large. In 1858 the sheriff seized stock in execution of a judgment against the husband. The trial court found for the defendant sheriff. The plaintiff wife appealed.

The defendant argued that where a wife permits her property to be blended for the purposes of trade with merchandise belonging to her husband, it is liable to seizure for his debts. The court rejected this argument since the merchandise was the sole property of the wife. The court, relying on *Knapp* v. *Smith*, liberally construed the statute by holding that a wife having separate property could lawfully employ her insolvent husband as agent.[14]

A similar case reached the highest court of New York the following year. *Gage* v. *Dauchy*[15] was an action for trespass brought by a married woman against a sheriff's aide who had attached some property belonging to her. She charged the defendant with taking and converting a pair of her bobsleds and eight of her hogs. The defendant's theory was that if a farm was carried on by a husband, with the consent of a wife, in the absence of any agreement to compensate him for his services, the law will imply that the farm was cultivated for the benefit of the husband and he will be entitled to the produce and profit of the business, the proceeds of which could be attached by the man's creditors. The court refused to imply such a benefit. The attachment was held void.

In so doing, the court had to construe the act strictly as it reasoned that there could exist no contract between husband and wife for wages even after the act; therefore, the farm proceeds belonged to her alone. As a result, the court found for the plaintiff in accord with the intent of the 1848 and 1849 laws, which were designed to protect the wife's property from the husband's creditors and which never changed the common-law rule prohibiting contracts between husband and wife.[16] The interesting thing about this case is that it demonstrates that broad generalizations alleging that courts were more conservative than legislatures, because they restrictively construed the statutes, are not substantiated when a close look at the facts is taken. To protect the wife's property from the creditors of the husband, the court *had* to construe the statute restrictively on at least one point.

In 1867, a case reached the Court of Appeals in which the creditor of a married woman prevailed. In *Owen* v. *Cawley*[17] the plaintiff was a lawyer, rather than a lay businessman. This 1867 action was for professional services rendered to a married woman for the benefit of her separate estate. An examination of the facts shows that the instant plaintiff did not fall into the trap of legal technicalities of other creditors. The married woman in this case already owned a separate business at the time the debt was incurred and the services were rendered for the benefit of this separate business.

The court acknowledged that the "disabilities arising from the conjugal relations were not wholly removed"[18] by the Married Women's Property Acts of 1848 and 1849. After this tribute was paid to the stability of family law, the court stated the limits of the legal capacity of a married woman after these acts.

She was still left without capacity to bind herself *personally* by a naked promise, note or bond; but she could exercise the right of an owner, by subjecting her *separate estate* to charges in equity, for services rendered at her request for the benefit of such estate; or she could dedicate it to other purposes if she chose to evince her intention by a formal and deliberate pledge.[19]

The trial court found that the attorney plaintiff rendered his services to the married woman through the agency of her husband, and that the services were rendered for the benefit of her separate estate. Therefore, he was within the limits of the rule and was able to obtain an equitable lien on her separate estate so his payment due could be appropriated.

In the 1870 case of *The Corn Exchange Insurance Company* v. *Babcock,*[20] the Court of Appeals, in a twenty-five-page decision, made its clearest statement of the rule of married women's right to contract after the 1848, 1849, 1860, and 1862 Married Women's Property Acts. The action was brought by a creditor on a promissory note endorsed by a married woman and made by her husband. Mrs. Babcock had made her endorsement as surety for her husband. Unlike the facts of *Owen* v. *Bellows*, in *Corn Exchange* v. *Babcock*, the married woman had no interest in the transaction and there was no benefit to her separate estate. The sole benefit of the note went to the principal debtor, Mr. Babcock, the maker of the note.

Mr. Babcock was insolvent and the creditor sought repayment out of the separate estate of Mrs. Babcock, the solvent accommodation party, or cosigner. At the trial, the plaintiff creditor alleged the ownership by Mrs. Babcock of a separate estate at the time of endorsement, which had continued ever since, and her intent to charge that separate estate by her endorsement. The trier of fact gave judgment for plaintiff-creditor but the intermediate appellate court reversed. The creditor, therefore, appealed to the Court of Appeals.

On appeal, it was the creditor who asserted the rights of married women as derived from the Married Women's Property Acts and the married woman who asked for strict construction. The creditor argued that before the act of 1862, the surety contract of a married woman could be enforced by a court of equity, providing that she execute a contract for that purpose which evinced an intention to charge her separate estate with its payment, but since the legislature had passed the act of 1862, this remedy was available at law. This was the rule of *Yale* v. *Dederer*, and the creditor argued that rule was applicable to the instant contract. Moreover the insurance company contended, "[t]he Act of 1860, as amended in 1862, is a remedial statute, and its provisions should receive a liberal construction, so that the intent of the legislature may be carried into effect."[21] The question, of course, was: who was to be the beneficiary of the new remedy? The title of the acts indicated an intent to protect married women's property. But protect it from whom was the question. If the answer was "not from the husband," could it have been from the husband's creditors?

The defendant, Mrs. Babcock, was not eager to assert the rights the codifiers and feminists had won for married women. Rather she argued that "[t]he enabling statutes as contravening the common law, are to be strictly construed,"[22] and "it is not to be presumed, that the legislature intended to make innovation upon the common law, further than the case absolutely requires."[23] In fact the defendant married woman's argument implied that married women were better protected by Blackstone's common law than by the statutes, if liberally applied to the facts of this case, passed allegedly for the protection of married women. Her counsel argued that:

The legislature may eventually, adopt a suggestion made by the Civil Code commissioners, and give wives all the rights and corresponding obligations of single women; but until it does, courts cannot by implication enlarge the few rights given, especially as the enabling statutes, already enacted, purport to provide for "the more effectual *protection* of married women."[24]

The Court of Appeals found the plaintiff-creditor's arguments persuasive and rejected the defendant's attempt to keep the rule confined to the facts of the *Owen* case, that is, that for a contract of a married woman effectively to bind her separate property, it must be made for the benefit of her separate estate. Rather the court made it clear that the equity rule codified by the Acts of 1848, 1849, 1860, 1862 included two ways for a contract to bind the separate estate of a married woman.

Under our decisions, the liability arises *ipso facto* where the debt is for the benefit of her estate. Where she incurs liability for another, there is required the further condition that the intent to make the charge must be declared in the contract creating the indebtedness.[25]

Since the instant contract evinced the requisite intent to charge her separate estate, she was held liable on the note despite the fact that the money did not benefit her estate. Thus in this case, the beneficiary of the remedial act was the creditor, not the married woman. Nevertheless the rule remained a trap for future creditors with less carefully drawn contracts.

The 1877 case of *Grosman* v. *Cruger*[26] is illustrative of the problem. The action was brought upon a bond executed by a defendant married woman as surety. The plaintiff creditor alleged that the defendant, Mrs. Cruger, was, at the time of execution of the bond, a married woman, having a separate estate, and that the bond was executed in compliance with an order of the court by which she signed an affidavit to the effect that she possessed enough estate to make her a sufficient surety. The creditor's theory was that, due to the existence of this affidavit, it was not necessary that the intention to charge her separate estate be expressed in the contract, in this case the bond itself, since the intention to charge the separate estate was necessarily to be implied from its terms.[27]

The defendant married woman insisted that the rule of *Yale* v. *Dederer* mandated that the intention to charge her separate estate be expressed in the contract itself before she incurs any liability.[28] The court agreed with Mrs. Cruger and held that the rule was "that the intention to charge the separate estate must be expressed in the contract, or implied in the terms of it."[29] The affidavit was not part of the contract or its terms and, although the creditor relied on it, the defendant escaped liability.

An interesting case demonstrating the problems this rule wrought for the businessman not schooled in the law was *Taddiken* v. *Cantrell*.[30] In that 1877, case, a married woman executed a promissory note neither for the benefit of nor expressing an intent to charge her separate estate. However, she gave to the creditor an authority to have his legal counsel add anything to the note that would make the note "right, legal and proper." The attorney added the expression of an intent to charge her separate estate to the contract signed by the married woman.

The defendant married woman argued that the alterations were material and vitiated the notes in suit.[31] The court held the married woman liable, despite the fact that the alteration was material, since the jury found that the authority to alter was in fact given. Without the advice of counsel, however, the creditor would have lost his debt forever since the original contract, like that made by Mrs. Cruger, included no intent to charge her separate estate.

Another harsh gloss on the rule of equity construed into the new statutes is found in the 1877 case of *Eisenlord* v. *Snyder*.[32] The action was brought by an employee of a deceased married woman against the executors of her will for wages due. The employee had rendered services to the deceased since 1839, when she was twelve years old. The services were domestic and not for the benefit of the married woman's separate estate; therefore, the employee was forced to produce a contract exhibiting an intent on the part of the married woman employer to pay the wages out of her separate estate. The plaintiff's only contract with the married woman was an agreement by her to pay for the value of many years of past unpaid service in her will. The court held the plaintiff could not collect the wages due, reasoning that the rule of *Yale* v. *Dederer* meant that to charge the separate estate of a married woman for services not rendered for the benefit of the estate, an agreement so to charge must be included in the original contract of hiring. The court concluded that an agreement by her to charge the value of past services upon her estate was insufficient.[33] Clearly to impose such a duty of contracting properly on a twelve-year-old employee working for an obviously propertied woman was a heavy burden.

The 1877 case of *Nash* v. *Mitchell*[34] demonstrated the other burdens imposed upon creditors by a legal system that sought only to extend old equity rules to all married women in order to keep family law unchanged. In this case, the defendant, a married woman, executed to her husband a power of attorney, authorizing him "to make, sign, endorse and accept all checks, notes, drafts and bills of exchange" for her. The power of attorney was deposited with the bank where she kept an account. She was the owner of real estate from which she received rents, but was not carrying on a trade or business. Her husband gave to the plaintiffs a check in the defendant married woman's name in exchange for their check, payable to his order. The plaintiffs presented the check at maturity, but the payment was refused due to insufficient funds. Thereupon, this action was brought to recover the amount of the check.

The defendant married woman contended that she was not liable for payment of the check since she was a married woman. The plaintiff creditor argued that the defendant, although a married woman, had power to perform all the acts delegated to her husband as agent. The plaintiff had presumed that the money was borrowed for the benefit of the defendant's separate estate. His theory was that the law should share his presumption and place the burden on the debtor to disprove it. The court, however, did not share plaintiff's theory. Rather it decided that the

onus was upon plaintiffs to show ... that it was in a transaction and for a consideration in respect of which the disabilities of the defendant as a *feme covert* were removed, and she at liberty to contract and assume liabilities as if she were *feme sole*.[35]

Thus a creditor who dared to contract with a married woman, even after the Married Women's Property Acts of 1848, 1849, 1860, and 1862, could not assume the party with whom he was dealing was competent to make the contract she was making. Rather creditors were held "bound to know ... [t]he legal capacity of the defendant to contract,"[36] unless the "charge upon the estate of the defendant is created by the terms of the check."[37] In the instant case, the court held that the plaintiff creditor did not meet this burden. Consequently the innocent, yet ignorant, creditor was left bearing the loss of a nonsufficient funds check, while the estate of Mrs. Mitchell was left intact.

Because of this and similar principles that traditionally place the burden of proving the validity of a contract on the party who is asserting its validity, it would certainly have facilitated commercial transactions if married women were as competent to make all contracts as were men and single women. By 1884, to the benefit of the entire commercial world, married women gained that right. In that year another Married Women's Property Act was passed by the New York legislature.[38] This act enabled married women to enter into contracts as if unmarried, whether such contracts related to their separate property or not. By this act, the confusions wrought by a bifurcated legal system and a codification of old equity principles were at last removed for creditors, while the legislature simultaneously specified a commitment to the doctrine of unity by refusing to extend the right to contract between husband and wife.[39]

Notes

1. A. DICEY, LECTURES ON THE RELATION BETWEEN LAW AND PUBLIC OPINION IN ENGLAND DURING THE NINTEENTH CENTURY 381 (1st ed. 1905).
2. 1. N.Y. 452 (1848).
3. *Id.* at 462-72.
4. *Id.* at 472.
5. 18 N.Y. 265 (1858).

6. *Id.* at 272.
7. *Id.*
8. *Id.*
9. 24 N.Y. 381 (1862).
10. *Id.* at 384.
11. 27 N.Y. 277 (1863).
12. *Id.* at 279.
13. 33 N.Y. 517 (1865).
14. *Id.* at 521, 524.
15. 34 N.Y. 293 (1866).
16. *Id.* at 297.
17. 36 N.Y. 600 (1867).
18. *Id.* at 602.
19. *Id.* at 603 (emphasis in original).
20. 42 N.Y. 613 (1870).
21. *Id.* at 622.
22. *Id.* at 615 in argument of respondent.
23. *Id.* at 615-616 in argument of respondent.
24. *Id.* at 616 (emphasis in original) in argument of respondent.
25. *Id.* at 638-39 (emphasis in original).
26. 69 N.Y. 87 (1877).
27. *Id.* at 88 in argument of appellants.
28. *Id.* in argument of respondent.
29. *Id.* at 90.
30. 69 N.Y. 597 (1877).
31. *Id.* at 598 in argument of appellant.
32. 71 N.Y. 45 (1877).
33. *Id.* at 47.
34. 71 N.Y. 199 (1877).
35. *Id.* at 201-02 (emphasis in original).
36. *Id.* at 202.
37. *Id.* at 203.
38. 1884 N.Y. Laws ch. 384 §1.
39. 1884 N.Y. Laws ch. 384 §2.

13 THE IMPACT OF THE JUDICIAL CONSTRUCTION ON WORKING WIVES

The New York State legislature in 1860 granted married women the right to own the product of their services in addition to gifts or bequests of fathers or other wealthy benefactors. This statute was intended to be an enabling act for working women. Section two provided:

A married woman may bargain, sell, assign and transfer her separate personal property, and carry on any trade or business, and perform any labor or services on her sole and separate account, and the earnings of any married woman, from her trade, business, labor or services shall be her sole and separate property, and may be used or invested by her in her own name.[1]

The courts had liberally construed the 1848 and 1849 acts to keep the property of fathers from being wasted by sons-in-law.[2] Courts, however, had not been as willing to construe liberally legislation for the protection of a married woman's earnings. They used the clause "on her sole and separate account" to qualify what had been intended to be an enabling act.

One of the first cases to construe the 1860 act was *Brooks* v. *Schwerin*.[3] In this 1873 case, the action was brought by a married woman to recover damages for personal injury done to her by being knocked down and run over by a defendant's horse and wagon through his careless driving in one of the streets of the city of New York on April 13, 1865. The plaintiff, before the injury, both took charge of her family and worked outside the home for wages. The defendant objected to the proof of these facts, which were to be used to demonstrate the amount of damages suffered through the defendant's negligence. He contended that the plaintiff's time and services belonged to her husband, whether performed inside or outside of the home.

The defendant's arguments compelled the court to construe the Married Women's Property Act of 1860. The court had two principles from which to reason. One principle was the common-law rule; the other was the language of the statute. "At common law," the court noted, "when a married woman was injured in her person, she was joined with her husband in an action for the injury, and in such action nothing could be recovered for loss of service or for the expenses to which the husband had been subjected in taking care of and curing her. For such loss of service and expenses the husband alone could sue."[4] Counteracting the common-law rule was section two of the 1860 act. To what degree this section derogated the common-law rule was an issue for the court. The clause "on her sole and separate account" was a codification of a prior equity term. It referred to married women who acted as *feme sole traders* (a married women who engage in business on their own account). It did not refer to whether this trade was carried on at home or on premises external to the home.

The court liberally construed the statute. In fact the opinion referred to the statute as "a radical change of the common law."[5] Although the court concluded that the statute did not affect "services of the wife in the household in the discharge of her domestic duties,"[6] it did emphasize the change in the law with regard to money earned outside the home. The court held the statute to mean that when a married woman "labors for another, her service no longer belongs to her husband, and whatever she earns in such service belongs to her as if she were a *feme sole*, and, so far as she is disabled to perform such service by any injury to her person, she can in her own name recover a compensation against the wrong-doer for such disability as one of the consequences of the injury."[7]

The case of *Reynolds* v. *Robinson*[8] brought the construction of the 1860 act before the Court of Appeals again. The action in this 1876 case was brought to recover the value of services performed by the plaintiff's wife in caring for a man who was dying of cancer. The decedent promised to pay what these services were worth by his will. The decedent bequeathed to the plaintiff's wife, who nursed him for six years, only about one quarter of what the plaintiff thought the services were worth.

The defendant, relying on *Brooks* v. *Schwerin*, argued on the theory that the wife was the proper plaintiff that this action could not be maintained by a husband as plaintiff.[9] The court was therefore faced with the alternative of construing the 1860 statute liberally, as it had done in *Brooks*, and consequently throwing the plaintiff out of court without reaching the merits of the case, or strictly construing the statute but allowing the plaintiff's case to be heard. The court chose the latter alternative. The result was that the same judge who wrote the *Brooks* opinion had to write another opinion distinguishing it. To do that he had to find some fact in the case at bar sufficiently different from the facts of the case that arguably was controlling precedent.

The meaning of the clause "on her sole and separate account" was again at issue. Mrs. Reynolds and Mrs. Brooks were both married women rendering services for someone other than their husbands. The nature of the services in both cases were other than those normally performed for husband and family. The only difference between the facts of the two cases was the place where those services were performed. Here was a distinction the court could use. Mrs. Brooks left her home to work while Mrs. Reynolds nursed her patient in her home. Thus it was held that services performed by a married woman within the confines of her home, although for a third person and of an extradomestic nature, were not services performed "on her sole and separate account." This reasoning was applied to obtain a just result in the case at bar, for the case was brought by a husband whose interests were identical to those of his wife. However, it reached this just result at the expense of restrictive construction of the statute, which was effectively to prevent working-class women from controlling their own wages for many years to come, thereby proving the truth of the judicial maxim warning that hard cases make bad law.

The 1843 and 1849 acts were beneficial only to a married woman who owned real or personal property passed on to her by a person other than her husband. That is, it was of value only to propertied women with wealthy benefactors, who were usually their fathers. These early acts did not change the common-law rule that gave the husband the right to the services and earnings of the wife in cases where she had no separate estate, and where her labor was not connected with the use of her separate property. Thus middle- and working-class women, whose only assets were their physical and mental abilities, were unaffected by the 1848 and 1849 statutes. The second section of the Married Women's Property Act of 1860 intended to remedy this defect in the law. However, by 1878 it was apparent that only middle-class married women, and not those of the working class, would in fact be benefited even by the later act.

In that year, the case of *Birkbeck* v. *Ackroyd*[10] reached the New York Court of Appeals. This was an action to recover for work and wages. It was brought by a married man for the value of his own services and those of his wife and minor children. They all worked in the defendant's woolen mill.

The defendant argued that the plaintiff was not entitled to maintain the action for his wife's services. To support his contentions, he cited *Brooks* v. *Schwerin* and the Laws of 1860 chapter 90, sections 2 and 7. The defendant was clearly correct to cite the statute and the *Brooks* case. Mrs. Birkbeck, just as Mrs. Brooks, worked outside of the home and for a third person and at nondomestic services. Surely if a citizen were able to rely on precedent and not *ex post facto* lawmaking, this defendant should have been able to rely on the 1860 statute and the case that construed it. Such, however, was not to be the case. Instead, the court further limited the effect of the statute by holding that:

The bare fact that [a married woman] performs labor for third persons, for which compensation is due, does not necessarily establish that she performed it, under the act of 1860, upon her separate account. The true construction of the statute is that she may elect to labor on her account, and thereby entitle herself to her earnings, but in the absence of such an election or of circumstances showing that she intended to avail herself of the privilege and protection conferred by the statute, the husband's common-law right to her earnings remains unaffected.[11]

The court reasoned that the clause "on her sole and separate account" meant earnings that were not used to maintain the family,[12] a connotation not before advanced to interpret that clause. The clause had, in the past, meant that a married woman under equity was not to be treated as disabled with respect to property to which she held equitable title with legal title in a trustee. It did not mean that she could not use the funds to help maintain her family. It only meant that her husband could not dissipate it as his own and that it was not liable for his debts. After *Birkbeck*, the clause meant that it was the presumption of law that all services of a wife belonged to her husband, and that this presumption could only be rebutted by evidence of an election on her part to labor on her sole and separate account.

The highest court of New York set out guidelines for determining what sets of facts would be sufficient to defeat the presumption. That is, examples of cases that could be deemed sufficient to demonstrate that a married woman had elected to labor on her own account, and thereby avail herself of the protection of the statute that would entitle her to her own earnings, were set out by the *Birkbeck* opinion. The court stated:

> Where the husband and wife are living together, and mutually engaged in providing for the support of themselves and their family, each contributing by his or her labor to the promotion of the common purpose—and there is nothing to indicate an intention on the part of the wife to separate her earnings from those of her husband, her earnings ... belong ... as at common law, to the husband ... Where the wife is engaged in a business, as that of a trader, and it, is conducted in her name, there would be no room to question her right to the avails and profits.[13]

The social class impact of such guidelines is clear. Working-class women sell their labor for the benefit of their husbands, and middle-class women own businesses for their own benefit.

A working-class woman could defeat the presumption in favor of her husband's ownership of her wages in three ways. If the contract for labor specified that payments were to be made to her alone, if the wife was separated from her husband, or if his conduct or habits necessitated her control over the money, the presumption was rebuttable.[14] The court probably feared the dissipated drunkard husband; however, it was unlikely that a nineteenth-century working wife would be able to negotiate a contract specifically giving to her her own wages. On the contrary, it was customary for farm and factory workers to be engaged through a contract between the employer and the husband for the services of his entire family. The aggregate wages were paid to the husband-father. In fact this was the case for the Birkbeck family. Even the wages earned through the labor of Mr. Birkbeck's sons' wives belonged to Mr. Birkbeck.[15] It would be quite unlikely that women of the working class, usually unable to speak English, and ignorant of the technicalities of the law, would be able to avail themselves of the right to elect to have wages for their services paid to them. Certainly this was not the intent of the legislature. Nevertheless it probably worked well enough to suit the needs of nineteenth-century employers. In that sense, it was not a feudal anachronism out of place in the commercial and industrial economy of post-Civil War America.

It cannot be said that this judicial construction was harmful to the Birkbeck family. Like the result in *Reynolds*, the result in *Birkbeck* was not unjust. Thus *Birbeck* was yet another "hard case" that made "bad law". Mr. Birkbeck had prevailed at the trial level. The defendant must have clearly been guilty of depriving the family of wages earned, for his only ground for appeal was procedural. The defendent-appellant was not advancing the cause of married women's rights for altruistic reasons. He asserted the *Brooks* rule because he could not win on the merits. It was his sole ground for appeal.[16] To have held that the defendant's interpretation of the statute was correct would have meant that a factory owner, guilty of not paying wages due, would have been able to use the procedural technicality of a "wrong" party as plaintiff, to cause the Birkbeck family much time and expense. He already caused them the added expense of two appeals. If the Court of Appeals had decided in his favor, the Birkbecks would have had to begin again at the trial level. This time they would have had to have his wife and daughters-in-law joined as plaintiffs if not barred by a statute of limitation. Certainly this added litigation would have been detrimental to a family who seemed to be getting along together. The head of that household had not deserted his family, nor had he dissipated the money needed for the family's support. It is unfortunate that Mr. Birkbeck did not join his wife and daughters-in-law in the initial suit. Perhaps if he had, a just decision would have resulted in "good law," that is, in a more liberal construction of the statute.

In 1884 another Married Women's Property Act was passed in New York State. Section one of that act provided:

A married woman may contract to the same extent, with like effect and in the same form as if unmarried, and she and her separate estate shall be liable thereon, whether such contract relates to her separate business or estate or otherwise, and in no case shall a charge upon her separate estate be necessary.[17]

In 1901 the Court of Appeals was called upon to decide if the new act ended the common-law right of a husband to the earnings and services of his wife as a plain reading of the statute would indicate. The case in which the question arose was *Holcomb* v. *Harris*.[18]

The action was brought by a married man to recover for services rendered by his wife and daughter to a testator and for damages arising from the breach of the contract of employment. The jury rendered a verdict for $2,000 in favor of the plaintiff. The defendant, a nephew of the testator and executor of his will, appealed to the Appellate Division. The intermediate appellate court affirmed the judgment below. The defendant then took the case to the Court of Appeals.

The plaintiff had proven to the satisfaction of the jury the following facts. The testator and his wife called on the plaintiff and his family in 1887. During the visit, the testator's wife asked the plaintiff and his wife, if she died before her husband, would they come to Troy and take care of her husband. They promised to do so. In consideration for this promise, the testator assured them that the plaintiff and his wife would never want for anything. In 1888 the wife died. At the funeral, the testator reaffirmed the contract. Upon his direction, the plaintiff sold everything he owned, relinquished his wagon-making business, and relocated himself and his family at the home of the testator. For four and one-half years, Mrs. Holcomb and her daughter nursed and cared for the testator. At that point, Charles W. Harris, the defendant, entered the scene. He was a poor nephew of the testator. Although the testator expressed no dissatisfaction with the services of the Holcombs, he let them go. Charles Harris and his wife replaced them.

Clearly Mrs. Holcomb and Mr. Harris had adverse interests, while she and her husband had similar interests. If Mr. Holcomb, the plaintiff, were to prevail, the defendant, Mr. Harris, would have a decreased estate to inherit and the plaintiff's family would have $2,000 to compensate them for four and one-half years of service and the disruption of the plaintiff's business. Yet it was Mr. Harris who was asserting the rights of married women as enlarged by the 1884 act.[19] The court was unpersuaded by defendant's argument that the judgment should be reversed because the wrong plaintiff brought suit. Rather, the court upheld the jury findings that the wife had rendered these services while living with her husband and under an unwritten contract made by the husband with the testator and, therefore, the action was properly brought in the name of Mr. Holcomb.[20] Consequently the 1884 Married Women's Property Act, although clearly drafted to relieve a married woman of the common-law disability to contract without the necessity of a separate estate or business, was construed to deprive a married woman of the right to her own earnings. Like the result in the *Birkbeck* case, however, the result in *Holcomb v. Harris* cannot be said to have done an injustice to the specific married woman involved in the case at bar since her interests and those of her husband were identical. Again a "hard case" made "bad law".

In 1901 a married woman, as plaintiff, asserted her own right to sue for lost wages. The case was *Klapper* v. *Metropolitan St. Ry. Co.*[21] Pauline Klapper, while living with her husband, worked outside of the home for wages. She was injured by defendant's negligence and, as a result of the injury, she lost wages. At the trial, the plaintiff offered testimony about the amount of lost wages. The defendant objected to this testimony and moved to strike it from the record. The motion was denied and the defendant appealed.

The intermediate appellate court reversed in favor of the defendant, agreeing that it was a reversible error to admit the testimony.[22] This court, taking its cues from the Court of Appeals, cannot be said to have decided the case against the weight of precedent. The court noted that:

At common law the husband was absolutely entitled to the services and earnings of his wife, and neither the enabling act of 1860, nor the broader one of 1884, has affected this right, unless the services and earnings were rendered or received expressly upon her sole and separate account.[23]

Citing cases decided by the Court of Appeals, the court in *Klapper* held that presumptively damages for diminishing negligently the earning capacity of a married woman belong to her husband, and when she seeks, as plaintiff, to recover such damages, her complaint must contain an allegation that for some reason she herself is entitled to the wages.[24] That is, she must show an election or circumstance rebutting the presumption.

The application of the narrow construction of the statutes in *Klapper*, in contrast to the cases that preceded it, led to an unjust result. Here an injured plaintiff went without redress and a negligent defendant was relieved of paying some damages on the procedural technicality of who should be the proper plaintiff. Perhaps Mr. and Mrs. Klapper though it was best for her to be the plaintiff. This would make sense if her damages for pain and suffering were likely to be greater than damages for lost wages. Nevertheless the result in *Klapper* at best meant that a new trial would have to be held with Mr. Klapper as plaintiff in an action for Mrs. Klapper's lost wages.

Shortly after the *Klapper* decision, the legislature again amended the law. The Laws of 1902, chapter 289,[25] finally ended the discrepancy between working-class married women and married women of the propertied classes. That law revised the presumption of the law in favor of a wife's right to her own earnings. It provided that in any action or proceeding in which a married woman or her husband seeks to recover earnings resulting from her services, the presumption of the law is that such married woman alone is entitled thereto, unless the contrary expressly appears.

Notes

1. 1860 N.Y. Laws ch. 90 § 2.
2. Construction was strict only when vested rights were at issue. If a husband's rights were vested before the Married Women's Property Acts, courts declared the acts to be unconstitutional as applied to them. *See, e.g.,* Westervelt v. Gregg, 12 N.Y. 202 (1854).
3. 54 N.Y. 343 (1873).
4. *Id.* at 348.
5. *Id.*
6. *Id.*
7. *Id.* at 348-49.
8. 64 N.Y. 589 (1876).
9. *Id.* at 592 in Synopsis of Respondent's brief.
10. 74 N.Y. 356 (1878).
11. *Id.* at 358.
12. *Id.* at 359.
13. *Id.*

14. *Id.*
15. *Id.* at 360.
16. *Id.* at 357 in Synopsis of Appellant's brief.
17. 1884 N.Y. Laws ch. 381 §1.
18. 166 N.Y. 257, 59 N.E. 820 (1901).
19. *Id.* at 258 in Synopsis of Appellant's brief & 260.
20. *Id.* at 261.
21. 34 Misc. 528, 69 N.Y.S. 955 (Sup. Ct. 1901).
22. *Id.* at 956.
23. *Id.* at 955.
24. *Id.*
25. 1902 N.Y. Laws ch. 289, now N.Y. GEN. OBLIGATIONS LAW §3-315.

14 HUSBANDS AND WIVES AS ADVERSE PARTIES: THE DEMISE OF THE COMMON-LAW DOCTRINE OF UNITY—THE LEGAL FOUNDATION OF INTERGENDER EQUALITY

Although most conflicts between creditors and married women were settled by the 1884 Married Women's Property Act, the concept of unity remained viable. Accordingly, cases reaching the courts under the Married Women's Property Acts were no longer dominated by questions involving commercial law. Rather, questions of family law and of the nature of the marital relationship were to be litigated as husbands and wives began appearing as adverse parties.

The 1889 case of *Bennett v. Bennett*[1] was a tort action, that is, an action prompted by a civil wrong done by a tortfeasor to another person, brought by a married woman in her own name, without joining her husband as party. At common law, due to the fiction of unity, a married woman could not sue for damages without joinder of, that is, without joining, her husband. However, the latest Code of Civil Procedure[2] had given to married women the right to sue alone or be joined with other parties as if she were single. Nevertheless the defendant tortfeasor made the argument for a conservative judicial approach to questions involving a possible change in the traditional notions of husband-wife relations. The tortfeasor argued that "[t]he common-law unity of husband and wife has not been altered by the statutes beyond the exact letter, and that a strict construction is to be given to the letter of the statute."[3]

It is interesting to note that the instant tortfeasor, who argued for the retention of the doctrine of unity, was being sued for enticing the plaintiff's husband from her, alienating his affection, and depriving her of his society. Judge Bradley apparently recognized this irony and the fact that the instant husband and wife had adverse interests when he reasoned that:

The cause involves the misconduct of the husband, and there is no propriety in permitting him to join with his wife in prosecuting an action for such cause and to realize a pecuniary benefit as the result of his own wrong.[4]

Certainly if the married woman could not sue for alienation of affection without joinder of her husband, she would be virtually without remedy for the wrong done to her, for such joinder is not likely to occur. Judge Vann, as well as Judge Bradley, recognized this fact. In reply to the defendant's claim that to allow this plaintiff to prevail would be an unprecedented departure, he responded:

> Moreover, the absence of strictly common-law precedents is not surprising, because the wife could not bring an action alone, owing to the disability caused by coverture, and the husband would not be apt to sue, as by that act he would confess that he had done wrong in leaving his wife.[5]

Rejecting the defendant's claim that the doctrine of unity should be left intact, Judge Vann held that "[e]very step in legislation . . . has been in the direction of the complete abrogation of the common-law unity of husband and wife"[6] and, therefore, the plaintiff's cause of action in a suit alone was good.

One aspect of the marital relationship that was avidly conserved by a judiciary that had the doctrine of unity to rely on was the duty of a husband to support his wife. The 1889 case of *Hendricks* v. *Isaacs*[7] involved the question of whether a husband and wife could contract with regard to that duty. Mr. and Mrs. Hendricks were separated. Although the nature of the difficulty between these spouses was not disclosed in the case, it could be inferred that Mr. Hendricks was more probably the party guilty of marital misconduct. This conclusion can be deduced from two factors. First, the children resided with their mother, which was not a common occurrence in the nineteenth century. Second, Mr. Hendricks's father had disowned this son and left what would have been the son's share of his estate to his daughter-in-law and the grandchildren for their support and maintenance.

While separated, Mr. Hendricks made advances of money to his wife for her and the children's support upon her written promise to reimburse him once she received her interest in her father-in-law's estate. The action was brought on this contract by the husband against the administrator of his father's estate. The court held that the contract was void and not legally enforceable. Although willing to acknowledge the changes in the common law with regard to married women's rights vis-à-vis third persons, the court nevertheless held the marital relationship unchanged.

> [A married woman] may now, under our laws, purchase real and personal property and carry on business on her own account, and, as incident to these rights, she may enter into contracts with third persons for the purchase and sale of property, or in the prosecution of her separate business, enforceable in a legal action to the same extent as though she was a *feme sole*. But the disability to deal with her husband, or to make a binding contract with him, remains unchanged. Contracts between husband and wife are invalid as contracts in the eye of a court of law to the same extent now as before the recent legislation.[8]

The court, in deciding *Hendricks,* as has been demonstrated, used the doctrine of unity as its rationale. Under the doctrine of unity of husband and wife, the legal existence of the wife was deemed to be merged in that of her husband, thus preventing them from contracting with each other as if they were two separate individuals. The fiction of unity had been disregarded in equity, however, which allowed for contracts between husband and wife under some circumstances. The *Hendricks* case was remitted to the surrogate for further proceedings on the question of whether the contract resulted in equity to the plaintiff's claim.

An exposition of what types of contracts between husbands and wives were valid in equity was presented by the Court of Appeals in deciding the 1908 case of *Winter* v. *Winter.*[9] Presumably, if the Hendricks's contract met the traditional equitable test as expressed by *Winter,* the surrogate would be obliged to hold their contract valid. The husband and wife were separated and attempted to make a contract for separate maintenance of the wife. The action was brought by Mrs. Winter to enforce the contract, since Mr. Winter was in default on the payments. The defendant husband admitted the execution of the contract but alleged that it was illegal, null, and void at law because of the doctrine of merger or unity and in equity because it was made without the intervention of a trustee.

The court, in an opinion written by Judge Vann, conceding that the defendant's contention was at one time the rule, held that the Married Women's Property Act of 1896[10] "[c]hanged and codified ... previous statutes, each of which had advanced further than any of its predecessors toward the complete commercial emancipation of married women."[11] The Married Women's Property Acts, Judge Vann pointed out, "very cautiously [severed] the merger of identity"[12] and by the 1896 act granted married women the right to contract, as long as a husband and wife do not contract to "alter or dissolve the marriage or to relieve the husband from his liability to support his wife."[13] Thus as Judge Vann viewed the history of women's emancipation, the legislature intended to emancipate women commercially, while leaving the relations between spouses intact.

Nevertheless before the legislation that gave married women general power to make contracts, it was the law that if the parties had actually separated, an agreement valid in equity might be made through the medium of a trustee for an allowance from the husband to the wife for her support. Therefore, the court reasoned, this equitable doctrine is now available to all women at law and a contract for separate maintenance is valid without a trustee's intervention since

the only reason for resorting to a trustee was the ancient rule that a husband and wife were one person, but both the reason and the rule ceased to exist when the common law was supplanted by statute.[14]

The court held Winter's contract valid and enforceable and conceded the demise of the common-law fiction of unity. Again, it was due to equitable principles brought into law through legislative reform. As Judge Vann concluded:

Courts of law now recognize the separate existence of a husband and wife the same as courts of equity and give to each the same rights and remedies.[15]

Despite the fact that the court in *Winters* held that the 1896 Married Women's Property Act had demolished the doctrine of unity, vestiges of the doctrine remained in automobile negligence law. A husband, and consequently his insurance company, could not be held liable for his wife's injuries caused by his negligence due to the fact that a husband could not be liable in damages to himself for injuring himself.[16] Finally, in 1937 a special statute was passed to provide a spouse with an actionable remedy for negligent injury by her husband to her person or property.[17]

In 1954 the New York courts were faced with a question even more challenging to the marital relation than a contract not to support a wife or a tort action by a wife against her husband. In the case of *People* v. *Morton,*[18] a wife had her husband arrested for larceny of her property. The husband's defense was that, due to the fiction of unity, it was legally impossible for a husband to steal his wife's property.

Involved here was a conflict between two statutes, two principles behind the statutes, and two approaches to statutory construction. The defendent drew the court's attention to the fact that larceny had been carefully defined by the legislature and that, since it is a penal statute, it should be strictly construed lest anyone be punished for an act committed without clear notice that it was forbidden and, therefore, punishable. An 1829 statute provided that "every person who shall be convicted of the felonious taking and carrrying away the personal property of another"[19] shall be guilty of grand larceny if the value of the property was more than $25. The property allegedly stolen in this case was $350. A wife, the defendant contended, was not "another" person within the meaning of the statute.

In conflict with the larceny statute were the Married Women's Property Acts. These acts, and the cases construing them, had gradually whittled away at the fiction of unity of husband and wife. Nevertheless the legislature had never expressly stated that the doctrine was abrogated. In denying the husband's defense, the Appellate Division (2d Dep't) reasoned in a way the early nineteenth-century codifiers would have applauded, that is, by analogy from the principles behind the Married Women's Property Acts. Instead of merely applying the language to the facts of the case before it, the court applied the reasons for the language. Recognizing that "law is not static,"[20] the court determined that, "the language, literally construed, included undiscovered, as well as existing modes of operation,"[21] and that:

It would be an unjust reflection upon the wisdom and intelligence of the law-making body to assume that they intended to confine the scope of their legislation to the present, and to exclude all consideration for the developments of the future. If any presumption is to be indulged in, it is that general legislative enactments are mindful of the growth and increasing needs of society, and they should be construed to encourage, rather than embarrass the... progressive tendency of the people.[22]

After so reasoning, the court concluded that defendant's motion to dismiss the indictment be denied since, "It would not be consonant with our present social concepts of husband and wife to say that one is not a person separate from the other."[23]

The concurring opinion was even more explicit regarding its methodology of reasoning by analogy from the principles behind the Married Women's Property Acts.

We see no reason why the rule under consideration should survive the reasons for its existence,... the reasons for its existence having been removed by the Legislature, the rule has ceased to exist.[24]

When the Court of Appeals affirmed this decision,[25] the doctrine of unity, or the fiction of civil death so despised by the drafters of the *Declaration of Sentiments*, was officially dead in New York.

Notes

1. 116 N.Y. 584, 23 N.E. 17 (1889).
2. 876 N.Y. Laws ch. 448 §450.
3. 116 N.Y. at 586 in argument of appellant.
4. *Id.* at 598, 23 N.E. 21.
5. *Id.* at 590, 23 N.E. at 18.
6. *Id.* at 594, 23 N.E. at 20.
7. 117 N.Y. 411, 22 N.E. 1029 (1889).
8. *Id.* at 416-17, 22 N.E. at 1030.
9. 191 N.Y. 462, 84 N.E. 382 (1908).
10. 1896 N.Y. Laws ch. 272 §21.
11. 191 N.Y. at 467, 84 N.E. at 384.
12. *Id.* at 467, 84 N.E. at 384.
13. *Id.* at 467, 84 N.E. at 384.
14. *Id.* at 472-73, 84 N.E. at 386.
15. *Id.* at 475, 84 N.E. at 387.
16. *See, e.g.,* Newton v. Weber, 119 Misc. 240, 196 N.Y.S. 113 (1922); Wadsworth v. Webster, 237 App. Div. 319, 261 N.Y.S. 670 (3d Dep't 1932).
17. *See* Stonborough v. Preferred Accident Ins. Co. of N.Y., 180 Misc. 339, 40 N.Y.S. 2d 480, *aff'd* 266 App. Div. 838, 43 N.Y.S. 2d 512, *aff'd* 292 N.Y. 154, 54 N.E. 2d 342 (1944).
18. 284 App. Div. 413, 132 N.Y.S. 2d 302 (2d Dep't 1954).

19. 1830 N.Y. Revised Statutes ch. 1 §63.
20. 284 App. Div. at 417, 132 N.Y.S. 2d at 307.
21. *Id.* at 417, 132 N.Y.S. 2d at 307.
22. *Id.* at 417, 132 N.Y.S. 2d at 307.
23. *Id.* at 418, 132 N.Y.S. 2d at 308.
24. *Id.* at 420, 132 N.Y.S. 2d at 310.
25. People v. Morton, 308 N.Y. 96, 123 N.E. 2d 790 (1954).

CONCLUSION

Any discussion of the history of women's legal status would be incomplete if it did not address itself to two fundamental questions: Why did the Married Women's Property Acts come when they did, and why did they come with so little resistance? To answer these questions, it is important to note that what little resistance existed was couched in terms of fears of innovations in family law and intergender relationships. Only the fact that by the midnineteenth century there existed a widespread belief in the urgent need to defeudalize real property law and, thereby, make land into an item of commerce can explain why even the very legislator who spoke against the innovations in family law (which were necessary incidents of the 1848 New York Married Women's Property Act) could vote for it. Furthermore only this widespread belief can explain why the new act received so little attention by contemporary newspapers, both lay and legal.

Some attention, however, was given to the question of married women's property before the acts were passed. In the very years in which Elizabeth Cady Stanton, Ernestine Powtowski Rose, and Paulina Wright Davis were hard put to obtain signatures for their petitions, circulated with an intent to change intergender relationships, the New York State legal profession discussed the question of married women's property within a more narrow context. Their concern was with the uncertain state of the law. For example, an 1843 edition of the *New York Legal Observer* carried an article on "Husband and Wife." The article sought to inform practitioners that setting up a trust for the benefit of a married woman's separate use was tricky business. Substantiating Senator Geddes's fear that a married woman's separate estate was not secured even by a carefully drawn trust instrument, the article illustrated how such instruments had been held by courts not to have created a trust for separate use of a married woman without a husband's disclaimer.[1]

In the 1845 edition of this same legal newspaper, an article[2] was written to warn practitioners of the technicalities of doctrines surrounding a married woman's equitable right to contract with regard to her separate estate. The complex equity rules laid out in this article were those later construed into the Married Women's Property Acts before the enactment of the 1884 act, which was passed with the intention of guaranteeing to a married woman the same capacity to contract as that of a man or a single woman.

That the legal profession was not entirely in favor of having those complex equity rules construed into the new legislation is demonstrated by an 1854 letter to the editor of this same periodical.[3] The letter began by noting that "there has been some difference in the profession as to the power of a woman to make a covenant"[4] under the 1848 and 1849 Married Women's Property Acts. The remainder of the letter set out the arguments to support a position that the acts should be construed to mean that a married woman could now make contracts. Among other axioms, the author of the letter proposed that the statute had provided that the property of a married woman shall be her own as if she were a single female. Since a single female can make a *covenant*, or a written agreement, and since, to make full use of her property, it is necessary to make a convenant in relation to it, then the power to make a convenant, the author reasoned, is given by necessary implication to married women, incident to their right to own property. Despite this and other persuasive arguments presented in the letter, the New York Court of Appeals, when the question arose four years later in the case of *Yale* v. *Dederer,*[5] chose to read the complications of equity into the statutes, instead of the granting of a complete legal capacity to contract. If this letter was indicative of the feelings of the legal profession, the result in *Yale* was one the legal profession probably wished to avoid.

Despite judicial conservatism, the legislature, over the next decades, expanded the legal capacity of married women by slowly ridding the statutes of equitable glosses. The forces to which the legislature was responding included more than the pressure of feminist lobbyists and commentators within the legal profession. Some very real market forces were also involved. One such force was the effect of the Revised Statutes on the law of real property. These and other acts effected the abolition of primogeniture, whereby the first son inherits everything, and land entails, which restricted inheritance to lineal descendants. These reforms resulted in an expanded class of people who benefited from descent and distribution laws. Along with second sons, daughters were added to the class of distributees. The result was more property being inherited, and therefore owned, by women. It was logical for fathers to become concerned with how this property would be managed once married women took more and more property. As Elizabeth Cady Stanton observed, the fathers in the Dutch aristocracy "desired to see their life-long accumulations descend to their daughters and grandchildren rather than pass into the hands of dissipated, thriftless sons-in-law."[6] If this were true, it might shed some light on why the early acts were entitled "for the more effectual protection of the property of married women."[7]

In the nineteenth century sound commercial reasons existed for a desire to protect married women's property. The economy had been developing rapidly, bringing with it concomitant speculation, business failures, and general fluctuations in the business cycle. Insolvencies became frequent. Protection of a married women's property, more often than not, meant protection from the husband's creditors, rather than from the husband.

Despite fears by opponents of the Married Women's Property Acts in the legislature and at the New York State Constitutional Convention of 1846 that the acts would damage the family, in fact the acts strengthened the family at least as an economic unit. Most litigation under the acts involved debtor-creditor relations rather than husband-wife relations and, in most cases, the family property was kept safe from creditors by judges who interpreted the acts. Like the corporation's protection of shareholders from personal liability, the Married Women's Property Acts limited the family's liability to only those assets in the name of the husband. But also like the corporation, the Married Women's Property Acts, by decreasing the risk of investment, probably increased the volume of investment and contributed to the growth of the economy.

Another fundamental issue in the history of women's legal status is: What was the impact of the Married Women's Property Acts? The acts are significant for their two-fold impact: the legal redefinition of women and the effect this redefinition had on the nineteenth-century women's rights movement.

James McCauley Landis was a professor of legislation at Harvard Law School when he wrote the article "Statutes and the Sources of Law"[8] in 1932. Landis expressed a civil-law predisposition rather than a typically American devotion to the separation of powers concept. To him, legislation should be viewed as a source for judicial creativity or analogical reasoning. Upon examining the interaction between courts and legislation regarding married women's property in several jurisdictions, Landis concluded that his research revealed "courts giving effects to statutes far beyond their express terms."[9] One example of this, Landis proposed, was the change in women's status.[10]

Landis pointed out that a concept of status is a solidification of "[d]octrines of common law dealing with the relationship between individuals . . . seen to hinge upon a conception as to the position that one party is to occupy in our social structure."[11] This result necessarily obtains because "status has no meaning apart from its incidents."[12] Because the incidents are important in "shaping the nucleus of status,"[13] an alteration in an incident "may call for a radical revision of the privileges or disabilities"[14] that actually comprise the status.

Landis suggested that changes in status are commonly the unconscious product of legislation. Because statutes "rarely directly make or alter status as such,"[15] they often do not see the "seamlessness of the pattern they seek to change."[16] Consequently, Landis concluded, "structural changes must of necessity be left to the courts."[17] Such was the method Landis claimed was "pursued in the married women's legislation."[18] With regard to this legislation, the courts used the "terse statutes" granting to married women powers merely to hold and convey property and sue and be sued,[19] as general principles or sources for the whole series of cases that ultimately gave to married women the status of an independent and competent adult citizen. Yet this result was a product of a dynamic interaction between courts and legislatures. The judgments that "sought to retain the older common-law limitations hostile to the aim of the statutes [had to be] overruled by subsequent legislation, more attuned to the principles of the married women's acts."[20]

This new method consisted of finding the content of law in the principles of a statute, rather than a judicial finding of the law in the spirit of the people on the one hand, or making decisions going no further than the express words of the statute on the other hand, that is, a redefinition of women resulting from what Landis called "an impressive edifice of law resting upon statute and yet not depending upon the express terms of the statutes for its content."[21] Surely this method is in accord with the principles of the nineteenth-century codifiers out of whose work the Married Women's Property Acts developed.[22]

The effect of the Married Women's Property Acts on the nineteenth-century women's rights movement is clear. Elizabeth Cadey Stanton noted the relationship. First, the bill "[gave] rise to some discussion of women's rights."[23] Then its passage "encouraged action on the part of women."[24] Stanton found it a useful political tool that "the demands made in the [Seneca Falls] convention were not entirely new to the reading and thinking public of New York."[25] Thus the only truly novel demand of the *Declaration of Sentiments*, Stanton admitted, was the demand for suffrage, which arose out of the discussions at the convention.[26]

Once suffrage became the focal point of the nineteenth-century women's movement, however, the question of married women's legal status received less and less attention. Since most adult women in the nineteenth and first three quarters of the twentieth century became married women, the neglect of their status left the women's revolution incomplete after 1920. The questions of a married woman's right to her own name, credit, domicile, a share in the assets of the marriage upon dissolution, and equal social and economic opportunity were left unanswered. The answers are finally coming with the twentieth-century women's movement.

Notes

1. 1 N.Y. Legal Observer, 1843, at 246, cols. 1 & 2.
2. 3 N.Y. Legal Observer, 1845, at 159, cols. 1 & 2.
3. 12 N.Y. Legal Observer 1854, at 31.
4. *Id.*
5. 18 N.Y. 265 (1858).
6. E. STANTON, EIGHTY YEARS AND MORE: REMINISCENCES 1815-1897, at 150 (Schocken paper ed. 1971, reprinted from Unwin ed. 1898) [hereinafter cited as E. STANTON'S REMINISCENCES].
7. *See, e.g.,* the titles of 1848 N.Y. Laws ch. 200, 1849 N.Y. Laws ch. 375, as distinguished from the titles of 1860 N.Y. Laws ch. 90 ("An act concerning the rights and liabilities of husband and wife") & 1884 N.Y. Laws ch. 381 ("An act in relation to the rights and liabilities of married women").
8. Landis, *Statutes and the Sources of Law*, 2 HARV. J. LEGIS. 7 (1965).
9. *Id.* at 15.
10. *Id.* at 15-17.
11. *Id.* at 15.

12. *Id.* at 16.
13. *Id.*
14. *Id.*
15. *Id.*
16. *Id.*
17. *Id.*
18. *Id.*
19. *Id.* at 17.
20. *Id.*
21. *Id.*
22. *Cf.* People v. Morton, 284 App. Div. 413, 132 N.Y.S. 2d 309 (2d Dep't 1954), for a New York case that used the process described by Landis to redefine legally New York women as persons separate from their husbands.
23. E. STANTON'S REMINISCENCES 150.
24. *Id.*
25. *Id.* at 151.
26. *Id.*

EPILOGUE: WOMEN, WORK, AND THE LAW

On page one of her work, *Women in Industry*, Edith Abbott wrote:

Public opinion in this country has been recently concerned with the increase in gainful employment among women, and misapprehension has arisen from a failure to understand the complexity of the problem. . . . In the professions there are still to face the old questions of restriction of opportunity, of equal work for unequal pay. . . . In the group of occupations, including stenography, typewriting, bookkeeping and salesmanship . . . there is a long series of problems of which perhaps the most pressing is the effect of the pinmoney worker who makes of her occupation a "parasitic trade."[1]

Although Abott's observations were made in 1909, these issues were still not only alive after the last New York Married Women's Property Act passed in 1902 granted to working women the right to the wages they earned, but also are alive even today, after nearly two decades of federally mandated equal employment opportunity.

If the right to own the property one earns is the cornerstone of civil capacity, and thus the most fundamental of civil rights of free people, the story of the attainment of that right by female American citizens is not complete without at least a glance at the history of women and work in America. This history is best presented in relation to the issues isolated by Abbott as far back as 1909. More specifically, the questions in need of exposition are: what has been the relationship between the notion of "women's work" and the pay women have historically been able to command in the labor market, and what are the basic problems remaining to be solved affecting working women after a generation of legally created equal employment opportunity?

The history of women and work in America can be conveniently divided into five episodes: (1) the preindustrial period; (2) the "industrial revolution" and the establishment of the factory system; (3) the rise of the service industries and the "professionalization" of services; (4) World War II, its aftermath, and the era of equal employment opportunity; and (5) beyond equal opportunity.

I.

Before the so-called industrial revolution, women worked primarily, but not exclusively, in the home. In the colonial period, in fact, what little manufacturing was done in North America was done by women at home, and both women and men performed necessary argicultural tasks. Female heads of households received their portions of the planting land in colonial New England and, for at least a time, "maid's lots" were also granted.[2] In colonial New York, women had been known to manage estates of some several thousand acres,[3] and in the southern colonies women could manage a plantation.[4] The wills recorded in the New York Surrogate's Office during this period suggest that women could inherit property and functioned independently as a result.[5] Moreover women, under either voluntary or indentured contracts for service, learned skilled crafts as apprentices.[6]

Colonial women, however, did not limit their industry to manual labor. They also were active in commerce and the professions. Elizabeth Anthony Dexter, a historian of women's work, through the perusal of colonial newspapers, diaries, and court records, found colonial women engaged in varied trades such as tavern keepers, "she-merchants," artificers, avocational medical doctors, midwives, teachers in Dame schools, writers, and printers.[7] The "she-merchants" sold groceries, tobacco, apparel, window glass, wine, shoes, linens, jewelry, seeds, china, spectacles, books, hardware, cutlery, braziery, and sundry other goods.[8] The female artifacer created samplers, babies' bonnets, quilts, gowns, coats, hats, dresses, fans, furniture, mirrors, soap, candles, horseshoes, tea kettles, coffeepots, and other pots and pans.[9]

With the industrial revolution came the rise of the factory system of production. This change in the mode of production began in America in the late eighteenth and early nineteenth centuries. Edith Abbott, one of the earliest historians of women's work, usefully subdivided this era into two periods. The years 1760-1808 she characterized as "the period of transition," and the actual inauguration of the industrial revolution of America she dated with the Embargo and Non-Intercourse Acts of 1808.[10]

While the American period of transition was taking place, the English "industrial revolution" had already materialized. The transition to which Abbott refers is that from the old domestic system of production to the modern factory system. During this time Yankee entrepreneurs were striving to transplant the machines and machinists of England. Since England, in her effort to become the world's workshop, had prohibited both the exportation of any of the machinery used in manufacturing and the emigration of working people who had learned to operate the new machines, the transplantation process was slow and arduous. Finally, in 1789, after a quarter century of preliminary efforts, Samuel Slatter's cotton mill, with all of the machinery needed for spinning in place, was established in Rhode Island, thereby inaugurating the American industrial revolution.

During the "period of transition," societies for encouraging manufacturers were formed in cities such as Boston, New York, Philadelphia, and Baltimore, and so-called manufactories were established. Because neither the new machinery nor power were in operation in these manufactories, Abbott considered them to be transitional arrangements. It was nevertheless in these manufactories that women were employed or otherwise paid for doing the work that had been their province for ages.

Abbott describes the manufactories as "merely rooms where several looms were gathered and where a place of business could be maintained."[11] The spinning was often done by women in their own homes and the yarn delivered to the manufactory where they were paid for their work. Sometimes the participating women wove the yarn at home and brought the finished cloth to the manufactory for sale; yet often the manufactory employed several hundred women to weave on the premises.[12]

With the transition from manufactories to factories, came a transition in employment patterns. After the transition, women continued to do the work they had done for centuries, but for the first time in American history the majority of them did it away from home.

Although the textile industry was the first industry to be modernized, as the nineteenth century progressed, the manufacture of boats and shoes, cigars, ready-made clothing, and printed materials also accommodated itself to the new mode of production. Although shoemaking had historically been "man's work," women became employed in this work after the introduction of the division of labor had "revolutionized" this age-old craft. Women also were engaged as cigar makers, operators of the new sewing machines in the ready-made clothing industry, and in the early typesetting rooms.[13]

It is commonly believed that as the nineteenth century progressed, the quality of life for people working in factories deteriorated. In the initial years, the owners provided for the economic, educational, and social needs of female and child laborers, the first factory workers. As Abbott pointed out, the first mill girls formed "Improvement Circles" and attended Emerson's lyceum lectures and their granddaughters heavily populated women's colleges by the turn of the century.[14] However, as American employers began to import immigrants to work in the mills, which were rapidly becoming "sweat shops," the quality of life for factory workers declined while the educated grand-daughters of native factory workers of the early nineteenth century began taking their places in new occupations open to women in the first decades of the twentieth century. This tendency was accelerated by the Civil War, which drew educated women out of the mills and into teaching, nursing, and clerking positions in the newly developing services industries.[15]

As two classes of female workers evolved, both faced a similar problem. Although the working conditions of the immigrant factory worker were substantially less pleasant than those of her educated, native-born sisters, both groups of women labored for low wages and with little hope of advancement. Two conditions ensured the continued evolution of this phenomenon. Trade unions ignored the needs of female production workers, and "professionalization" of the occupations of educated women forced them into the lowest echelons of professions becoming increasingly more stratified.[16]

Elizabeth Dexter pointed out that although women in all ages have considered it their duty to be a "ministering angel" to the sick, and that female monopolization of health-care duties was quite the norm even into the eighteenth century in America, by the early nineteenth century the highest places in the medical profession were being taken by males.[17] By this time the need for training of physicians in the burgeoning science of medicine was recognized; yet the nature of this training was deemed unfit for females. It was believed that if a woman were allowed into the dissecting room her moral qualities of character would be quickly destroyed.[18]

The growth of professionalization and the requirement of higher education (not accessible to women), which worked to drive females out of the professions they had freely practiced in the colonial period, came at a time when new attitudes toward women in general and toward women as workers were developing. In the colonial days, idleness of any person (man, woman, or child) was considered to be a sin[19] and due to the ramifications of such a religious belief, a working woman even up to the middle of the eighteenth century was considered on her own merits. However, after the turn of the nineteenth century, such a woman was beginning to be viewed as a "self-conscious" deviant who had "stepped out of the 'graceful and dignified retirement' which so well became her sex."[20] She was also beginning to be regarded as a less than rational being not worthy of advanced education,[21] someone who was frail and prone to ill health.[22] As such, she was deemed unfit for the work that in the nineteenth century had begun to be professionalized, that is, to require formal training and education.

Although women were also barred from law, architecture, engineering, and other professions, the greatest loss of job status resulting from these restrictions was in the professionalization of the healing arts, for it was there that women lost the ability to continue what had formerly been deemed to be "women's work" rather than the right to encroach upon traditionally male prerogatives. Nevertheless the nineteenth century brought new opportunities in the service industry where women worked as sales clerks and as clerks and secretaries in offices.[23] Similarly the nursing and teaching professions were receptive to women workers,[24] and by the end of the century, pioneers such as Elizabeth Blackwell and Alice Hamilton in medicine, and Myra Bradwell and Belva Lockwood in law, had put a crack in the door that would eventually lead to the opening of the professions to women.[25]

The record of organized labor's relationship to female and other-than-white workers had not been completely praiseworthy.[26] Abbott was perhaps one of the first historians to examine the question with regard to women workers. Her close look at the treatment of women by the printers' unions provides a case study.[27] Abbott found the study of this industry to be important from the point of view of women's work because of the large number of women engaged in it and because it was one of the old skilled hand trades. Moreover the employment of women in that trade had a very long history.[28] In America several colonial newspapers, books, and pamphlets were published by women.[29] However, Abbott pointed out that printing has "never been a trade which women have made their own."[30] She blamed men in this trade for the union policy that had "always been hostile to the employment of women."[31] Abbott supported her generalization with examples of union activity directed against the advancement of women. In the early nineteenth century the typographic unions of cities such as Philadelphia, Boston, Washington, New York, and Baltimore, responding to rumors and newspaper ads and articles, foiled employers' plans to engage female compositors throughout the nineteenth century.[32] Furthermore the Printers' National Union adopted resolutions from 1854 forward vowing that the union would not encourage the employment of female compositors.[33]

Recognizing the impossibility of keeping females out of the industry, by the latter part of the nineteenth century the labor movement slowly began to tolerate union membership for females as long as they were segregated into women's unions.[34] Evidently the unions had rejected female solidarity because they feared the suppression of the wage rate; however, little if anything was demanded by the unions to improve the training and therefore the wages of females.[35]

The research of Elliot and Mary Brownlee supported that of Abbott. In their documentary history of women in the American economy, they showed that during the period from 1870 to 1929, as organized labor gained strength among working men, the unionization of women made little headway except in the garment industry.[36] In fact the Brownlees accused unions of abstaining from the general consensus of reform organizations that supported the protection of working women.[37] Only the Knights of Labor had an interest in organizing women,[38] as the American Federation of Labor excluded women well into the twentieth century.[39] Only in recent years have unions begun to show an interest in organizing female workers and helping them to attain higher wages for the work they do.[40]

Although feminists organizations and some labor unions clamored for equal pay for women in the late nineteenth and early tweintieth centuries, it was not until World War II brought large numbers of women into the labor force that an era of equal opportunity for women could be ushered in.[41] During World War II, women worked as production workers in aircraft plants, shipyards, steel mills, artillery and ammunition plants, on the railways, and as farm laborers.[42] They worked as welders, mechanics, riveters, assemblers, inspectors, laboratory technicians, and chemists; however, they were rarely supervisors.[43] Performance reports indicated that females performed as well as the male warriors they filled in for.[44] Nevertheless the women were often paid less than men for doing substantially similar work.[45] This resulted in agitation for an equal-pay bill and an equal rights amendment.[46] Neither materialized during the war years or in the following two decades.

II.

After nearly two decades of postwar doldrums, Congress passed the Equal Pay Act of 1963 mandating that:

No employer . . . shall discriminate, within any establishment in which such employees are employed, between employees on the basis of sex by paying wages to employees in such establishment at a rate less than the rate at which he pays wages of employees of the opposite sex in such establishment for equal work on jobs the performance of which requires equal skill, effort, and responsibility, and which are performed under similar working conditions, except where such payment is made pursuant to (i) a seniority system; (ii) a merit system; (iii) a system which measures earnings by quantity or quality of production; or (iv) a differential based on any factor other than sex.[47]

The Equal Pay Act was passed after extensive legislative committee hearings demonstrating widespread wage discrimination against women. Although the original act applied only to hourly employees subject to the minimum-wage law[48] to which the act was amended, Title IX of the Educational Amendments of 1972[49] extended the act's coverage to professional and other employees exempted from the wage and hour laws.

The Equal Pay Act, a direct result of the federal government's desire to correct the injustices suffered by women working in the war effort,[50] solved only part of the problem of equal employment opportunity for women. A year later, another step was taken when Title VII of the Civil Rights Act of 1964[51] was passed. By Title VII, it became illegal for a private employer of fifteen or more employees to discriminate on the basis of race, religion, sex, color, or national origin. The ban on discrimination reached not only wages, but all other employment practices or policies affecting any term or condition of employment.

The 1960s provided female workers with yet another weapon in the equal employment opportunity arsenal. By Executive Order 11246, as amended by 11375,[52] private employers who do business with the United States Government acquired responsibilities toward female workers that went far beyond those enumerated by Title VII or the Equal Pay Act. In signing a government contract or subcontract in excess of $10,000, the contractor agrees that it "will not discriminate against any employee or applicant for employment because of . . . sex . . ." and that it "will take affirmative action to ensure that applicants are employed and that employees are treated during employment" without regard to sex. In the event that the contractor is deemed by the Department of Labor to be in a state of noncompliance with these nondiscrimination clauses of the agreement, the contract may be cancelled, terminated, or suspended in whole or in part and the contractor may be declared ineligible for further government contracts.

The nondiscrimination clauses require that the contractor: (1) will not discriminate in recruitment, selection, placement, upgrading, demotion, transfer, layoff, termination, rates of pay, or selection for training; (2) will post notices of its nondiscrimination policy; (3) will state in all solicitations or advertisements for employees that it is an equal opportunity employer; (4) will advise any labor union with which it has an agreement of understanding of its equal opportunity commitments; (5) will furnish all required information and reports; (6) will develop an affirmative-action compliance program including a written affirmative-action plan with goals and timetables if the contractor has contracts in excess of $50,000.[53]

Once Congress prohibited discrimination based on sex by passing Title VII, it became incumbent upon the executive and judicial branches to develop the parameters of sex discrimination. That is, Congress outlawed discrimination but did not define discrimination.

Section 705 of Title VII established the Equal Employment Opportunity Commission (EEOC) as a federal agency charged with responsibility to administer Title VII. Pursuant to this authority, the EEOC issued its first set of sex-discrimination guidelines on November 22, 1965. These guidelines were subsequently revised and refined by the guidelines of February 21, 1968, August 19, 1969, and April 4, 1972, which were partially rejected by the United States Supreme Court on December 7, 1976. Due to the Court's action, on October 31, 1978, President Carter signed into law a pregnancy disability amendment to Title VII that reinstated the EEOC's definition of sex discrimination.[54] A closer examination of this process of creating and refining a definition of sex discrimination is of import.

The EEOC guidelines had informed employers that the commission will find that certain practices would constitute forbidden sex discrimination rather than permitted distinctions based upon a bona fide occupational qualification. Some of the forbidden practices outlined in the EEOC guidelines were: (1) the refusal to hire a woman because of her sex based on assumptions about the comparative employment characteristics of women in general; (2) the refusal to hire an individual based on stereotyped characterizations of the sexes; (3) the refusal to hire an individual because of the preferences of coworkers, the employer, clients, or customers; (4) the maintenance of separate lines of progression or separate seniority lists based on sex; (5) the maintenance of an employment rule that forbids or restricts the employment of married women and that is not applicable to married men; (6) the placement of advertisements in columns classified by publishers on the basis of sex; (7) discrimination between men and women with regard to fringe benefits; (8) discrimination on the basis of pregnancy or the treatment of pregnancy as different from any other temporary disability. Also prohibited by these guidelines was the reliance on state laws, such as state protective legislation, that discriminate on the basis of sex. The commission determined that such laws were preempted or superseded by Title VII, a federal statute.

Until December 7, 1976, the federal courts tended to facilitate the EEOC in its protection of female workers from discrimination on the basis of their sex.

In line with this tendency, the United States Supreme Court, in the 1971 case of *Phillips* v. *Martin Marietta Corporation,*[55] rejected the argument that an employer was permitted under Title VII to discriminate on the basis of sex plus something else. That is, the Court found it unconvincing for an employer to argue that it could eliminate from consideration women with preschool-age children as long as it hired women who had no preschool-age children along with men who were hired regardless of whether or not they had preschool-age children.[56]

Despite the Supreme Court's early cooperation with the EEOC in its attempt to define sex discrimination, the Court of the mid-1970s, with its several Nixon appointees, began to take issue with the agency whose duty it is to enforce Title VII. Discrimination on the basis of sex plus pregnancy was held by the High Court in the 1976 case of *General Electric Company* v. *Gilbert*[57] not to fall within the definition of sex discrimination. The great significance of this case can only be grasped if one considers *Gilbert* in the light of another landmark case, *Griggs* v. *Duke Power Co.*[58] According to the EEOC, discrimination could be defined as the use of an employment practice that has a disparate effect on a class protected by Title VII and could not be demonstrated to be significantly related to job performance.[59] Reaching the Supreme Court in 1971, *Griggs* put the imprimatur of the judicial branch on the EEOC's definition of discrimination. Reasoning that "[t]he administrative interpretation of the Act by the enforcing agency is entitled to great deference,"[60] the Court found acceptable the EEOC's definition.

Griggs was also important for its landmark discussion with regard to whether an employer must intend to discriminate in order to be found in violation of Title VII. On this issue the Court said:

Under the Act, practices, procedures, or tests neutral on their face, and even neutral in terms of intent, cannot be maintained if they operate to "freeze" the status quo of prior discriminatory employment practices.[61]

and explained that:

[G]ood intent or absence of discriminatory intent does not redeem employment procedures or testing mechanisms that operate as "built-in headwinds" for minority groups and are unrelated to measuring job capability.[62]

It certainly is indisputable that the image of women as childbearers has operated as a barrier to the hiring, promoting, and otherwise advancing, of female employees. Moreover it is this capacity to become pregnant that primarily differentiates females from males and is likely to precipitate sex-role stereotyping. Consequently for the Court to sanction an employer's discrimination against female employees on the basis of pregnancy would seem to fly in the face of both *Griggs* and *Phillips*. How then did the Court rationalize this apparent departure from precedent?

The General Electric Company (GE) provided for all of its employees a disability plan that paid weekly nonoccupational sickness and accident benefits. Excluded from coverage, however, were disabilities arising only from pregnancy. All other disabilities were covered. Female employees brought their complaint to the EEOC in the belief that GE's policy of treating pregnancy different from other temporary disabilities fell within the definition of proscribed sex discrimination. Relying on the *Griggs* definition of discrimination, the EEOC, the federal district court,[63] and the federal court of appeals[64] agreed. The United State Supreme Court did not.

Writing for the majority, Justice Rehnquist, reasoning that since GE insured against "no risk from which men are protected and women are not," apparently rejected the "disparate impact" test of *Griggs* and left intact only a "disparate treatment" definition of sex discrimination. In so doing, the Court seemed to be unmoved by the fact that GE's policy resulted in the subjection of only women to a substantial risk of total loss of income because of a temporary disability.[65] Since "the rule at issue places the risk of absence caused by pregnancy in class by itself,"[66] one would think that the Court would have had to distinguish this case from *Phillips*, wherein the employer attempted to place the risk of mothering small children in a class by itself. It did not do so.

Justices Blackmun and Stewart concurred in Rehnquist's rendition of the Supreme Court's *Gilbert* decision. In so doing, however, each felt the necessity of addressing the problem of defining discrimination in terms of effect or impact. Justice Stewart, joinging in "the opinion of the Court holding that General Electric's exclusion of benefits for disability during pregnancy is not a *per se* violation of §703 (a) (1) of Title VII, and that the respondents have failed to prove a discriminatory effect,"[67] made it a point to say that he did "not understand the opinion to question either *Griggs* v. *Duke Power Co.,* specifically, or the significance generally of proving a discriminatory effect in a Title VII case."[68]

Justice Blackman concurred only in part.

I join the judgment of the Court and concur in its opinion insofar as it holds (a) that General Electric's exclusion of disability due to pregnancy is not, *per se*, a violation of §703(a) (1) of Title VII; (b) that the plaintiffs in this case therefore had at least the burden of providing disciminatory effect; and (c) that they failed in that proof.[69]

After concurring in part, Justice Blackmun specifically declined to join in "any inference or suggestion in the Court's opinion—if any such inference or suggestion is there—that effect may never be a controlling factor in a Title VII case, or that *Griggs* v. *Duke Power Co.*, is no longer good law."[70]

Since it takes five justices to make a majority of the Court, Stewart's vote was decisive. (Rehnquist declared the opinion of the Court in which Burger, Stewart, White, and Powell joined and in which Blackmun joined in part. Brennan filed a dissenting opinion, in which Marshall joined. Stevens filed a dissenting opinion.) Consequently it might be persuasively argued that the

Griggs test for defining discrimination is still good law even with regard to sex discrimination. Nevertheless it can hardly be denied that pregnancy had received very different treatment by the Supreme Court than any other condition only or primarily found among members of any one protected class. This conclusion is all the more evident if one examines the Supreme Court's reasoning in two more cases decided by the Court in the following year.

One year after the U.S. Supreme Court rendered its *General Electric* v. *Gilbert* decision, it decided yet another case involving discrimination on the basis of pregnancy. This was *Nashville Gas Co.* v. *Satty.*[71] The Nashville Gas Company maintained a sick-leave plan from which coverage of disability due to pregnancy had been excluded. The company also required pregnant employees to take formal leaves of absence without receiving pay. While on such leaves, the pregnant employees lost all accumulated job seniority. As a result, the employees returning from maternity leaves were reemployed in a premanent position only if no other employee also applied for the job. The United States District Court held that these policies violated Title VII,[72] and the Court of Appeals for the Sixth Circuit affirmed.[73] The Supreme Court granted *certiorari* (a request to make sure) to decide, in light of its *General Electric* v. *Gilbert* decision, whether the lower courts properly applied Title VII to the company's policies.

In deciding the issues before it, the High Court bifurcated the concept of discrimination on the basis of pregnancy. With regard to the denial of seniority because of pregnancy, Justice Rehnquist, again writing for the majority, declared:

We conclude that petitioner's policy of denying accumulated seniority to female employees returning from pregnancy leave violates §703(a)(2) of Title VII.[74]

Reasoning that the company's "decision not to treat pregnancy as a disease or disability for the purposes of seniority retention is not on its face a discriminatory policy,"[75] Rehnquist conceded that the company "has imposed on women a substantial burden that men need not suffer."[76] This concession was despite the fact that Rehnquist did not abandon his *Gilbert* reasoning. Relying on *Gilbert*, Rehnquist reaffirmed his position that women have "differing roles in 'the scheme of human existence.' "[77] Therefore he deduced that the company's policy of not awarding sick-leave pay to pregnant employees is "legally indistinguishable from the disability insurance program upheld in *Gilbert*."[78] Thus Rehnquist concluded that Title VII does not require that greater economic benefits be paid to one sex over the other by applying the conclusion he had already reached in *Gilbert*, wherein it was deemed controlling that no evidence had been produced to suggest that men received more benefits from General Electric's disability insurance fund than did women.

If *Gilbert* makes it appear that the Supreme Court has abandond the "sex-plus" test for determining whether an employment practice or policy discriminates on the basis of sex, the case of *City of Los Angeles Department of Water and Power* v. *Manhart,*[79] decided by the U.S. Supreme Court on April 25, 1978, does little to belie that appearance.

The facts of *Manhart* were rather straightforward. As a class, women live longer than men. For this reason, the employer required its female employees to make larger contributions to its pension fund than its male employees. Characterizing the issue as "whether this practice discriminated against individual female employees because of their sex,"[80] the Court held that the employer's practice created a facial violation of §703(a)(1) of Title VII.

In *Manhart,* Justice Stevens, who had dissented in *Gilbert,* delivered the opinion of the Court. Stevens was joined in part by Justice Marshall who had also dissented in *Gilbert.* Justices Stewart, White, and Powell joined in the majority decision. Chief Justice Burger and Justice Rehnquist dissented. For Justice Blackmun, the fact that Justices Stewart, White, and Powell participated in the majority opinion supported his conclusion that the *Manhart* decision "cuts back on *General Electric,*" thereby making the recognition of that case as continuing precedent "somewhat questionable."[81] Blackmun based his conclusion on an examination of the majority's stated rationale.

Congress, by Title VII ... intended to eliminate, with certain exceptions, ... sex ... as factors upon which employers may act. ... A program such as the one challenged here does exacerbate gender consciousness ... [while] the program under consideration in *General Electric* did exactly the same thing and yet was upheld against challenge.[82]

Despite the soundness of Blackmun's reasoning, he overlooked a "sex-plus" analysis. Rejecting as "just too easy"[83] the majority's distinction between *Gilbert* and *Manhart* permitting employees to be divided into two classes (pregnant women and nonpregnant persons of both sexes), but not permitting employers to classify employees into two groups each composed entirely and exclusively of members of the same sex, Blackmun would have made himself clearer if he had couched his criticism in terms of an uneasiness with the unreasoned departure from the *Phillips* v. *Martin Marietta* precedent.

On October 31, 1978, President Carter signed into law a pregnancy disability amendment[84] to Title VII of the 1964 Civil Rights Act. The impetus for amending Title VII to prohibit discrimination because of pregnancy was, of course, the impact of *General Electric* v. *Gilbert* and *Nashville Gas* v. *Satty* on disability and sick-pay policies. The net effect of this legislative process, however, was the outlawing of any disparate treatment of pregnant women for all employment-related purposes.

The amendment, expanding the definition of sex discrimination to include discrimination on the basis of pregnancy, childbirth, or related medical conditions, accomplished the following: (1) required employers to treat pregnancy and childbirth the same as other causes of disability under fringe-benefit plans; (2) prohibited terminating or refusal to hire or promote a woman solely because she is pregnant; (3) prohibited mandatory leaves for pregnant women arbitrarily set at a certain time in their pregnancy and not based on their inability to work; (4) protected the reinstatement rights of women on leave for pregnancy-related reasons, including credit for previous service and accrued retirement benefits and accumulated seniority.[85]

The only exception to the mandate of equal treatment of pregnant workers is a provision stating that employers are not requred to pay for health insurance benefits for abortion, except when the life of the mother would be endangered if the fetus was carried to term or when medical complications have arisen from an abortion. The Senate-House Conference Committee Report,[86] however, stressed that the basic language of the amendment covers decisions by women who terminate their pregnancy for nonmedical reasons. That is, it is the intent of the legislature to preclude an employer from firing or refusing to hire a women simply because she has had an abortion or plans to have one.

The fundamental purpose of the amendment was to set forth the opinion of Congress that it was the dissenting justice in *Gilbert* who had correctly interpreted Title VII.[87] The House Committee sought to end the incongruity in the act's interpretation created by the Supreme Court with its *Gilbert* and *Satty* decisions. To accomplish this, the House sought to make clear that "distinctions based on pregnancy are *per se* violations of Title VII" and thereby eliminate the need to analyze the impact of a pregnancy-related employment policy.[88] The problem, as summarized by the committee, was that by using the disparate-impact test, the Court had relied upon the distinction that there was no proof that the disability package was worth more to men than to women in the *Gilbert* case, and in *Satty* the employer had not merely refused to extend to women a benefit that men cannot receive, but had imposed on women a substantial burden that men need not suffer. What the committee found to be inexplicable was: why the Court's " 'burden' approach did not apply in *Gilbert*, where only women were burdened with paying their living expenses out of their own savings during a disability period, and why the right to retain one's seniority while absent from work is not a 'benefit.' "[89] Since the testimony received by the committee demonstrated that "the assumption that women will become pregnant and leave the labor force leads to the view of women as marginal workers, and is at the root of the discriminatory practices which keep women in low-paying and deadend jobs,"[90] the committee report made explicit that the intent of HR 6075 was "unmistakably [to] reaffirm that sex discrimination includes discrimination based on pregnancy, and specifically define standards which require that pregnant workers be treated the same as other employees on the basis of their ability or inability to work."[91]

The text of the Senate Committee Report[92] reveals a legislative intent identical to that of the House. Because of the testimony received by the Senate committee demonstrating that "the assumption that women will become pregnant and leave the labor market is at the core of the sex stereotyping resulting in unfavorable disparate treatment of women in the workplace,"[93] it recommended passage of S. 995 with an intent "to amend Title VII of the Civil Rights Act of 1964 by adding to section 701 a new subsection (k) which makes clear that the prohibitions against sex discrimination in the act include discrimination in employment on the basis of pregnancy or pregnancy-related disabilities."[94]

On April 20, 1979, the Equal Employment Opportunity Commission issued official guidelines[95] for interpreting the new amendment. Interestingly, the commission applied Rehnquist's reasoning to the detriment of employers such as General Electric who had fought for and capitalized upon the judicial acceptance of the "benefit-burden" dichotomy. The EEOC did this when it directed employers whose benefit plan pays doctor and hospital bills for medical conditions for husbands of pregnant workers also to provide pregnancy coverage for wives of male employees to avoid a situation in which "male employees are receiving a less favorable fringe benefit package"[96] than female employees. It might be safe to assume that General Electric will soon regret the day it advanced the contorted argument that Title VII means not giving to one sex a benefit that the other sex does not enjoy as marked by the value of the fringe-benefit package. So, too, is it safe to assume that other employers will regret their rejoicement in Rehnquist's acceptance of such a departure from the Title VII case precedent.

Discrimination on the basis of pregnancy has been, at least for the moment, resolved, but two other significant areas of discrimination against female workers remain that have yet to be declared to be within the legal definition of sex discrimination. These are the rights to be paid equally for work of equal value to the employer and to be free from sexual harassment in the workplace.

III.

The standard used by the Department of Labor's (DOL) Wage and Hour Division as it has enforced the Equal Pay Act can be summarized by the maxim "equal pay for equal work." Essential to a determination that the act has been violated is, therefore, a finding that the job performed by a female has the same content as a comparable but higher paying job performed by a male.

The Wage and Hour *Interpretive Bulletin* states this rule positively by its directive that "application of the equal pay standard is not dependent on job classifications or titles but depends rather on actual job requirements and performance."[97] To determine whether equality of job content obtains, the Labor Department investigators measure the jobs in question against three separate standards. In so doing, "equal" is not thought to mean "identical," but rather to mean "substantially similar" in skill, effort, and responsiblity.[98] Once it is established that the jobs in question have a substantially similar job content, the DOL investigator must determine if the work is performed under similar working conditions. If the jobs are so performed, a violation of the act is found and the salaries of the lower paid employees are brought to the level of those employees of the opposite sex receiving the higher wage rate.

It is important to note, however, that the DOL position holds that

the fact that jobs performed by male and female employees may have the same total point value under an evaluation system in use by the employer does not in itself mean that the jobs concerned are equal according to the terms of the statute.[99]

It is with this position that modern feminists have recently taken exception. Feminists of the late 1970s believe that a major problem for female workers is that work traditionally done by women has historically been underpaid and that the standard of "equal pay for equal work" must therefore be supplemented with another notion of justice—"equal pay for work of equal value."

A case embodying this struggle is *Christensen* v. *Iowa.*[100] The action was brought by representatives of a class of female clerical employees at the University of Northern Iowa (UNI)who believed that UNI's practice of paying clerical workers, who are exclusively female, less than the amount it pays physical plant workers, who are predominantly male, for jobs of equal value to the university creates a violation of Title VII of the Civil Rights Act of 1964.

The facts of this case reflect the historical predicament of female workers. Since employment opportunities first opened for them outside of the home, females have been hired only for jobs that males shunned because of their low pay. Such jobs came to be thought of as "women's work," which perpetuated sex segregation in the marketplace. Simultaneously, trade unions ignored these job classifications in their organizational efforts until after "male" jobs had been unionized. All of these forces worked together to keep the market value of the positions artificially low, that is, lower than their actual value to the employer. In 1974 the University of Northern Iowa took cognizance of this situation and attempted to remedy it.

Before 1974 the university determined the wage scales for nonprofessional jobs by reference to wages paid for similar work in the local labor market. Two sets of factors were applied, one for the clericals and one for plant employees. Although all positions at the university were open to persons of both sexes, the nonprofessional jobs were segregated by sex. All of the employees in the clerical classification were female, and the majority of the physical plant department employees were male. The local labor market was, of course, similarly sex segregated.

In 1974 the university employer instituted a new pay scheme under which compensation was to be based upon an objective evaluation of each job's relative worth to the organization. This pay system would have gone substantially farther along the road of equal pay for women than those systems to which the Labor Department had already given its imprimatur. That is, the system used by the university assigned points and established pay grades according to value to the employer rather than job content. Jobs with similar points were placed in the same "labor grade" regardless of the actual content of the job. Then the "pay range" for each "labor grade" was determined by reference to the market rates in the vicinity of the university for similar jobs. The system then divided each labor grade into sixteen pay steps to provide increases based on length of service. As stated above, such an approach had not been mandated by the Department of Labor.

The new system, after raising expectations of female workers, failed to operate as anticipated. Due to the high local pay scales for the jobs performed by physical plant employees, the university found it necessary to provide for advanced-step starting pay for many of its physical plant employees, but not for its entry-level clerical employees who were paid about the local average for clerical work. As a result, predominantly male physical plant employees continued to be paid an average rate that was higher than the rate for female clerical employees despite equivalent longevity and classification within the same labor grade. Moreover every individual female clerical worker was paid less than every individual male of equivalent longevity in the same labor grade.[101]

After finding the above-outlined facts, the district court[102] determined that there was no violation of Title VII, whose compensation provisions were deemed equivalent to those of the Equal Pay Act. The plaintiffs appealed to the United States Court of Appeals for the Eighth Circuit.[103] On appeal, they argued that the university paid their female clerical employees "less than their jobs are worth when compared to the pay received by male Plant Department employees because the Clerical Department employees are female."[104] More specifically, the appellants contended that the university's policy of paying male plant workers more than female clerical workers where the women's jobs are of equal value to those of the men under the university's own objective job-evaluation plan violates section 703(a) of Title VII,[105] and that the university has no valid defense to its section 703(a) violation.[106]

To make these arguments, appellants had to deal first with the threshold question of whether Title VII required an analysis essentially the same as that of the Equal Pay Act when a compensation violation was alleged. Appellants argued that such identical analysis was not required despite the Bennett Amendment,[107] which provides that:

It shall not be an unlawful employment practice . . . for any employer to differentiate upon the basis of sex in determining the amount of the wages or compensation paid or to be paid to employees . . . if such differentiation is authorized by the [Equal Pay Act].

Rather, they pointed out that the language of Title VII was significantly broader than that of the Equal Pay Act.[108] In addition to proscribing the payment of lower wages to females than to males, the appellants contended that Title VII "forbids employers to classify employees *in any way* which would even *tend to deprive* them of employment opportunities or adversely affect their status as employees on the basis of sex."[109]

At the heart of the appellants' case rested the argument that the entire job market tends to discriminate against those seeking positions that are predominately occupied by women and to allow the defendant to do so, too, would be to accept the notion that if other employers in the community pay women less than men, the university may do so also.[110] In advancing this line of reasoning, the appellants used sociological authorities whose work takes up where that of Abbott, the Brownlees, and Dexter leaves off.[111] That is, they sought to instruct the appellate court on the history of women and work that amounted to long-standing discriminatory practices that channeled women workers into a small number of jobs, thereby creating an oversupply of workers and depressed wages in those jobs. Their theory was that the violation of Title VII committed by the employer was its policy of relying upon prevailing wage rates in determining beginning pay scales for jobs of equal worth to the organization that had the effect of transplanting the sex discrimination of the marketplace into the wage policies of the college.

Rejecting the appellants' reasoning that the higher wages paid to physical plant jobs are merely a continuation of a long history of sex discrimination in the local job markets, UNI argued that the higher wages for plant employees are justified, because to base wages on local market wage surveys that reflect comparable wages for similar work is neither contrary to the Equal Pay Act nor to Title VII, which, due to the Bennett Amendment, requires a showing of "equal work" in claims of sex discrimination in compensation.[112]

In deciding the case in favor of the employer, the federal appeals court saw no necessity to resolve the conflict presented over the interpretation of the Bennett Amendment. The court was "convinced that, apart from the Bennett Amendment, appellants [had] failed to make a *prima facie* case."[113] In so determining, the court acknowledged the fact that UNI's pay system perpetuated the traditional disparity between wages paid to women and those paid to men.[114] Despite the admittedly deleterious effects of history, the court concluded that the female employees "failed to demonstrate that the difference in wages paid to clerical and plant employees rested upon sex discrimination and not some other legitimate reason,"[115] one of which was the right of an employer to consider the market in setting wage rates for genuinely different work classification.[116] In rejecting the appellants' reasoning, the court was persuaded in part by the fact that the female employees "are not locked into clerical positions by any University policy or practice."[117] and therefore equality of opportunity, the federal policy embodied in Title VII, was not really at issue in this case.[118]

The Equal Employment Opportunity Commission (EEOC), the agency charged with enforcing Title VII, not surprisingly took issue with the Eighth Circuit Court of Appeals. The commission had already issued several decisions in which it found to be discriminatory the use by employers of prevailing community wage systems that establish a lower schedule of wages for clerical jobs than craft jobs. They also filed an *amicus* brief in *Christensen* v. *Iowa* as well as other cases on this issue. Moreover the EEOC contracted with the National Academy of Science to assess the feasibility of developing objective and comprehensive methods of determining job comparability in an effort to meet this issue head-on.

In a speech before the delegates of the Federal Bar Association meeting in Washington, D.C., on June 9, 1978, Daniel E. Leach, vice chairman of the EEOC, set forth the commission's position on the issue of equal pay for work of equal value. He explained that the EEOC reads Title VII's section 703(a) and its underlying legislative history to mean that

Congress understood that discrimination is often subtle and complex—and intended the law to root out and remedy that discrimination which is not readily apparent ...[and therefore] Title VII is broad enough in scope to reach this form of wage inequality.[119]

With regard to the Bennett Amendment, Vice Chairman Leach presented the commission's view that the amendment "speaks only to the defenses which are available under the Equal Pay Act ... [and] does not define the standards for making out a prima facie violation of Title VII."[120] Finally, Leach summarized the mission of Title VII and, therefore, the EEOC.

Title VII was enacted to make changes in the very fabric of the workplace—to eliminate the stereotypes. To that end job comparability—structure bias—must be explored and pursued.[121]

Women today await higher authority's choice between the conflict of opinion in the reasoning of the circuit court and that of the EEOC.

IV.

As noted above, when Congress passed Title VII with an intent to end adverse employment discrimination based upon sex, it failed to define the concept of sex discrimination, thereby leaving the job of refining the term to the courts. The defining process begins when a plaintiff, feeling that some injustice has befallen her brings her grievance to the judiciary. The complaint outlines the facts of perceived injustice and states the harm that befell her due to the injustice. It also names the party (defendant) who allegedly perpetrated the harm. The defendant, feeling unjustly accused of violating the act, brings a motion to dismiss the complaint for failure to state a cause of action or a motion for summary judgment contending that even if all that the plaintiff has alleged were true, there would be no violation of the law. Then the court is forced to decide—given what the plaintiff claims is true, should such alleged acts causing such alleged harm be legally deemed to constitute sex discrimination? In the early 1970s, women's groups, themselves believing that sexual harassment on the job constituted discrimination in employment, sought to convince the public and the judiciary of the soundness of their opinion.[122]

Among the earliest cases alleging a theory that violation of Title VII's ban on sex discrimination occurs when a female subordinate is sexually harassed by a supervisor was a case decided by the U.S. District Court, District of Columbia on August 9, 1974. In *Barnes* v. *Train*,[123] the plaintiff, a female federal employee, claimed that her job was abolished and she was reassigned because she refused to have sexual relations with her supervisor. Not surprisingly, the defendant (the United States Government) moved for summary judgment.

Assuming *arguendo* that the plaintiff's job was in fact abolished and she in fact reassigned because she refused to have sexual relations with her supervisor, the court was forced to decide whether a retaliatory employment action by a male supervisor toward a female subordinate because she refused his request for a sexual affair is the type of forbidden conduct contemplated by Title VII. The court, taking its standard from the case of *Sprogis* v. *United Airlines*,[124] decided that "the instant actions which plaintiff complains of, plainly fall wide of the mark set by the court in *Sprogis*."[125] Acknowledging that the proper test (that is, the *Sprogis* test) of whether complained-of actions state a cognizable claim under the statute is whether such actions fall within "the entire spectrum of disparate treatment of men and women resulting from sex stereotypes,"[126] the court reasoned that "the substance of plaintiff's complaint is that she was discriminated against not because she was a woman, but because she refused to engage in a sexual affair with her supervisor" and therefore was not harmed by an "arbitrary barrier to continued employment based on plaintiff's sex."[127] Rather the court characterized the complained-of acts as a mere "inharmonious personal relationship."[128]

The weaknesses of the court's analysis are clear. Certainly the court would acknowledge that the problem presented involves the abuse of power and position in an organization to extort sexual gratification from a subordinate. However, the court blinded itself to facts of which it should have taken judicial notice; that is, that the working world is by and large one in which females are supervised by males and that the vast majority of males are heterosexual.

If notice had been taken of these facts, the court could have logically concluded that being subjected to the unbridled risk of sexual harassment by a supervisor creates an artificial barrier having a disparate effect on the employment of females that cannot be justified by business necessity and is not a bona fide occupational qualification. That is, the court could have easily concluded that the actions compained of fell squarely within the definition of forbidden discrimination as formulated by the U. S. Supreme Court in *Griggs* v. *Duke Power Co.* Furthermore once the court conceded that at least one proper test for the existence of discrimination on the basis of sex was "disparate treatment of men and women resulting from sex stereotypes," it defies both logic and common sense not to recognize that conditioning employment opportunities on willingness to gratify the sexual desires of a supervisor, rather than on willingness and ability to satisfy the business-related duties of the job, is equivalent to treating women according to the sexual stereotype of females as sexual objects. That is, the sexual stereotype in question is the perception of a woman as an object (nonworker) whose primary value is to provide sexual gratification to males, thereby reducing her willingness and ability to perform the duties of her job to a mere irrelevancy. This interpretation is given further credence by the fact that as a worker, the plaintiff was expendable as long as her "primary duty" as sexual object was not performed. This is not a risk that male subordinates must run.

Implicit in the court's "inharmonious personal relationship" analysis is the assumption that some day a female supervisor might abolish the job of a male subordinate who refused to gratify her sexually. Yet this, too, constitutes both faulty logic and an ignorance of the equal opportunity case precedent. No claim that someone was harrassed because of his race or religious beliefs has been barred from the courts on the basis that someday, somewhere, members of the harassee's race or religious group might also be supervisors. Moreover Title VII has been interpreted to reach those influences that subtly affect the atmosphere of the working environment.

Finally, the court overlooked the possibility of "reverse discrimination" when it dismissed the plaintiffs' claim. It could have been held that once sexual advances are made by a supervisor, a Title VII cause of action is created for one of the two sexes. A female who accepts the offer avails herself of an employment practice (opportunity) that discriminates on the basis of sex in favor of females and against similarly situated males. On the other hand, if she declines the offer, and is retaliated against, she becomes subject to an employment practice (barrier) that discriminates on the basis of sex against her.

For several years after *Barnes* v. *Train*, courts remained reluctant to recognize a cause of action under Title VII on the theory of sexual harassment. In the 1975 case of *Corne* v. *Bausch and Lomb, Inc.,*[129] the district court, reasoning that "the only sure way an employer could avoid such charges would be to have employees who were asexual,"[130] refused to hold that an employer should be found liable for putting a male in a supervisory position over female employees where the male supervisor persistently takes unsolicited and unwelcome sexual liberties with female subordinates.[131]

By 1976 judicial reasoning with regard to the issue of whether sexual harassment constituted sex discrimination had begun to become more precise, thus indicating that the theory of the plaintiffs was being taken more seriously. In *Miller* v. *Bank of America,*[132] a 1976 case, the district court granted the defendant's motion for summary judgment where the female plaintiff failed to bring the matter to the employer's attention. Without so doing, the court reasoned, there exists no employer practice of imposing a condition of sexual submission on female employees. In order for the plaintiff to state a claim, the court held, "specific factual allegations describing an employer policy which in its application imposes or permits a consistent, as distinguished from isolated, sex-based discrimination on a definable employee group"[133] must be made. The employer was secure from liability where it could demonstrate that on occasions, when it had received complaints of sexual harassment, it had investigated such complaints, taken appropriate action, and made no reprisals against the female subordinate making the complaint[134] or where it could demonstrate both lack of knowledge of the male supervisor's alleged misbehavior and a firm rule against sexual fraternalization among its employees.[135]

Williams v. *Saxbe*,[136] decided in April 1976, was one of the first cases to support a sexual-harassment theory of discrimination. In *Williams*, the plaintiff alleged a causal connection between the rejection of the supervisor's sexual advances and an adverse employment condition (a retaliatory termination). Where future plaintiffs' theories conformed to that of the one sustained in *Williams*, their claims have likewise been upheld as within Title VII's definition of forbidden sex discrimination.[137] However, where a plaintiff does not set forth facts that, if true, would indicate that her employment was conditioned on acquiescence to romantic advances, or that the supervisor had authority to retaliate, her claim has not withstood a motion to dismiss or a motion for summary judgment.[138] Of course, the question still left open is: How much sexual harassment must females withstand from job-related encounters with men who are not their supervisors? The higher women climb up organizational charts, the more significant this question becomes.

V.

Some would hold that the status of women is rooted in the nature of things. Justice Rehnquist reflects the belief of many when he colors his interpretation of Title VII on a preconception that irrespective of the act, women, with their potential for becoming pregnant, have a different role in "the scheme of human existence" than do men and therefore it is natural that they be treated differently from their male counterparts in the workplace. On the opposite side of the philosophical spectrum, others hold that it is unnatural for females to be treated differently from males, and that although their current oppression is related to the irrationalities of the capitalist mode of production, their eventual progress is as inevitable as is the destruction of the economic order that necessitates the unnatural condition of female oppression.

It is difficult to assess which world view is more insidious. Both are detrimental to female liberation. The former theory makes it a crime against nature for women to strive for acceptance as human beings capable of more than merely procreating. The latter theory, while overlooking the historical fact that women were oppressed long before capitalism and remain so oppressed in noncapitalist societies, labels women as "reactionary" if they strive for equality of opportunity rather than expend their time and energy hastening the coming of the inevitable revolution.

Perhaps it is counterproductive to debate the causes of female oppresion when a solution to the problem has yet to materialize. No matter what the etiology of this social disorder, it is today the symptoms with which one must deal. The most significant of these symptoms is the barrier to full female humanity created by sex-role stereotyping and its necessary corollary, the segregation of males and females into two different worlds. With the legal rights to own property and to equal employment opportunity, the barrier has begun to crumble. Only time will tell how this equality under the law will affect social relations in a culture in which law is but one of many of the norms that determine the behavior of human beings.

Notes

1. E. ABBOTT, WOMEN IN INDUSTRY 1 (1909) [hereinafter cited as ABBOTT].
2. *Id.* at 11.
3. E. BROWNLEE & M. BROWNLEE, WOMEN IN THE AMERICAN ECOMONY 43-50 (1976) [hereinafter cited as BROWNLEE].
4. *Id.* at 50-63.
5. *Id.* at 64-71.
6. *Id.* at 72-78.
7. E. DEXTER COLONIAL WOMEN OF AFFAIRS *passim* (1931) [hereinafter cited as DEXTER].
8. *Id.* at 18-38.
9. *Id.* at 39-57.
10. ABBOTT, *supra* note 1, at 35-62.
11. *Id.* at 37.
12. *Id.* at 37-42.
13. *Id. passim.*
14. *Id.* at 110, 137-40.
15. *Id.* at 141.
16. For a closer examination of the history of women workers and trade unionism, *see generally* P. FONER, WOMEN AND THE AMERICAN LABOR MOVEMENT (1979); A. HENRY, WOMEN AND THE LABOR MOVEMENT (1923); J. O'SULLIVAN & R. GALLICK, WORKERS AND ALLIES (1975); P. FONER, HISTORY OF THE LABOR MOVEMENT IN THE UNITED STATES (1955) [hereinafter cited as FONER]; ABBOTT, *supra* note 1, at 146, 170, 206-08, 250-58; BROWNLEE, *supra* note 3, at 31-35, 160-69, 184-85, 213-18, 216-28.
17. DEXTER, *supra* note 7, at 59-60.
18. *Id.*
19. ABBOTT, *supra* note 1, at 32-34; DEXTER *passim.*
20. E. DEXTER, CAREER WOMEN OF AMERICA 1776-1840, at 219 (1950).
21. *Id.* at 222.
22. *Id.*

23. BROWNLEE, *supra* note 3, at 256-62; R. SMUTTS, WOMEN AND WORK IN AMERICA 21-24 (1959) [hereinafter cited as SMUTTS].

24. BROWNLEE, *supra* note 3, at 266-70; SMUTTS, *supra* note 23, at 1-37.

25. For an account of the efforts of these women, *see* BROWNLEE, *supra* note 3, at 270-307.

26. *See, e.g.*, 2 FONER, *supra* note 16, at 61-66, 364-68; SMUTTS, *supra* note 23, at 120; BROWNLEE, *supra* note 3, at 213; ABBOTT, *supra* note 1, at 146, 170, 206-08, 250-58; C. GREGORY, WOMEN IN DEFENSE WORK DURING WORLD WAR II 166 (1974) [hereinafter cited as GREGORY].

27. ABBOTT, *supra* note 1, at 246-61.

28. *Id.* at 246.

29. *Id.* at 246-47.

30. *Id.* at 249-50.

31. *Id.* at 250-51.

32. *Id.* at 250-52.

33. *Id.* at 252-53.

34. *Id.* at 253.

35. *Id.* at 254-61.

36. BROWNLEE, *supra* note 3, at 184.

37. *Id.* at 186.

38. *Id.* at 209.

39. 2 FONER, *supra* note 16, at 364-68.

40. New York Times, July 9, 1979, at A14.

41. *See* GREGORY, *supra* note 26, at 165-207.

42. *Id.* at 67-139.

43. *Id.*

44. *Id.* at 152-64.

45. *Id.* at 167-69.

46. *Id.* at 165-91.

47. 29 U.S.C. §206(d) (1) (1970).

48. 29 U.S.C. §201 *et seq.* (1970).

49. 20 U.S.C. §§1681-1686 (1976).

50. GREGORY, *supra* note 26, at 169-91; *accord* DEPARTMENT OF LABOR WAGE AND HOUR DIVISION, Interpretive Bulletin, EQUAL PAY FOR EQUAL WORK UNDER THE FAIR LABOR STANDARDS ACT 29 C.F.R. §800.114 (1967).

51. 42 U.S.C. §2000e *et seq.* as amended, 86 Stat. 103 (Nov. 24, 1972).

52. 3 C.F.R. §684 (1966-1970).

53. 41 C.F.R. §60-1.4 and §60-1.40 (1978).

54. Act of Oct. 31, 1978, Pub. L. No. 95-555 (1978) (to be codified in 42 U.S.C. §2000e §701(k)).

55. 400 U.S. 542 (1971).

56. The prohibition against discrimination on the basis of "sex plus" something else has been applied to sex plus marriage. Sprogis v. United Airlines, 444 F.2d 1194 (7th Cir.), *cert. denied*, 404 U.S. 991 (1971), and to sex plus age, EEOC Dec. 6-6-5762, CCH EEOC Dec. ¶6001 (1968), GC Opinion No. 22 (1976).

57. 429 U.S. 125 (1976).

58. 401 U.S. 424 (1971).

59. *Id.* at 433-34.

60. *Id.*

61. *Id.* at 430.

62. *Id.* at 432.

63. Gilbert v. General Electric Co., 375 F. Supp. 367 (E. D. Va. 1974).

64. Gilbert v. General Electric Co., 519 F. 2d 661 (4th Cir. 1975).

65. Such was the fear of the dissenters in General Electric Co. v. Gilbert, 429 U.S. 125 (1976).

66. 429 U.S. 161 (Stevens, J., dissenting).

67. *Id.* at 146 (Stewart J., concurring).

68. *Id.*

69. *Id.* (Blackmun, J., concurring in part).

70. *Id.*

71. 434 U.S. 136 (1977).

72. Satty v. Nashville Gas Co., 384 F. Supp. 765 (M.D. Tenn. 1974).

73. Satty v. Nashville Gas Co., 522 F. 2d 850 (6th Cir. 1975).

74. 434 U.S. 139.

75. *Id.* at 140.

76. *Id.* at 142.

77. *Id.*

78. *Id.* at 143.

79. 435 U.S. 702 (1978).

80. *Id.* at 704.

81. *Id.* at 725 (Blackmun, J., concurring in part and concurring in the judgment).

82. *Id* at 724-25.

83. *Id.* at 725.

84. Act of Oct. 31, 1978, Pub. L. No. 95-555 (1978) (to be codified in 42 U.S.C §2000e §70 (k)).

85. *Id.*

86. H.R. & S. CONF. REP., 95th Cong., 2d Sess. (1978).

87. H.R. REP. NO. 948, 95th Cong., 2d Sess. (1978).

88. *Id.*

89. *Id*

90. *Id*

91. *Id.*

92. S. REP. NO. 331, 95th Cong., 1st Sess. (1977).

93. *Id.*

94. *Id.*

95. Appendix to 29 C.F.R. 1604.

96. *Id.*

97. 29 C.F.R. §800.121 (1967).

98. *Id.* at §800.122.

99. *Id.* at §800.121.

100. 417 F. Supp. 423 (N.D. Iowa 1976).

101. Brief for Appellants, Christensen v. State of Iowa, 563 F. 2d 353 (8th Cir. 1977) 21.

102. Christensen v. State of Iowa, 417 F. Supp. 423 (N.D. Iowa 1976).

103. Christensen v. State of Iowa, 563 F.2d 353 (8th Cir. 1977).

104. Brief for Appellants, *supra* note 101, at 8.

105. *Id.* at 41.

106. *Id.* at 55.

107. The Bennett Amendment refers to the last sentence of Section 703(h) of Title VII, 42 U.S.C. §2000e-2(h) (1972).

108. Brief for Appellants, *supra* note 101, at 24.

109. *Id* at 27 (emphasis in original).

110. *Id.* at 56-61.

111. *See* table of "Other Authorities Cited", *id.* at iv-vi.

112. Brief for Respondents, Christensen v. State of Iowa, 563 F.2d 353 (8th Cir. 1977) at 14.

113. Christensen v. State of Iowa, 563 F.2d 353 (8th Cir. 1977) at 355.

114. *Id.* at 356-57.

115. *Id.* at 355.

116. *Id.* at 356.

117. *Id.*

118. *Id.*

119. Address by EEOC Vice Chairman Daniel E. Leach, Federal Bar Association Meeting, Washington, D.C. (June 9, 1978), *reprinted in* C.C.H. EMPLOYMENT PRACTICES ¶5070.

120. *Id.*

121. *Id.*

122. One of the foremost of such women's groups is the Working Women United Institute. Formed in 1975, its first major project consisted of tackling sexual harassment on the job through extensive public education, social science research, intervention counseling, and amicus briefs. *See Project Statement: Sexual Harassment on the Job*, by Susan Meyer, executive director, and Karen Sauvigné, project director, Working Women United Institute. By the late 1970s women's labor groups also addressed this issue. For example, in 1979 the United Auto Workers (U.A.W.), a union with an active women's department, supported the Detroit hearings on sexual harassment. *See* Solidarity (the newspaper of the U.A.W.), July 2, 1979, at 15.

123. Barnes v. Train, [1974] 13 FEP Cases 123 (D.C.D.C. 1974).

124. 444 F.2d 1194 (7th Cir. 1971).

125. 13 FEP Cases 124.

126. *Id.*

127. *Id.*

128. *Id.*

129. 390 F. Supp. 161 (D. Ariz. 1975).

130. *Id.* at 163-64.

131. *Id.*

132. 418 F. Supp. 233 (N.D. Cal. 1976).

133. *Id.* at 236.

134. *See, e.g.,* Neeley v. American Fidelity Ass. Co. [1978] EMPLOY. PRAC. DEC. (C.C.H.) ¶8395 (W. D. Okla. Feb. 21, 1978).

135. *See, e.g.,* Price v. John F. Lawhorn Furniture Co. [1978] EMPLOY. PRAC. DEC. (C.C.H.) ¶ 8342 (N.D. Ala. May 16, 1978).

136. 413 F. Supp. 654 (D.D.C. 1976).

137. *See, e.g.,* Rinkel v. Assoc. Pipeline Contractors Inc. [1978] EMPLOY. PRAC. DEC. (C.C.H.) ¶8331 (D. Alas. April 6, 1978); Heelan v. Johns-Manville Corp., 451 F. Supp. 1382 (D. Colo. 1978); Tompkins v. Pub. Service Electric & Gas Co., 568 F.2d 1044 (3d Cir. 1977); Munford v. James T. Barnes & Co., 441 F. Supp. 459 (E.D. Mich. 1977); Barnes v. Castle, 561 F.2d 983 (D.C. Cir. 1977); Garber v. Saxon Bus. Prod. Inc., 552 F.2d 1032 (4th Cir. 1977).

138. Fisher v. Flynn [1979] EMPLOY. PRAC. DEC. (C.C.H.) ¶9204 (D. Mass. May 8, 1979).

STATUTORY APPENDIX

The following is the bill introduced in the assembly by Judge Herttell, relative to the rights and property of married women April, 1837.

An act for the protection and preservation of the rights and property of married women.

The people of the state of New York, represented in Senate and Assembly, do enact as follows.

§1. That the property, both real and personal, belonging to any woman at the time of her marriage, and who shall or may become covert after the passing of this act; and also that to which she shall or may thereafter become entitled by inheritance, gift, bequest or devise, and also that which she may acquire by her own industry and management, shall of right continue to be vested in such owner, in the same manner and to the same or like extent, after, as before her coverture. Nor shall such personal estate, or any part thereof, nor the income thereof, nor shall the rents, issues or profits of the real estate of such married woman, or any part of the income thereof, inure to the husband or be vested in him during the life time of the wife by virtue of her marriage, unless by her voluntary consent, duly and properly obtained.

§2. That on the demise of the wife during the lifetime of her husband, he shall be entitled to such portion of the property owned and possessed by his wife at the time of her demise, in like manner and to the same or like extent, as by the laws of this state the widow is entitled to have and possess of the property possessed by her husband at the time of his demise.

§3. That it shall not be lawful for any married woman, who shall or may become covert after the passing of this act, directly or indirectly to assign, transfer or convey to her husband, her real or personal estate, or any part thereof, of which she shall or may be possessed in her own right, except the rents, issues, profits and income thereof or of any part thereof, unless by order of a chancellor or vice-chancellor, on application to him in writing, signed by the husband and wife, and unless the chancellor or vice-chancellor shall be satisfied on due proof that the voluntary consent of the wife shall have been properly obtained and that the object of the proposed transfer, and the uses and purposes to which the money arising from such sale, are intended to be applied, appear to be proper, just and necessary, and beneficial to the wife.

§4. All property both real and personal which shall or may hereafter be transferred or conveyed to or vested in any married woman by deed, gift, bequest or devise, and also all property which shall or may be earned or acquired by any married woman by her personal labor, industry and management, and the income, rents, issues and profits of all such real and personal estate as aforesaid, shall be held and deemed to be her own separate estate and be subject to her own control and disposal, in like manner and as effectually as if she were feme sole, [a single woman.]

§5 That it shall be lawful for any married woman to dispose of her estate both real and personal by her last will and testament in writing to be executed in like manner and with the like formalities and restrictions as other persons are by law authorised to do.

§6. This law shall take effect immediately after the passage thereof.

Chap. 200.

AN ACT *for the more effectual protection of the property of married women.*

Passed April 7, 1848.

The People of the State of New York, represented in Senate and Assembly, do enact as follows:

§1 .The real and personal property of any female who may hereafter marry, and which she shall own at the time of marriage, and the rents issues and profits thereof shall not be subject to the disposal of her husband, nor be liable for his debts, and shall continue her sole and separate property, as if she were a single female.

§2. The real and personal property, and the rents issues and profits thereof of any female now married shall not be subject to the disposal of her husband; but shall be her sole and separate property as if she were a single female except so far as the same may be liable for the debts of her husband heretofore contracted.

§3. It shall be lawful for any married female to receive, by gift, grant devise or bequest, from any person other than her husband and hold to her sole and separate use, as if she were a single female, real and personal property, and the rents, issues and profits thereof, and the same shall not be subject to the disposal of her husband, nor be liable for his debts.

§4. All contracts made between persons in contemplation of marriage shall remain in full force after such marriage takes place.

Chap. 375.

AN ACT *to amend an act entitled "An act for the more effectual protection of the property of married women," passed April 7, 1848.*

Passed April 11, 1849,

The People of the State of New York, represented in Senate and Assembly, do enact as follows:

§1. The third section of the act entitled "An act for the more effectual protection of the property of married women," is hereby amended so as to read as follows:

§3. Any married female may take by inheritance or by gift, grant, devise or bequest, from any person other than her husband and hold to her sole and separate use and convey and devise real and personal property, and any interest of estate therein, and the rents, issues and profits thereof in the same manner and with like effect as if she were unmarried, and the same shall not be subjec to the disposal of her husband nor be liable for his debts.

§2. Any person who may hold or who may hereafter hold as trustee for any married woman, any real or personal estate or other property under any deed of conveyance or otherwise, on the written request of such married woman accompanied by a certificate of a justice of the supreme court that he has examined the condition and situation of the property, and made due enquiry into the capacity of such married woman to manage and control the same, may convey such married woman by deed or otherwise, all or any portion of such property, or the rents issues or profits thereof, for her sole and separate use and benefit.

§3. All contracts made between persons in contemplation of marriage shall remain in full force after such marriage takes place.

Chap. 90.

AN ACT concerning the rights and liabilities of husband and wife.

Passed March 20, 1860.

The People of the State of New York, represented in Senate and Assembly, do enact as follows:

SECTION 1. The property, both real and personal, which any married woman now owns, as her sole and separate property; that which comes to her by descent, devise, bequest, gift or grant; that which she acquires by her trade, business, labor or services, carried on or performed on her sole or separate account; that which a woman married in this state owns at the time of her marriage, and the rents, issues and proceeds of all such property, shall, notwithstanding her marriage, be and remain her sole and separate property, and may be used, collected and invested by her in her own name, and shall not be subject to the interference or control of her husband, or liable for his debts, except such debts as may have been contracted for the support of herself or her children, by her as his agent.

§2. A married woman may bargain, sell, assign and transfer her separate personal property, and carry on any trade or business, and perform any labor or services on her sole and separate account, and the earnings of any married woman, for her trade, business, labor or services, shall be her sole and separate property, and may be used or invested by her in her own name.

§3. Any married woman posssessed of real estate as her separate property, may bargain, sell and convey such property, and enter into any contract in reference to the same, but no such conveyance or contract shall be valid without the assent, in writing, of her husband, except as hereinafter provided.

§4. In case any married women possessed of separate real property, as aforesaid, may desire to sell or convey the same, or to make any contract in relation thereto, and shall be unable to procure the assent of her husband, as in the preceding section provided, in consequence of his refusal, absence, insanity, or other disability, such married woman may apply to the county court in the county where she shall at the time reside, for leave to make such sale, conveyance or contract, without the assent of her husband.

§5. Such application may be made by petition, verified by her, and setting forth the grounds of such application. If the husband be a resident of the county, and not under disability, from insanity or other cause, a copy of said petition shall be served upon him, with a notice of the time when the same will be presented to the said court, at least ten days before such application. In all other cases the county court to which such application shall be made, shall, in its discretion, determine whether any notice shall be given, and if any, the mode and manner of giving it.

§6. If it shall satisfactorily appear to such court, upon such application, that the husband of such applicant has willfully abandoned his said wife, and lives separate and apart from her, or that he is insane, or imprisoned as a convict in any state prison, or that he is an habitual drunkard, or that he is any way disabled from making a contract, or that he refuses to give his consent, without good cause therefor, then such court shall cause an order to be entered upon its records, authorizing such married women to sell and convey her real estate, or contract in regard thereto without the assent of her husband, with the same effect as though such conveyance or contract had been made with his assent.

§7. Any married woman may, while married, sue and be sued in all matters having relation to her property, which may be here sole and separate property, or which may hereafter come to her by descent, devise, bequest, or the gift of any person except her husband, in the same manner as if she were sole. And any married woman may bring and maintain an action in her own name, for damages, against any person or body corporate, for any injury to her person or character, the same as if she were sole; and the money received upon the settlement of any such action, or recovered upon a judgment, shall be her sole and separate property.

§8. No bargain or contract made by any married woman, in respect to her sole and separate property, or any property which may hereafter come to her by descent, devise, bequest or gift of any person except her husband, and no bargain or contract entered into by any married woman in or about the carrying on of any trade or business under the statutes of this state, shall be binding upon her husband, or render him or his property in any way liable therefore.

§9. Every married woman is hereby constituted and declared to be the joint gardian of her children, with her husband, with equal powers, rights and duties in regard to them, with the husband.

§10. At the decease of husband or wife, leaving no minor child or children, the survivor shall hold, possess and enjoy a life estate in one-third of all the real estate of which the husband or wife died seised.

§11. At the decease of the husband or wife intestate, leaving minor child or children, the survivor shall hold, possess and enjoy all the real estate of which the husband or wife died seised, and all the rents, issues and profits thereof during the minority of the youngest child, and one-third thereof during his or her natural life.

Chap. 172.

AN ACT to amend the act entitled "An act concerning the rights and liabilities of husband and wife," passed March twentieth, eighteen hundred and sixty.

Passed April 10, 1862; three-fifths being present.

The People of the State of New York, represented in Senate and Assembly, do enact as follows:

SECTION 1. The third section of the act entitled "An act concerning the rights and liabilities of husband and wife," passed March twentieth, eighteen hundred and sixty, is hereby amended so as to read as follows:

§3. Any married woman possessed of real estate as her separate property, may bargain, sell and convey such property and enter into any contract in reference to the same, with the like effect in all respects as if she were unmarried, and she may in like manner enter into such covenant or covenants for title as are usual in conveyances of real estate, which covenants shall be obligatory to bind her separate property, in case the same or any of them be broken.

§2. The fourth, fifth, sixth, ninth, tenth and eleventh sections of the said act are hereby repealed.

§3. The seventh section of the said act is hereby amended so as to read as follows:

§7. Any married woman may, while married, sue and be sued in all matters having relation to her sole and separate property, or which may hereafter come to her by descent, devise, bequest, purchase, or the gift or grant of any person in the same manner as if she were sole; and any married woman may bring and maintain an action in her own name, for damages, against any person or body corporate, for any injury to her person or character, the same as if she were sole; and the money received upon the settlement of any such action or recovered upon a judgment, shall be her sole and separate property. In case it shall be necessary in the prosecution or defence of any action brought by or against a married woman, to enter into any bond or undertaking, such bond or undertaking may be executed by such married woman with the same effect in all respects as if she were sole, and in case the said bond or undertaking shall become broken or forfeited the same may be enforced against her separate estate.

§4. The eighth section of the said act is hereby amended so as to read as follows:

§8. No bargain or contract made by any married woman, in respect to her sole and separate property, or any property, which may hereafter come to her by descent, devise, bequest, purchase, or the gift or grant of any person (except her husband,) and no bargain or contract entered into by any married woman in or about the carrying on of any trade or business, under any statute of this state, shall be binding upon her husband, or render him or his property in any way liable therefor.

§5. In an action brought or defended by any married woman in her name, her husband shall not neither shall his property be liable for the costs thereof, or the recovery therein. In an action brought by her for an injury to her person, character or property, if judgment shall pass against her for costs, the court in which the action is pending shall have jurisdiction to enforce payment of such judgment out of her separate estate, though the sum recovered be less than one hundred dollars.

§6. No man shall bind his child to apprenticeship or service or part with the control of such child or create any testamentary guardian therefor, unless the mother if living, shall in writing signify her assent thereto.

§7. A married woman may be sued in any of the courts in this state, and whenever a judgment shall be recovered against a married woman the same may be enforced by execution against her sole and separate estate in the same manner as if she were sole.

§8. This act shall take effect on the first day of July next.

Chap. 381.

AN ACT in relation to the rights and liabilities of married women.

PASSED May 28, 1884; three-fifths being present.

The People of the State of New Yok, represented in Senate and Assembly, do enact as follows:

SECTION 1. A married woman may contract to the same extent, with like effect and in the same form as if unmarried, and she and her separate estate shall be liable thereon, whether such contract relates to her separate business or estate or otherwise, and in no case shall a charge upon her separate estate be necessary.

§2. This act shall not affect nor apply to any contract that shall be made between husband and wife.

§3. This act shall take effect immediately.

Article III. Domestic Relations Law of 1896

Certain Rights and Liabilities of Husband and Wife.
Section 20. Property of married woman.
21. Powers of married women.

Section 20. Property of married women.—Property, real or personal, now owned by a married woman, or hereafter owned by a woman at the time of her marriage, or acquired by her as prescribed in this chapter, and the rents, issues, proceeds and profits thereof, continues to be her sole and separate property as if she were unmarried, and is not subject to her husband's control or disposal nor liable for his debts.

§21. Powers of married woman.—A married woman has all the rights in respect to property, real or personal, and the acquisition, use, enjoyment and disposition thereof, and to make contracts in respect thereto with any person including her husband, and to carry on any business, trade or occupation, and to exercise all powers and enjoy all rights in respect thereto and in respect to her contracts, and be liable on such contracts, as if she were unmarried; but a husband and wife can not contract to alter or dissolve the marriage or to relieve the husband from his liability to support his wife.

§22. Insurance of husband's life.—A married woman may, in her own name, or in the name of a third person, with his consent, as her trustee, cause the life of her husband to be insured for a definite period, or for the term of his natural life. Where a married woman survives such period or term she is entitled to receive the insurance money, payable by the terms of the policy, as her separate property, and free from any claim of a creditor or representative of her husband, except, that where the premium actually paid annually out of the husband's property exceeds five hundred dollars, that portion of the insurance money which is purchased by excess of premium above five hundred dollars, is primarily liable for the husband's debts. The policy may provide that the insurance, if the married woman dies before it becomes due and without disposing of it, shall be paid to her husband or to his, her or their children, or to or for the use of one or more of those persons; and it may designate one or more trustees for a child or children to receive and manage such money until such child or children attain full age. The married woman may dispose of such policy by will or written acknowledged assignment to take effect on her death, if she dies thereafter leaving no descendant surviving. After the will or the assignment takes effect, the legatee or assignee takes such policy absolutely.

A policy of insurance on the life of any person for the benefit of a married woman, is also assignable and may be surrendered to the company issuing the same, by her, or her legal representative, with the written consent of the assured.

§23. Contracts in contemplation of marriage.—A contract made between persons in contemplation of marriage, remains in full force after the marriage takes place.

§24. Liability of husband for ante-nuptial debts.—A husband who acquires property of his wife by ante-nuptial contract or otherwise, is liable for her debts contracted before marriage, but only to the extent of the property so acquired.

§25. Contract of married woman not to bind husband.—A contract made by a married woman does not bind her husband or his property.

§26. Husband and wife may convey to each other or make partition.—Husband and wife may convey or transfer real or personal property directly, the one to the other, without the intervention of a third person; and may make partition or division of any real property held by them as tenants in common, joint tenants or tenants by the entireties. If so expressed in the instrument of partition or division such instrument bars the wife's right to dower in such property, and also, if so expressed, the husband's tenancy by curtesy.

§27. Right of action by or against married woman for torts. A married woman has a right of action for an injury to her person, property or character or for an injury arising out of the marital relation, as if unmarried. She is liable for her wrongful or tortious acts; her husband is not liable for such acts unless they were done by his actual coercion or instigation; and such coercion or instigation shall not be presumed but must be proved. This section does not affect any right, cause of action or defense existing before the eighteenth day of March 1890.

§28. Pardon not to restore marital rights.—A pardon granted to a person sentenced to imprisonment for life within this state, does not restore that person to the rights of a previous marriage or to the guardianship of a child, the issue of such a marriage.

§29. Compelling transfer of trust property.—A person who holds property as trustee of a married woman, under a deed of conveyance or otherwise, on the written request of such married woman, accompanied by a certificate of a justice of the supreme court, that he has examined the condition and situation of the property, and made inquiry into the capacity of such married woman to manage and control the same, may convey to such married woman all or any portion of such property, or the rents, issues or profits thereof.

Chap. 289.

AN ACT to amend the domestic relations law, in relation to the rights of married women.

Became a law, April 2, 1902, with the approval of the Governor. Passed, three-fifths being present.

The People of the State of New York, represented in Senate and Assembly, do enact as follows:

Section 1. Chapter two hundred and seventy-two of the laws of eighteen hundred and ninety-six, entitled "An act in relation to the domestic relations, constituting chapter forty-eight of the general laws," is hereby amended by adding the following section to article three:

§30. Married woman's right of action for wages, et cetera.—A married woman shall have a cause of action in her own sole and separate right for all wages, salary, profits, compensation or other remuneration for which she may render work, labor or services, or which may be derived from any trade, business or occupation carried on by her, and her hsuband shall have no right or action therefor, unless she, or he, with her knowledge or consent, has otherwise expressly agreed with the person obligated to pay such wages, salary, profits, compensation or other remuneration. In any action or proceeding in which a married woman or her husband shall seek to recover wages, salary, profits, compensation or other remuneration for which such married woman has rendered work, labor, or services, or which was derived from any trade, business or occupation carried on by her or in which the loss of such wages, salary, profits, compensation or other remuneration shall be an item of damage claimed by a married woman or her husband, the presumption of law in all such cases shall be that such married woman is alone entitled thereto, unless the contrary expressly appears.

§2. The foregoing section shall not affect any right, cause of action or defense existing before the date when this act shall take effect.

§3. This act shall take effect immediately.

SELECTED BIBLIOGRAPHY

Manuscripts and Collections

Stanton, Elizabeth Cady, Papers, Library of Congress, Washington, D.C.
Stanton, Elizabeth Cady, Papers, Vassar College Library, Poughkeepsie, N.Y.

Documents

New York Assembly Document Number 189 (1842).
New York Assembly Document Number 96 (1844).

Miscellaneous Reports and Proceedings

BISHOP, WILLIAM, & ATTREE, WILLIAM. REPORT OF THE DEBATES & PROCEEDINGS OF THE CONVENTION FOR THE REVISION OF THE CONSTITUTION OF THE STATE OF NEW YORK. Albany: Albany Evening Atlas, 1846.
CROSWELL, C., & SUTTON, R. DEBATES AND PROCEEDINGS IN THE NEW YORK STATE CONVENTION FOR THE REVISION OF THE CONSTITUTION. Albany: Albany Argus, 1846.
FIELD, DAVID. PROPOSED CIVIL CODE 1865.
HOUSE REPORT NO. 948, 95th Congress, 2d Session (1978).
HOUSE REPORT & SENATE CONFERENCE REPORT, 95th Congress, 2d Session (1978).
Livingston, Edward. Report of the Commission on Revision of the Louisiana Civil Code. 1823.
New York Assembly Commission on Practice and Pleadings. Report of the Commission. 1848.
New York Assembly Committee on the Judiciary. Report of the Committee on Petitions Asking for an Act for the More Effectual Protection of the Rights of Property of Married Women. Assembly Document No. 96. February 26, 1844.
New York Assembly Committee on the Judiciary. Report of the Committee on Petitions Asking for an Act to Protect the Rights of Property of Married Women. Assembly Document No. 189. April 12, 1842.
NEW YORK STATE ASSEMBLY JOURNAL 1837, 1842, 1848, 1852, 1860, 1862, 1884, 1896, 1902.
NEW YORK STATE SENATE JOURNAL 1848, 1849, 1860, 1862, 1884, 1896, 1902.
Report of the Commissioners of the Code. David Dudley Field, Chairman. Albany, N.Y.: Weed, Parsons Co., 1865.
SENATE REPORT NO. 331, 95th Congress, 1st Session (1977).

Statutes, Orders, and Regulations

CIVIL RIGHTS ACT, 42 UNITED STATES CODE §2000e *et seq.* (1964).

DEPARTMENT OF LABOR, OFFICE OF FEDERAL CONTRACT COMPLIANCE PROGRAMS, AFFIRMATIVE ACTION PROGRAMS OF GOVERNMENT NONCONSTRUCTION CONTRACTORS (revised Order #4), 41 CODE OF FEDERAL REGULATIONS §60-2 (1978).

DEPARTMENT OF LABOR, OFFICE OF FEDERAL CONTRACT COMPLIANCE PROGRAMS, EQUAL EMPLOYMENT OPPORTUNITY DUTIES OF GOVERNMENT CONTRACTORS, 41 CODE OF FEDERAL REGULATIONS §60-1 (1978).

DEPARTMENT OF LABOR, OFFICE OF FEDERAL CONTRACT COMPLIANCE PROGRAMS, SEX DISCRIMINATION GUIDELINES FOR GOVERNMENT CONTRACTORS, 41 CODE OF FEDERAL REGULATIONS §60-20 (1978).

DEPARTMENT OF LABOR, OFFICE OF FEDERAL CONTRACT COMPLIANCE PROGRAMS, STANDARDIZED CONTRACTOR EVALUATION PROCEDURES FOR NONCONSTRUCTION CONTRACTS (revised order #14). 41 CODE OF FEDERAL REGULATIONS §60-60 (1978).

DEPARTMENT OF LABOR, WAGE AND HOUR DIVISION, EQUAL PAY FOR EQUAL WORK UNDER THE FAIR LABOR STANDARDS ACT, 29 CODE OF FEDERAL REGULATIONS §800; (1967).

13 Edw. 1, c. 1 (1285).

13 Edw. 1, c. 18 (1285).

18 Edw. 1, c. 1 (1290).

EQUAL EMPLOYMENT OPPORTUNITY COMMISSION, QUESTIONS AND ANSWERS ON PREGNANCY DISCRIMINATION, Appendix to 29 CODE OF FEDERAL REGULATIONS §1604 (1979).

EQUAL EMPLOYMENT OPPORTUNITY COMMISSION, SEX DISCRIMINATION GUIDELINES, 29 CODE OF FEDERAL REGULATIONS §1604 (1972).

EQUAL EMPLOYMENT OPPORTUNITY COMMISSION, SEX DISCRIMINATION GUIDELINES, 29 CODE OF FEDERAL REGULATIONS §60-20 (1978).

EQUAL PAY ACT OF 1963, 29 UNITED STATES CODE §206 (d) (1) (1970).

EXECUTIVE ORDER 11246 as amended by 11375, 3 CODE OF FEDERAL REGULATIONS §684 (1966-1970).

FAIR LABOR STANDARDS ACT, 29 UNITED STATES CODE §201 *et seq.,* (1964).

52 Hen. 3, c. 23 (1267).

27 Hen. 8, c. 10 (1536).

27 Hen. 8, c. 16 (1536).

NEW YORK CIVIL PRACTICE LAW AND RULES §302 (b) (McKinney 1974).

NEW YORK CONSTITUTION (1846).

NEW YORK DOMESTIC RELATIONS LAW §32 (McKinney 1958).

NEW YORK DOMESTIC RELATIONS LAW §231 (McKinney 1963).

NEW YORK DOMESTIC RELATIONS LAW §236 (McKinney 1963).

NEW YORK ESTATES, POWERS AND TRUSTS LAW §6-1.2 (McKinney 1782).

NEW YORK EXECUTIVE LAW §§290-301 (McKinney 1969).

NEW YORK EXECUTIVE LAW §296 (McKinney 1974).

NEW YORK LAWS ch. 200 (1848).

NEW YORK LAWS ch. 379 (1848).

NEW YORK LAWS ch. 375 (1849).

NEW YORK LAWS ch. 90 (1860).

NEW YORK LAWS ch. 172 (1862).

NEW YORK LAWS ch. 450 (1876).
NEW YORK LAWS ch. 381 (1884).
NEW YORK LAWS ch. 272 §§20-29 (1896).
NEW YORK LAWS ch. 289 (1902).
NEW YORK REVISED STATUTES (1828).
NEW YORK REVISED STATUTES (1830).
NEW YORK REVISED STATUTES (1836).
NEW YORK REVISED STATUTES (1846).
STATUTE OF USES, 27 Hen. 8, c. 10 (1536).
TITLE VII OF THE CIVIL RIGHTS ACT OF 1964, 42 UNITED STATES CODE § 2000e *et seq.*, as amended, 86 Stat. 103 (Nov. 24, 1972).
TITLE IX OF THE EDUCATION AMENDMENTS OF 1972, 20 UNITED STATES CODE §§ 1681-686 (1976).

Cases

Abbey V. Deyo, 44 N.Y. 343 (1871).

Babcock v. Eckler, 24 N.Y. 623 (1862).

Barnes v. Castle, 561 F. 2d 983 (D.C. Cir. 1977).

Barnes v. Train [1974] 13 FEP Cases 123 (D.C.D.C. 1974).

Bennett v. Bennett 116 N.Y. 584, 23 N.E. 17 (1889).

Bertles v. Nunan, 92 N.Y. 152 (1883).

Blood v. Humphrey, 17 Barb. 660 (1854).

Bool v. Mix, 17 Wend. 119 (1842).

Bradley, v. Walker, 138 N.Y. 291, 33 N.E. 1079 (1893).

Brooks v. Schwerin, 54 N.Y. 343 (1873).

Buckley v. Wells, 33 N.Y. 518 (1865).

Cashman v. Henry, 75 N.Y. 103 (1878).

Caudrey's Case, 5 Coke Rep. 1 (Queen's Bench 1595).

Christensen v. State of Iowa, 417 F. Supp. 423 (N.D. Iowa 1976), *aff'd* 563 F. 2d 353 8th Cir. 1977).

City of Los Angeles Department of Water and Power v. Manhart, 435 U.S. 702 (1978).

Coleman v. Burr, 93 N.Y. 17 (1883).

Corne v. Bausch and Lomb, Inc., 390 F. Supp. 161 (D. Ariz. 1975).

Cropsey v. McKinney, 30 Barb. 47 (N.Y. Sup. Ct. 1859).

Darcy v. Allein, 44 Eliz., 11 Rep. 84b.

DeBrauwere v. DeBrauwere, 203 N.Y. 406, 96 N.E. 772 (1911).

Dickerson v. Rogers, 114 N.Y. 405, 21 N.E. 992 (1889).

Duke of Norfolk's Case, 3 Ch. Cas. 1 (1682).

Edwards v. Woods, 131 N.E. 350, 30 N.E. 237 (1897).

Fisher v. Flynn [1979] Employ. Prac. Dec. (C.C.H.) —9204 (D. Mass. May 8, 1979).

Fuller's Case, 12 Coke Rep. 41 (1607).

Gage v. Dauchy, 34 N.Y. 293 (1866).

General Electric Company v. Gilbert, 429 U.S. 125 (1976).

Gardner v. Gardner, 22 Wend. 526 (1839).

Gilbert v. General Electric Co., 375 F. Supp 367 (E.D. Va. 1974), 519 F. 2d 661 (4th Cir. 1975), *revs'g* 429 U.S. 125 (1976).

Graber v. Saxon Bus. Prod. Inc., 552 F. 2d 1032 (4th Cir. 1977).

Griffen v. Banks, 37 N.Y. 621 (1868).

Griggs v. Duke Power Co., 401 U.S. 424 (1971).

Heelan v. Johns-Manville Corp., 451 F. Supp. 1382 (D. Colo. 1978).

Hendricks v. Isaacs, 117 N.Y. 411, 22 N.E. 1029 (1889).

Hiles v. Fisher, 144 N.Y. 306 (1895).

Holcomb v. Harris, 166 N.Y. 257, 59 N.E. 820 (1901).

Hunt v. Johnson, 44 N.Y. 27 (1890).

In re Callister, 153 N.Y. 294, 47 N.E. 268 (1897).

In re Gillingham's Estate, 55 Hun. 604, 8 N.Y.S. 385 (1889).

Jackson *ed dem.* Clowes v. Vanderhyden, 17 Johns 167 (1820).

Jones v. Patterson, 11 Barb. 572 (N.Y. Sup. Ct. 1852).

Klapper v. Metropolitan St. Ry. Co., 34 Misc. 528, 69 N.Y.S. 955 (Sup. Ct. 1901).

Knapp v. Smith, 27 N.Y. 277 (1863).

Lennon v. Eldred, 65 Barb. 410 (N.Y. Sup. Ct. 1873).

McIlvaine v. Kadel, 3 Robt. 429 (1865).

Marbury v. Madison, 1 Cranch. 137, 2 L.Ed. 60 (1803).

Martin v. Dwelly, 6 Wend. 9 (1832).

Martin v. Martin, 1 N.Y. 473 (1848).

Martin v. Rector, 101 N.Y. 77, 4 N.E. 183 (1886).

Matter of Mitchell, 61 Hun. 372, 16 N.Y.S. 180

Maxwell v. Lowther, 59 Hun. 617, 13 N.Y.S. 169 (1891).

Miller v. Bank of America, 418 F. Supp. 233 (N.D. Cal. 1976).

Munford v. James T. Barnes & Co., 441 F. Supp. 459 (E.D. Mich. 1977).

Mygatt v. Coe, 124 N.Y. 212, 26 N.E. 611 (1891).

Nashville Gas Co. v. Satty, 434 U.S. 136 (1977).

Neeley v. American Fidelity Ass. Co. [1978] Employ. Prac. Dec. (C.C.H.) —8395 (W. D. Okla. Feb. 21, 1978).

Newton v. Weber, 119 Misc. 240, 196 N.Y.S. 113 (1922).

Niccloy v. Treasure, 115 N.Y.S. 1030 (1909).

Nostrand v. Ditmis, 127 N.Y. 355, 28 N.E. 27 (1891).

Oishei v. Gilbert, 9 N.Y.S. 402 (1890).

Paxton v. Marshall, 18 Federal Reporter 361 (N.D. Ill. 1883).

People v. Law, 31 App. Div. 2d 554, 294 N.Y.S. 2d 394 (1968).

People v. Morton 284 App. Div. 413, 132 N.Y.S. 2d 302 (1954).

People v. Morton, 308 N.Y. 96, 123 N.E. 2d 790 (1954).

Phillips v. Martin Marietta Corporation, 400 U.S. 542 (1971).

Porter v. Dunn, 131 N.Y. 314, 30 N.E. 122 (1892).

Power v. Lester, 23 N.Y. 527 (1861).

Price v. Holman, 135 N.Y. 124 (1892).

Price v. John F. Lawhorn Furniture Co. [1978] Employ. Prac. Dec. (D.D.H.) ¶8342 (N.D. Ala. May 16, 1978).

Rawson v. Pennsylvania R. Co., 48 N.Y. 212 (1872).

Rinkel v. Assoc. Pipeline Contractors Inc. [1978] Employ. Prac. Dec. (C.C.H.) ¶8331 (D. Alas. April 6, 1978).

Ryder v. Hulse, 24 N.Y. 372 (1862).

Sammis v. McLaughlin, 35 N.Y. 647 (1866).

Savage v. O'Neil, 44 N.Y. 298 (1871).

Schlitz Brewing Co., v. Ester, 86 Hun. 22, 33 N.Y.S. 143, *aff'd*, 157 N.Y. 714, 53 N.E. 1126 (1895).

Sheldon v. Sheldon, 133 N.Y. 1, 30 N.E. 730 (1892).

Shelley's Case, 1 Rep. 88 (b) (1581).

Sherman v. Elder, 24 N.Y. 381 (1862).

Shirley v. Shirley, 9 Paige 361 (Ch. 1841).

Smith v. Kane, 2 Paige 302 (Ch. 1830).

Spencer v. Board of Registration, 8 D.C. Reports 169, 171, 1 McArth. 8 M. 160, 171 (1873).

Sprogis v. United Airlines, 444 F. 2d 1194 (7th Cir.), *cert. denied*, 404 U.S. 991 (1971).

Stanley v. National Union Bank, 115 N.Y. 122, 22 N.E. 29 (1889).

Stonborough v. Preferred Accident Ins. Co. of N.Y., 180 Misc. 339, 40 N.Y.S. 2d 480, *aff'd* 226 App. Div. 838, 43 N.Y.S. 2d 512, *aff'd* 292 N.Y. 154, 54 N.E. 2d 342 (1944).

Taltarum's Case, Y.B. 12 Edw. 4, 19 (1472).

Thurber v. Townsend, 22 N.Y. 517 (1860).

Tompkins v. Pub. Service Electric & Gas Co., 568 F. 2d 1044 (3d Cir. 1977).

Torrey v. Torrey, 14 N.Y. 430 (1856).

Vanderheyden and Wife v. Mallory and Hunter, 1 N.Y. 452 (1848).

Van Duzer v. Van Duzer, 6 Paige 366 (Ch. 1837).

Vanneman v. Powers, 56 N.Y. 39 (1874).

Wadsworth v. Webster, 237 App. Div. 319, 261 N.Y.S. 670 (3d Dep't 1932).

Westervelt v. Gregg, 12 N.Y. 202 (1854).

White v. White, 5 Barb. 474 (1849).

Whiton v. Snyder, 88 N.Y. 299 (1882).

Williams v. Saxbe, 413 F. Supp. 654 (D.D.C. 1976).

Winter v. Winter, 191 N.Y. 462, 84 N.E. 382 (1908).

Wood v. Wood, 83 N.Y. 575 (1881).

Woodworth v. Sweet, 51 N.Y. 8 (1872).

Woolsey v. Henn, 85 App. Div. 331, 83 N.Y.S. 394 (1903).

Yale v. Dederer, 18 N.Y. 265 (1858).

Books and Articles

ABBOTT, EDITH. WOMEN IN INDUSTRY: A STUDY IN AMERICAN ECONOMIC HISTORY. New York: D. Appleton and Co., 1909.

Abram, A. *Women Traders in Medieval London.* 26 THE ECONOMIC JOURNAL 276 (June 1916).

ACWORTH, EVELYN. THE NEW MATRIARCHY. London: Victor Gollancz Ltd., 1965.

ADAMS, CHARLES. FAMILIAR LETTERS OF JOHN ADAMS AND HIS WIFE ABIGAIL ADAMS, DURING THE REVOLUTION. 2nd ed. Freeport, N.Y.: Books for Libraries Press, 1970.

ADAMS, GEORGE. COUNCIL AND COURTS IN ANGLO-NORMAN ENGLAND. New York: Russell & Russell (1965).

———. *The Origin of English Equity.* 16 COLUMBIA LAW REVIEW 87 (1916).

Adoption of the Principles of Equity Jurisprudence into the Administration of Our Common Law. 8 AMERICAN LAW REGISTER 708 (1860).

Alexander, William H. *Jeremy Bentham, Legal Philosopher and Reformer.* 7 NEW YORK UNIVERSITY LAW REVIEW 141 (1929).

Amram, David Werner. *A Lawyer's Studies in Biblical Law: The Position of Women.* 14 THE GREEN BAG 343 (July 1902).

ANTHONY, KATHERINE. SUSAN B. ANTHONY: HER PERSONAL HISTORY AND HER ERA. Garden City: Doubleday Co., 1954.

ARIES, PHILIPPE. CENTURIES OF CHILDHOOD: A SOCIAL HISTORY OF FAMILY LIFE. New York: Vintage Books, 1962.

ATKINSON, CHARLES. JEREMY BENTHAM, HIS LIFE AND WORK. New York: AMS Press, 1971.

BACON, MATTHEW. A NEW ABRIDGMENT OF THE LAW. 1st American ed. from 6th English ed. Philadelphia: Farrand and Nicholas, 1811.

BEARD, MARY R. ON UNDERSTANDING WOMEN. New York: Longmans, Green and Co., 1931.

———. WOMAN AS FORCE IN HISTORY. New York: Macmillan Co., 1946.

BEBEL, AUGUST. WOMEN UNDER SOCIALISM. New York: Schocken Books, 1971.

Beers, George E. *Real Property.* IN TWO CENTURIES GROWTH OF AMERICAN LAW 1701-1901. Edited by Members of the Yale Law Faculty. New York: Charles Scribner's Sons, 1902.

BENTHAM, JEREMY. THE WORKS OF JEREMY BENTHAM. 11 vols. Edited by John Bowring. London: Simpkin, Marshall & Co., 1843.

BERGIN, THOMAS F., & HASKELL, PAUL G. *Preface to* ESTATES IN LAND AND FUTURE INTERESTS. Brooklyn: Foundation Press, 1966.

BIRD, CAROLINE. ENTERPRISING WOMEN. New York: W. W. Norton & Co., 1976.

BISHOP, JOEL PRENTIS. COMMENTARIES ON THE LAW OF MARRIED WOMEN UNDER THE STATUTES OF THE SEVERAL STATES AND AT COMMON LAW AND IN EQUITY. Boston: Little, Brown, and Co., 1873.

BLACKSTONE, SIR WILLIAM. COMMENTARIES ON THE LAWS OF ENGLAND, Philadelphia: William, Birch, Young and Abraham, 1803.

Bloomfield, Maxwell. *William Sampson and the Codifiers: The Roots of American Legal Reform, 1820-1830.* 11 AMERICAN JOURNAL OF LEGAL HISTORY 234 (1967).

BOWEN, CATHERINE. THE LION AND THE THRONE: THE LIFE AND TIMES OF SIR EDWARD CE. Boston: Little, Brown and Co., 1957.

BRIGHT, JOHN. A TREATISE ON LAW OF HUSBAND AND WIFE AS RESPECTS PROPERTY. New York: Banks, Gould & Co., 1850.

BROUGHAM, HENRY. OPINIONS OF LORD BROUGHAM ON POLITICS, THEOLOGY, LAW, SCIENCE, EDUCATION, LITERATURE AS EXHIBITED IN HIS PARLIAMENTARY AND LEGAL SPEECHES, AND MISCELLANEOUS WRITINGS. 2 vols. Philadelphia: Lea & Blanchard, 1838.

BROWNLEE W. ELLIOT & BROWNLEE, MARY M. WOMEN IN THE AMERICAN ECONOMY. New Haven: Yale University Press, 1976.

BRUCE, H. ADDINGTON. WOMAN IN THE MAKING OF AMERICA. Boston: Little, Brown and Co., 1928.

BUTLER, WILLIAM. THE REVISION OF THE STATUTES OF THE STATE OF NEW YORK AND THE REVISERS. New York and Albany: Banks & Brothers, 1889.

CALHOUN, ARTHUR. W. A SOCIAL HISTORY OF THE AMERICAN FAMILY FROM COLONIAL TIMES TO THE PRESENT. New York: Barnes & Noble, 1945.

CAM, HELEN. ENGLAND BEFORE ELIZABETH. 2d ed. New York: Hutchinson House, 1952.

CARTER, JAMES. THE PROVINCES OF THE WRITTEN AND THE UNWRITTEN LAW. New York: Banks & Brothers, 1889.

CASNER, A. J. AMERICAN LAW OF PROPERTY. 1952.

CHESTER, ALDEN, & WILLIAMS, E. MELVIN. COURTS AND LAWYERS OF NEW YORK: A HISTORY 1609-1925. New York: American Historical Society, 1925.

CHRISTIE, GEORGE. JURISPRUDENCE: TEXT AND READINGS ON THE PHILOSOPHY OF LAW. St. Paul: West Publishing, 1973.

CHRISTIE, JANE JOHNSTONE. THE ADVANCE OF WOMAN FROM EARLIEST TIMES TO THE PRESENT. Philadelphia: J. B. Lippincott Co., 1912.

CHUTE, MARCHETTE. THE FIRST LIBERTY: A HISTORY OF THE RIGHT TO VOTE IN AMERICA, 1619-1850. New York: E. P. Dutton & Co., 1969.

CLARK, ALICE. WORKING LIFE OF WOMEN IN THE SEVENTEENTH CENTURY. New York: E. P. Dutton & Co., 1919.

CLARKE, HELEN I. SOCIAL LEGISLATION. 2d ed. New York: Appleton-Century-Crofts, 1957.

Codification and Reform of the Law—No. 7. 21 AMERICAN JURIST 352 (1839).

Codification and Reform of the Law—No. 8. 22 AMERICAN JURIST 282 (1840).

Couch, John Andrew. *Woman in Early Roman Law*. 8 HARVARD LAW REVIEW 39 (1894).

CROMWELL, OTELIA. LUCRETIA MOTT: THE STORY OF ONE OF AMERICA'S GREATEST WOMEN. Cambridge: Harvard University Press, 1958.

CROSS, SUSAN. THE RIGHTS OF WOMEN. New York: Avon, Discuss Books, 1973.

CROSS, WHITNEY R. THE BURNED-OVER DISTRICT: THE SOCIAL AND INTELLECTUAL HISTORY OF ENTHUSIASTIC RELIGION IN WESTERN NEW YORK, 1800-1850. New York: Harper & Row, 1965; Ithaca: Cornell University Press, 1950.

DAVIS, PAULINA W. A HISTORY OF THE NATIONAL WOMEN'S RIGHTS MOVEMENT. New York: Journeymen Printers' Co-op., 1871.

DEXTER, ELIZABETH ANTHONY. CAREER WOMEN OF AMERICA 1776-1840. Francestown, N. H.: Marshall Jones Co., 1950.

———. COLONIAL WOMEN OF AFFAIRS. Cambridge, Mass.: The Riverside Press, 1931.

DICEY, A. V. LECTURES ON THE RELATION BETWEEN LAW AND PUBLIC OPINION IN ENGLAND DURING THE NINETEENTH CENTURY. London: Macmillan & Co., 1905.

DICKENS, CHARLES. BLEAK HOUSE. New York: Literary Guild of America, 1953.

DIGBY, KENLEM EDWARD. AN INTRODUCTION TO THE HISTORY OF THE LAW OF REAL PROPERTY. Oxford, England: Oxford University Press (Clarendon Press), 1897.

DONALDSON, JAMES. WOMAN: HER POSITION AND INFLUENCE IN ANCIENT GREECE AND ROME, AND AMONG THE EARLY CHRISTIANS. New York: Longmans, Green and Co., 1907.

ELLIS, DAVID; FROST, JAMES; SYRETT, HAROLD; & CARMAN, HARRY J. A HISTORY OF NEW YORK STATE. Ithaca: Cornell University Press, 1967.

ELTON, GEOFFREY RUDOLPH. THE TUDOR REVOLUTION IN GOVERNMENT. Cambridge, England: Cambridge University Press, 1953.

ENGELS, FREDERICK. THE ORIGIN OF THE FAMILY, PRIVATE PROPERTY AND THE STATE. Moscow: Progress Publishers. 1968.

Fenberg, Matilda. *Blame Coke and Blackstone.* 34 WOMEN LAWYERS JOURNAL 7 (1948).

FIELD, HENRY. THE LIFE OF DAVID DUDLEY FIELD. New York: Charles Scribner's Sons, 1898.

Field's Bills for Judicial Reform. 27 AMERICAN JURIST 214 (1842).

FLAHERTY, DAVID, ed. ESSAYS IN THE HISTORY OF EARLY AMERICAN LAW. Chapel Hill: University of North Carolina press, 1969.

FLEXNER, ELEANOR. CENTURY OF STRUGGLE. New York: Atheneum, 1968.

FLICK, ALEXANDER. HISTORY OF THE STATE OF NEW YORK. Port Washington, L.I., N.Y.: Ira J. Friedman, 1962.

Fluegal, James, *Woman's Legal Status in Ancient and Modern Times.* 11 THE AMERICAN LAWYER 332 (1903).

FONER, PHILIP. HISTORY OF THE LABOR MOVEMENT IN THE UNITED STATES New York: International Publishers, 1947-1955.

_____. WOMEN AND THE AMERICAN LABOR MOVEMENT. New York: Macmillan & Co., 1979.

Fowler, Robert Ludlow. *Constitutional & Related Aspects from 1801 to the Constitution of 1894.* In 1 HISTORY OF THE BEWNCH AND BAR OF NEW YORK. Edited by David McAdam. New York: New York History Co., 1897.

Franklin, Mitchell. *Concerning the Historic Importance of Edward Livingston.* 11 TULANE LAW REVIEW 163 (1937).

_____. *Contribution to an Explication of the Activity of the Warren Majority of the Supreme Court.* 24 BUFFALO LAW REVIEW (1975).

_____. *The Eighteenth Brumaire in Louisiana: Talleyrand and the Spanish Medieval Legal System of 1806.* TULANE LAW REVIEW 514 (1942).

_____. *Equity in Louisiana: The Role of Article 21.* 9 TULANE LAW REVIEW 485 (1935).

_____. *The Historic Function of the American Law Institute: Restatement as Transition to Codification.* 47 HARVARD LAW REVIEW 1367 (1933-34).

_____. *A New Conception of the Relation Between Law and Equity.* 11 PHILOSOPHY AND PHENOMENOLOGICAL RESEARCH 201 (1951).

_____. *The Ninth Amendment as Civil Law Method and its Implications for Republican Form of Government: Griswold v. Connecticut; South Carolina v. Katzenbach.* 40 TULANE LAW REVIEW 486 (1966).

————. *Review* of THE CIVIL CODE OF THE STATE OF LOUISIANA. Edited by Benjamin Dart. 7 TULANE LAW REVIEW 632 (1932).

————. *Some Considerations on the Existential Force of Roman Law in the Early History of the United States.* 22 BUFFALO LAW REVIEW 62 (1972).

FRIEDMAN, LAWRENCE. A HISTORY OF AMERICAN LAW. New York: Simon & Schuster, Touchstone Book, 1973.

FRIEDMANN, WOLFGANG GASTON. LEGAL THEORY. 5th ed. New York: Columbia University Press, 1967.

FRIEDRICH, CARL. THE PHILOSOPHY OF LAW IN HISTORICAL PERSPECTIVE. 2d ed. Chicago: University of Chicago Press, Phoenix Books, 1963.

Gager, Edwin B. *Equity.* In TWO CENTURIES GROWTH OF AMERICAN LAW 1701-1901, by Members of the Yale Law Faculty. New York: Charles Scribner's Sons, 1902.

GRAVESON, R. H., & CRANE F. R. A CENTURY OF FAMILY LAW 1857-1957. London: Sweet & Maxwell, 1957.

GREGORY, CHESTER W. WOMEN IN DEFENSE WORK DURING WORLD WAR II. New York: Exposition Press, 1974.

HARPER, IDA. LIFE AND WORK OF SUSAN B. ANTHONY. Indianapolis: Hollenbeck Press, 1898.

Haskins, GEORGE L. *The Development of Common Law Dower.* 62 HARVARD LAW REVIEW 42 (1948).

————. *The Estate by the Marital Right.* 97 UNIVERSITY OF PENNSYLVANIA LAW REVIEW 345 (1949).

HATCHER, WILLIAM. EDWARD LIVINGSTON, JEFFERSONIAN REPUBLICAN AND JACKSONIAN DEMOCRAT. Baton Rouge: Louisiana State University Press, 1940.

HECKER, EUGENE A. A SHORT HISTORY OF WOMEN'S RIGHTS FROM THE DAYS OF AUGUSTUS TO THE PRESENT TIME WITH SPECIAL REFERENCE TO ENGLAND AND THE UNITED STATES. New York: G. P. Putnam's Sons, 1910.

HENRY, ALICE. WOMEN AND THE LABOR MOVEMENT. New York: George H. Doran Co., 1923.

HERTTELL, THOMAS. THE CONDITION, INFLUENCE, RIGHTS AND APPEAL OF WOMEN. 3d ed. Albany, 1845.

————. THE RIGHT OF MARRIED WOMEN TO HOLD AND CONTRACT PROPERTY SUSTAINED BY THE CONSTITUTION OF THE STATE OF NEW YORK. New York: Henry Durell, 1839.

HILL, CHRISTOPHER. INTELLECTUAL ORIGINS OF THE ENGLISH REVOLUTION. Oxford, England: Clarendon Press, 1965.

————. PURITANISM AND REVOLUTION. 2d ed. New York: Schocken Books, 1964.

————. SOCIETY AND PURITANISM IN PRE-REVOLUTIONARY ENGLAND. 2d ed. New York: Schocken Books, 1967.

————. THE WORLD TURNED UPSIDE DOWN: RADICAL IDEAS DURING THE ENGLISH REVOLUTION. New York: Viking Press, 1972.

Hodes, William. *Women and the Constitution: Some Legal History and A New Approach to the Nineteenth Amendment.* 25 RUTGERS LAW REVIEW 26 (1907).

Holdsworth, William. *Blackstone's Treatment of Equity.* 43 HARVARD LAW REVIEW 1 (1929).

————. CHARLES DICKENS AS A LEGAL HISTORIAN, New Haven: Yale University Press, 1928.

————. AN HISTORICAL INTRODUCTION TO LAND LAW. Oxford: The Clarendon Press, 2d ed., 1927.

———. A HISTORY OF ENGLISH LAW. Boston: Little, Brown, and Co., 1909.

HOLMES, OLIVER WENDELL. THE COMMON LAW. Edited by Mark DeWolfe Howe. Cambridge: Harvard University Press, Belknap Press, 1963.

HORTON, JOHN. JAMES KENT: A STUDY IN CONSERVATISM 1763-1847. New York: Appleton-Century, 1939.

Horwitz, Morton J. *The Conservative Tradition in the Writing of American Legal History*. 17 AMERICAN JOURNAL OF LEGAL HISTORY 275 (1973).

———. *The Rise of Legal Formalism*. 19 AMERICAN JOURNAL OF LEGAL HISTORY 251 (October 1975).

———. THE TRANSFORMATION OF AMERICAN LAW 1780-1860. Cambridge: Harvard University Press, 1977.

HUMPHREYS, JAMES. OBSERVATIONS ON THE ACTUAL STATE OF THE ENGLISH LAWS OF REAL PROPERTY WITH OUTLINE FOR A SYSTEMATIC REFORM. 2d ed. London: John Murray Co., 1827.

HUNT, CHARLES. LIFE OF EDWARD LIVINGSTON. New York: Appleton and Co., 1864.

HURST, J. WILLARD. LAW AND THE CONDITIONS OF FREEDOM IN THE NINETEENTH-CENTURY UNITED STATES. Madison: University of Wisconsin Press, 1956.

JAMES, EDWARD T., ed. NOTABLE AMERICAN WOMEN: A BIOGRAPHICAL DICTIONARY. 3 vols. Cambridge: Harvard University Press, Belknap Press, 1971.

JEFFERSON, THOMAS. PAPERS OF THOMAS JEFFERSON. Edited by Jullian Boyd. Princeton: Princeton University Press, 1958.

JESSUP, HENRY WYNANS. LAW FOR WIVES AND DAUGHTERS: THEIR RIGHTS AND THEIR OBLIGATIONS. New York: Macmillan Co., 1927.

Katz, Stanley N. *The Politics of Law in Colonial America: Controversies over Chancery Courts and Equity Law in the Eighteenth Century*, 5 PERSPECTIVES IN AMERICAN HISTORY 257 (1971).

KEETON, GEORGE W. THE NORMAN CONQUEST AND THE COMMON LAW. New York: Barnes & Noble, 1966.

KEMPLIN, FREDERICK. HISTORICAL INTRODUCTION TO ANGLO-AMERICAN LAW. St. Paul: West Publishing, 1973.

KENT, JAMES. COMMENTARIES ON AMERICAN LAW. 12th ed. Boston: Little, Brown and Co., 1873.

KHARAS, RALPH. *A Century of Law-Equity Merger in New York*. In SELECTED ESSAYS ON EQUITY. Edited by Edward D. Re. New York: Oceana Publications, 1955.

Kiralfy, A. K. R. *Law Reform by Legal Fictions, Equity and Legislation in English Legal History*. 10 AMERICAN JOURNAL OF LEGAL HISTORY 3 (1966).

Kirkwood, M.R. *Equality of Property Interests Between Husband and Wife*. 8 MINNESOTA LAW REVIEW 579 (1924).

KRADITOR, AILEEN S. THE IDEAS OF THE WOMAN SUFFRAGE MOVEMENT 1890-1920. New York: Columbia University Press, 1965.

———. MEANS AND ENDS IN AMERICAN ABOLITIONISM. New York: Random House, 1969.

———. UP FROM THE PEDESTAL: SELECTED WRITINGS IN THE HISTORY OF AMERICAN FEMINISM. Chicago: Quadrangle Books, 1968.

Landis. James. *Statutes and the Sources of Law*. 2 HARVARD JOURNAL ON LEGISLATION 7 (1965).

LANG, MAURICE. CODIFICATION IN THE BRITISH EMPIRE AND AMERICA. Amsterdam: H. J. Paris, 1924.

LANGDON-DAVIES, JOHN. A SHORT HISTORY OF WOMEN. New York: The Literary Guild of America, 1927.

Law of Real Property. Review of OBSERVATIONS ON THE ACTUAL STATE OF THE ENGLISH LAWS OF REAL PROPERTY: WITH OUTLINES FOR A SYSTEMATIC REFORM by JAMES HUMPHREYS. 1 AMERICAN JURIST 58 (1829).

The Law of Real Property as Affected by the Revised Statutes of the State of New York. 4 AMERICAN LAW MAGAZINE 310 (1844-45).

The Law of Real Property as Affected by the Revised Statutes of the State of New York. 5 AMERICAN LAW MAGAZINE 50 (1845).

Law Reform in America. Review of THE STATUTES AND ORDERS OF THE COURT OF CHANCERY AND THE STATUTE LAW OF REAL PROPERTY OF THE STATE OF NEW YORK, RECENTLY REVISED AND AMENDED. WITH A BRIEF ACCOUNT OF THE EQUITY JURISDICTIONS AND LAW OF REAL PROPERTY AND REGISTRATION IN THE UNITED STATES, NORTH AMERICA, by JOSEPH PARKES. 6 LAW MAGAZINE AND REVIEW 127 (1831).

Law Reform and Law Reformers. 3 AMERICAN LAW REGISTER 513 (1864).

LEGAL AND JUDICIAL HISTORY OF NEW YORK. New York: National American Society, 1911.

LERNER, GERDA. THE WOMAN IN AMERICAN HISTORY. Menlo Park, Calif.: Addison-Wesley, Co., 1971.

LETOURNEAU CHARLES JEAN MARIE. THE EVOLUTION OF MARRIAGE AND OF THE FAMILY. New York: Charles Scribner's Sons, 1891.

LEVY-ULLMANN, HENRI. THE ENGLISH LEGAL TRADITION, ITS SOURCES AND HISTORY. Translated by M. Mitchell. London: Macmillan & Co., 1935.

LOCKMILLER, DAVID. SIR WILLIAM BLACKSTONE. Chapel Hill: University of North Carolina Press, 1938.

Logingier, Charles. *The Franco-American Codes* 19 VIRGINIA LAW REVIEW 351 (1933).

LUTZ, ALMA. CREATED EQUAL: A BIOGRAPHY OF ELIZABETH CADY STANTON. New York: John Day Co., 1940.

MACK M. P. JEREMY BENTHAM: AN ODYSSEY OF IDEAS. New York: Columbia University Press, 1963.

MACKINNON, CATHARINE A. SEXUAL HARASSMENT OF WORKING WOMEN. New Haven: Yale University Press, 1979.

Mailet, Jean. *The Historical Significance of French Codification.* 44 TULANE LAW VIEW 681 (1970).

MAINE, HENRY. ANCIENT LAW: ITS CONNECTION WITH THE EARLY HISTORY OF SOCIETY AND ITS RELATION TO MODERN IDEAS. Boston: Beacon Press, 1963.

MAITLAND, FREDERIC. *Introduction to Memoranda de Parliamento, 1305.* In SELECTED HISTORICAL ESSAYS OF F. W. MAITLAND. Cambridge, England: Cambridge University Press, 1957.

Melder, Keith E. The Beginnings of the Women's Rights Movement in the United States 1800-1840. Unpublished Ph.D. dissertation, Yale University, 1964.

MESSER, MARY BURT. THE FAMILY IN THE MAKING: AN HISTORICAL SKETCH. New York: G. P. Putnam's Sons, 1928.

MILLER, PERRY. THE LIFE OF THE MIND IN AMERICA FROM THE REVOLUTION TO THE CIVIL WAR. New York: Harcourt, Brace & World, Harvest Book. 1965.

MILLETT, KATE. SEXUAL POLITICS. New York: Doubleday & Co., 1970.

MORRIS, RICHARD B. STUDIES IN THE HISTORY OF AMERICAN LAW WITH SPECIAL REFERENCE TO THE SEVENTEENTH AND EIGHTEENTH CENTURIES. New York: Columbia University Press, 1930.

Morrison JAMES J. *Legislative Technique and the Problem of Suppletive and Constructive Laws*. 9 TULANE LAW REVIEW 544 (1935).

Morrow, Clarence. *Louisiana Blueprint: Civilian Codification and Legal Method for State and Nation*. 17 TULANE LAW REVIEW 351, 537 (1943).

———. *Matrimonial Property Law in Louisiana*. 34 TULANE LAW REVIEW 3 (1959).

MULLER-LYER, FRANZ L. THE EVOLUTION OF MODERN MARRIAGE: A SOCIOLOGY OF SEXUAL RELATIONS. London: George Allen & Unwin Ltd., 1913, 1930.

NELSON, WILLIAM E. AMERICANIZATION OF THE COMMON LAW. Cambridge: Harvard University Press, 1975.

———. *The Legal Restraint of Power in Pre-Revolutionary America*. 18 AMERICAN JOURNAL OF LEGAL HISTORY 1 (January 1974).

———. *The Reform of Common Law Pleading in Massachusetts 1760-1830: Adjudication as a Prelude to Legislation*. 122 UNIVERSITY OF PENNSYLVANIA LAW REVIEW 97 (November 1973).

NEWMAN, RALPH. EQUITY AND LAW; A COMPARATIVE STUDY. New York: Oceana Publications, 1961.

O'NEILL, WILLIAM L. EVERYONE WAS BRAVE: A HISTORY OF FEMINISM IN AMERICA. Chicago: Quadrangle Books, 1969, 1971.

———. THE WOMAN MOVEMENT: FEMINISM IN THE UNITED STATES AND ENGLAND. Chicago: Quadrangle Books, 1971.

OSTROGORSKI, MOISEI. THE RIGHTS OF WOMEN: A COMPARATIVE STUDY IN HISTORY AND LEGISLATION. New York: Charles Scribner's Sons, 1908.

O'SULLIVAN, Judith, & GALLICK. Rosemary. WORKERS AND ALLIES. Washington, D.C. Smithsonian Institution Press, 1975.

PARKES, JOSEPH. NEW YORK COURT OF CHANCERY AND REAL PROPERTY LAW. London: Maxwell & Stevens, 1830.

PINCHBECK , IVY. WOMEN WORKERS AND THE INDUSTRIAL REVOLUTION 1750-1850. London: Thomas Nelson (Printers) Ltd., 1930.

PLUCKNETT, THEODORE. A CONCISE HISTORY OF THE COMMON LAW. Boston: Little, Brown and Co., 1956.

POCOCK, JOHN. THE ANCIENT CONSTITUTIONAL AND THE FEUDAL LAW: A STUDY OF ENGLISH HISTORICAL THOUGHT IN THE SEVENTEENTH CENTURY. New York: W. W. Norton & Co., 1967.

POLLOCK, FREDERICK, & MAITLAND, FREDERIC. THE HISTORY OF ENGLISH LAW BEFORE THE TIME OF EDWARD I. 2 vols. 2d ed. Cambridge, England: Cambridge University Press, 1968.

POMEROY, JOHN NORTON. A TREATISE ON EQUITY JURISPRUDENCE AS ADMINISTERED IN THE UNITED STATES OF AMERICA ADAPTED FOR ALL THE STATES AND TO THE UNION OF LEGAL AND EQUITABLE REMEDIES UNDER THE REFORMED PROCEDURE. 5th ed. Rochester: The Lawyers Co-operative Publishing Co., 1941.

POUND, ROSCOE. THE FORMATIVE ERA OF AMERICAN LAW. Boston: Little, Brown, 1938.

———. *The French Civil Code and the Spirit of Nineteenth Century Law*. 35 BOSTON UNIVERSITY LAW REVIEW 77 (1955).

———. JURISPRUDENCE. St. Paul: West Publishing, 1959.

———— . *Revival of Comparative Law.* 5 TULANE LAW REVIEW 1 (1930-31).

POWELL, RICHARD R. REAL PROPERTY. New York: Matthew Bender Co., 1949, 1969.

PRALL, STUART. THE AGITATION FOR LAW REFORM DURING THE PURITAN REVOLUTION 1640-1660. The Hague: Martinus Nijhoff, 1966.

———— . *The Development of Equity in Tudor England.* 8 AMERICAN JOURNAL OF LEGAL HISTORY 1 (1964).

PUTNAM, EMILY JAMES. THE LADY: STUDIES OF CERTAIN SIGNIFICANT PHASES OF HER HISTORY. Chicago: University of Chicago Press, 1969.

Radin, MAX. *The Rivalry of Common Law and Civil Law Ideas in the American Colonies.* 2 LAW—A CENTURY OF PROGRESS, 1835-1935. N.Y.: New York University Press, (1937).

Rapacz, M. P. *Progress of Property Law Relating to Married Women.* 11 THE UNIVERSITY OF KANSAS CITY LAW REVIEW 173 (1943).

Recent Revisions & C. of Statute Laws—New York. 18 AMERICAN JURIST 244 (1838).

Redfield, Amasa. *English Colonial Polity and Judicial Administration 1664-1776.* In 1 HISTORY OF THE BENCH AND BAR OF NEW YORK. Edited by David McAdam. New York: New York History Co., 1897.

Reform in Remedial Law, 17 AMERICAN JURIST 253 (1837).

REPPY, ALISON ed., DAVID DUDLEY FIELD: CENTENARY ESSAYS. New York: New York University Press, 1949.

The Revision of 1830—The Innovations of 1847 and 1848 6 NEW YORK LEGAL OBSERVER 49 (1848).

RICHARDSON, H. G., & SAYLES, G. O. THE GOVERNANCE OF MEDIAEVAL ENGLAND FROM THE CONQUEST TO MAGNA CARTA. Edinburgh, England: Edinburgh University Press, 1963.

———— . LAW AND LEGISLATION FROM AETHELBERHT TO MAGNA CARTA. Edinburgh, England: Edinburgh University Press, 1966.

Riddell, William Renwick. *Bentham on Blackstone: A Review.* 15 JOURNAL OF THE AMERICAN BAR ASSOCIATION 66 (1929).

Rogers, R. Vashon. *Legal Positions of Women in Ancient Greece.* 11 THE GREEN BAG: AN ENTERTAINING MAGAZINE FOR LAWYERS 209 (1899).

———— . *Woman and the Law in Babylonia and Assyria.* 15 THE GREEN BAG: AN ENTERTAINING MAGAZINE FOR LAWYERS 495 (1903).

———— . *Women Under Early Christian Law.* 14 THE GREEN BAG: AN ENTERTAINING MAGAZINE FOR LAWYERS 547 (1902).

RROWN, GEORGE FOREST. THW IMPORTANCE OF WOMEN IN ANGLO-SAXON TIMES. New York: Macmillan Co., 1919.

SAMPSON, WILLIAM. AN ANNIVERSARY DISCOURSE DELIVERED BEFORE THE HISTORICAL SOCIETY OF NEW YORK ON SATURDAY, DECEMBER 6, 1823 SHOWING THE ORIGIN. PROGRESS, ANTIQUITIES, CURIOSITIES & NATURE OF THE COMMON LAW. New York: Bliss & White, 1824.

Scarman Honorable Mr. *Codification and Judge-Made Law: A Problem of Coexistence.* 42 INDIANA LAW JOURNAL 355 (1967).

SCOFIELD, CORA. A STUDY OF THE STAR CHAMBER. Chicago: University of Chicago Press, 1900.

SCOTT, ANNE FIROR. THE AMERICAN WOMAN: WHO WAS SHE? Englewood Cliffs, N.J.: Prentice-Hall, 1971.

———— . WOMEN IN AMERICAN LIFE. New York: Houghton Mifflin Co., 1970.

SELTMAN, CHARLES. WOMEN IN ANTIQUITY. New York: St. Martin's Press, 1955.

Separate Estate of Married Women. 3 AMERICAN LAW MAGAZINE 296 (1844).

Severns, Roger. *Nineteenth Century Equity: A Study in Law Reform.* 12 CHICAGO-KENT LAW REVIEW 81 (1934). Part II in 13 CHICAGO-KENT LAW REVIEW 305 (1935).

SIMPSON, ALFRED WILLIAM BRIAN. INTRODUCTION TO THE HISTORY OF LAND LAW. London: Oxford University Press, 1961.

SINCLAIR, ANDREW. THE EMANCIPATION OF THE AMERICAN WOMAN. New York: Harper & Row, 1965.

SMITH, CYRIL J. TRADITION OF EVE. San Antonio, Texas: Naylor Co., 1961.

SMITH, MUNROE. THE DEVELOPMENT OF EUROPEAN LAW. New York: Columbia University Press, 1928.

SMITH, PAGE. DAUGHTERS OF THE PROMISED LAND: WOMEN IN AMERICAN HISTORY. Boston: Little, Brown and Co., 1970.

SMUTTS, ROBERT W. WOMEN AND WORK IN AMERICA. New York: Schocken Books (1959).

SPRUILL, JULIA. WOMEN'S LIFE & WORK IN THE SOUTHERN COLONIES. Chapel Hill: University of North Carolina Press, 1938.

STANTON, ELIZABETH CADY. EIGHTY YEARS AND MORE (1815-1897): REMINISCENCES OF ELIZABETH CADY STANTON. London: T. Fisher Unwin, 1898.

STANTON, ELIZABETH CADY; ANTHONY, SUSAN; & GAGE, MATILDA. THE HISTORY OF WOMAN SUFFRAGE. vol. 1 of 6 vols. Rochester, 1881-1922.

STANTON, HENRY. RANDOM RECOLLECTIONS. 3rd ed. New York: Harper & Brothers, 1887.

————. SKETCHES OF REFORMS AND REFORMERS OF GREAT BRITAIN AND IRELAND. New York: John Wiley, 1849.

STENTON, DORIS MARY. THE ENGLISH WOMAN IN HISTORY. New York: Macmillan Co., 1957.

STEPHENS, WINIFRED. WOMEN OF THE FRENCH REVOLUTION. New York: E. P. Dutton & Co., 1922.

Stevenson, Charles. *Influence of Bentham and Humphreys on the New York Property Legislation of 1828.* 1 AMERICAN JOURNAL OF LEGAL HISTORY 155 (1957).

STONE, JULIUS. LEGAL SYSTEM AND LAWYERS REASONINGS. Stanford: University Press, 1968.

STORY, JOSEPH. COMMENTARIES ON EQUITY JURISPRUDENCE AS ADMINISTERED IN ENGLAND AND AMERICA. Boston: Hilliard Gray and Co., 1836.

SUHL, YURI. ERNESTINE ROSE AND THE BATTLE FOR HUMAN RIGHTS. New York: Reynal & Co., 1959.

Tate, Albert. *Civilian Methodology in Louisiana.* 44 TULANE LAW REVIEW 672 (1970).

Telkampf, J. Louis. *On Codification, or the Systematizing of the Law.* 26 AMERICAN JURIST 113 (1841).

————. *On Codification, or the Systematizing of the Law: Objections Against Codification Answered.* 26 AMERICAN JURIST 283 (1842).

Thompson, W. D. *The Development of Woman's Rights in the Law.* 8 THE MARQUETTE LAW REVIEW 152 (1924).

THRUPP SYLVIA L. THE MERCHANT CLASS OF MEDIEVAL LONDON 1300-1500. Chicago: The University of Chicago Press, 1948.

TIFFANY, HERBERT. THE LAW OF REAL PROPERTY AND OTHER INTERESTS IN LAND. Saint Paul: Keefe-Davidson, 1861.

TYLER, ALICE FELT. FREEDOM'S FERMENT; PHASES OF AMERICAN SOCIAL HISTORY FROM THE COLONIAL PERIOD TO THE OUTBREAK OF THE CIVIL WAR. New York: Harper Torchbooks, 1944.

Uses and Trusts as Affected by the Revised Statutes of the State of New York. 6 AMERICAN LAW MAGAZINE 268 (1845-46).

USHER, ROLAND. THE RISE AND FALL OF THE HIGH COMMISSION. Oxford, England: Clarendon Press, 1913.

Waite, C. B. *Who Were Voters in the Early History of This Country?* Chicago Law Times, October 1888.

Wagner, Donald. *Coke and the Rise of Economic Liberalism.* 6 ECONOMIC HISTORY REVIEW 30 (1938).

Warbasse, Elizabeth. The Changing Legal Rights of Married Women, 1800-1861. Unpublished Ph. D. dissertation, Radcliffe College, 1960.

WARREN, CHARLES. A HISTORY OF THE AMERICAN BAR. New York: Little, Brown and Co., 1911.

Warren, Joseph. *Husband's Right to Wife's Services.* 38 HARVARD LAW REVIEW 421 (1925).

Waterman, Julius S. *Thomas Jefferson and Blackstone's Commentaries.* In ESSAYS IN THE HISTORY OF EARLY AMERICAN LAW 451. Edited by David H. Flaherty. Chapel Hill: University of North Carolina Press, 1969.

WESTERMARCK, EDWARD A. THE HISTORY OF HUMAN MARRIAGE. 5th rev. ed. 3 vols. London: Macmillan & Co., 1921, 1925.

WHITCOMB, MERRICK, ed., TYPICAL CAHIERS OF 1789. Vol. IV, no. V of TRANSLATIONS AND REPRINTS FROM THE ORIGINAL SOURCES OF EUROPEAN HISTORY. Philadelphia: Department of History, University of Pennsylvania, 1898.

Wigmore, John. *Louisiana: The Store of Its Legal System.* 1 SOUTHERN LAW QUARTERLY 1 (1916).

———. A PANORAMA OF THE WORLD'S LEGAL SYSTEMS. Washington, D.C.: Washington Law Book Company, 1928.

Wilson, Solon. *Courts of Chancery in the American Colonies.* In 2 SELECT ESSAYS IN ANGLO-AMERICAN LEGAL HISTORY 779. Boston: Little, Brown and Co., 1907-9.

WINFIELD, PERCY H. THE CHIEF SOURCES OF ENGLISH LEGAL HISTORY. Cambridge: Harvard University Press, 1925.

Written and Unwritten Systems of Laws. Review of DE LA CODIFICATION EN GENERAL, ET DE CELLE DE L'ANGLETERRE EN PARTICULIER, by M. MEYER; and CONTRE-PROJECT TO THE HUMPHREYSIAN CODE, AND THE PROCESS OF REDACTION OF MESSRS. HAMMOND, UNIACKE AND TWISS, by JOHN PARK. 9 AMERICAN JURIST 5 (1833).

YALE LAW FACULTY. TWO CENTURIES GROWTH OF AMERICAN LAW 1701-1901. New York: Charles Scribner's Sons, 1902.

INDEX

Abbott, Edith, 158-60, 161-62; *Women in Industry*, 158
Abolitionists, and women's movement, 3-4, 12
Abortion, 169
Active trusts, 48-49, 75, 77-78. *See also* Trusts
Admiralty court, 33
Affirmative action, 163-64
Albany, New York, women's rights convention in, 112-13
Alienability of property. *See* Land, transferability of
Alienation of affection, 147-48
Ambiguous laws. *See* Law
American Federation of Labor, 162
American feminism, origins of, 3-13, 106-17
American Jurist, 78, 102, 103
American law, formative era, 61-62
American Law Review, 17, 55
American legislature, supremacy of, 32, 40, 52
American Revolution, and law reform, 12, 36, 55, 61, 66; Sampson's views of, 44
Analogical interpretation. *See* Statutes
Ancient Law, Maine, 25-27
Anniversary Discourse, Sampson, 44-45
Anthony, Susan B., 4, 107
Antislavery movement, theory of, as origin of women's rights movement, 3-4
Aristotelian concept of equity, 25-26, 27, 32
Aristotle, 25
Association of the Bar of the City of New York, attack on codification, 56
Austin, John, 55-56, 103, 104
Automobile negligence law, 150

Bacon, Francis, 32, 35; codification by, 33; Humphreys influenced by, 45
Bankruptcy, 127, 129
Barnes v. *Train*, 175-76
Bascom, Ansel, 93
Beard, Mary: theory of nineteenth-century feminism, 5-7, 36; weaknesses of argument, 75, 76-77; *Women as Force in History*, 5
Bennett amendment, 172-74
Bennett v. *Bennett*, 147-48
Bentham, Jeremy, 40-42, 52, 54, 56, 103, 104, 109-10; Field influenced by, 54-55, 56; Revisers influenced by, 62, 63-64
Birkbeck v. *Ackroyd*, 141-43

Blackmun, Justice Harry A., 166, 168
Blackstone, William, 5, 119-21, 125, 130; Austin's view of, 56; *Commentaries on the Laws of England*, 6, 119; women's movement influenced by, 5-7, 121
Blackwell, Elizabeth, 161
Bleak House, Dickens, 17
Boston Investigator, 111
Bowdish, John, 92
Bradley, Judge, 148
Bradwell, Myra, 161
Brennan, Justice William, 166
Bright, John, *A Treatise on the Law of Husband and Wife as Respects Property*, 17
Brooks v. *Schwerin*, 139-40, 141
Brougham, Henry Peter, First Baron, 63, 64-65, 109-10; feminism of, 108-9; Revisers influenced by, 68, 76, 77
Brown, Antoinette L., 112
Brownlee, Elliot and Mary, 162
Buckley v. *Wells*, 132
Business enterprise of wife: claims against, 131, 132, 139, 142; common law disability of, 19
Burger, Chief Justice Warren E., 166, 168
Butler, Benjamin F., 62
Butler, William A., 52, 61, 62, 63

Cady, Daniel, 108
Canon law, 27
Carter, James C., 56, 58
Chancellors, 25: of New York State, 101-2; in Tudor England, 26
Chancery court, 25, 27, 32, 33, 35-36; abolition of, 82, 91-92, 97, 100-2; in America, 6; enforcement of women's separate estate, 21, 125; and law reform, 68, 77; *Vanderheyden and Wife* v. *Mallory and Hunter*, 126-29; and women's property rights, 81, 125-26
Childbearers, women as, 165
Children, guardianship of, 113
Christensen v. *Iowa*, 171-74
Chronological approach to legal reform, 25, 31
Churchmen, uses of, 45
Circuit judges, equity power of, 102
City of Los Angeles Department of Water and Power v. *Manhart*, 167-68
Civil Code, French. *See* French Civil Code

ABOUT THE AUTHOR

Peggy A. Rabkin holds both a Ph.D in history and a law degree. Now a labor lawyer practicing in New York City, she has taught at the State University of New York at Buffalo in the Department of History and at the University of Louisville School of Law.